Angels Along the Way

Angels Along the Way

My Life with Help from Above

Della Reese

with Franklin Lett
and Mim Eichler

G. P. Putnam's Sons
New York

G. P. Putnam's Sons

Publishers Since 1838

a member of

Penguin Putnam Inc.

200 Madison Avenue

New York, NY 10016

The author acknowledges permission to quote lyrics from the following:
"Turn to the Light," composed by Robert Mayes. Copyright © 1979,
Christ Universal Temple (Chicago, IL).
"A Window Open," by songwriters T. C. Campbell and Robbie Long.
Copyright © 1996 by T. C. Campbell, Window Pane Music, ASCAP;
and Robbie Long, Sumner Music, ASCAP.

Library of Congress Cataloging-in-Publication Data

Reese, Della.

Angels along the way : my life with help from above / Della Reese
with Franklin Lett and Mim Eichler.

p.   cm.

ISBN 0-399-14342-4 (alk. paper)

1. Reese, Della.   2. Christian biography—United States.
3. Singers—United States—Biography.   4. Actors—United States—
Biography.   5. Clergy—United States—Biography.   I. Lett,
Franklin.   II. Eichler, Mim.   III. Title.

BR1725.R384A3   1997   97-13399 CIP

782.42164'092—dc21

[b]

Printed in the United States of America

1 3 5 7 9 10 8 6 4 2

This book is printed on acid-free paper. ♾

BOOK DESIGN BY DEBORAH KERNER

This book is dedicated from the "Christ in me" to all the angels along the way, those mentioned and those not mentioned but by no far stretch of the imagination forgotten; to my darling daughter and my adorable son; and to this wonderful guardian angel that the Father has sent me to spend the rest of my life with, my magnificent husband, who makes the waking of each day a pleasurable anticipation of the joy and love that will fill it.

Acknowledgments

Before I embarked on this project, many people warned me that writing an autobiography would be a huge and difficult undertaking. That, however, has not been my experience at all. Yes, it was slow going at first, but once I got into the writing groove, I had so much fun, I really didn't want to stop. In fact, I'm already thinking about a sequel.

There are a handful of very special individuals without whom I wouldn't have had so much fun, let alone completed this book. To these I would like to express my heartfelt gratitude.

First, second, and last—to my husband and coauthor, Franklin Lett. Thank you for cajoling me into this project in the first place, for keeping it and me on schedule, for your writing and research contributions, for sharing in the laughter and the tears, for keeping all our fires burning.

To my coauthor Mim Eichler-Rivas . . . there's a whole lot of talent in this little adorable package. You've been an angel throughout this entire project.

To Dan Strone and Jeff Kolodny at William Morris. Thanks for your belief in my vision for this book and for your assistance in seeing that vision realized. To the team at Putnam—Nanscy Neiman-Legette, for championing this project in every respect. To my editor, Stacy Creamer, for ushering this book into its publishing home, for your energetic enthusiasm, and your understanding of angels. Thanks also to everyone else in the copyediting, design, production, marketing, and publicity departments at Putnam. And to all of you in shipping, too. I hope you ship a lot.

Love and everlasting gratitude to all my friends and family who assisted me in recollections. My deepest thanks go to my loving family at Understanding Principles for Better Living. A special thank-you to Jean Thompson, Patricia Whitehead, Bill E. Hall, and Dr. Charles Brown, for helping me locate information, paperwork, and audiotapes. And to my fellow ministers, staff, and all members, thank you for sharing your letters, your words, and your memories with me to be included in this book.

Thanks to my other family, the cast and crew of *Touched by an Angel,* in Salt Lake City. You are my church away from home.

Loving thanks go to my personal assistants, Ron Hearin and Shirley Williams, for making everything smooth sailing here in L.A.

To my fans—old and new—without whom I would not be here today with a story to tell. And finally, I'd like to say a word of acknowledgment to all of you readers and to all of you who encourage others to read. Thank you. Without you, to whom would I tell this story?

Contents

Prologue
Salt Lake City, Utah
1997 ∾ 1

part one
Learning
1931 – 1949 ∾ 7

part two
Singing
1949 – 1961 ∾ 101

part three
Acting
1961 – 1980 ∾ 183

part four
Teaching
1980 – 1997 ∾ 263

Epilogue
Los Angeles, California
1997 ∾ 333

Prologue

Not too long ago, on a bitter cold February morning—at an hour much too early for humans to be stirring—my husband, Franklin, tried to rouse me from a deep, contented sleep.

"Della, time to get up." Franklin's mellow voice cooed in my ear as he leaned over from his side of the bed. "Early call today."

"All right," I mumbled back, "I'm gettin' up." I meant it, too, but my body, having a will of its own that morning, slid further down underneath our warm comforter.

No matter how busy the day ahead is going to be for both of us, my husband, Franklin, and I try to have some time together before the phone starts ringing and the typical daily hustle and bustle begins. This is part of our morning routine. I cherish our morning time together above many things but I admit it is no small undertaking for Franklin to get me out of the bed—one of my favorite places to be, if not *the* favorite. (And not just for sleeping.)

I *love* the bed and I *hate* the cold. Hate it. I hate it almost as much as I hate the sound of someone singing offkey, something which sends a pain right through my body. After living through more than two decades of Detroit's winters as a child, I figure I have had more than my share of snow, ice, sleet, and hail. Give me the tropics any day. The hotter the better.

That said, you'll understand why the thought of putting myself into a snowsuit and running around in sub-arctic temperatures on that recent February morning was not especially enticing. "Ten more minutes," I begged, my eyes still shut.

"Five," he bargained back, leaving me as he went to get the coffee started.

Now, five minutes may not sound like much. But for me it's enough for the special time I like to have before I rise each morning, a time of communion with God. Just Him and me. In this place between sleep and awakening, this is my time to think over and be thankful for all the joyous things I am blessed with. This way, when I do get up to greet the day, I wake in a state of thanksgiving and praise. I might be thinking about Franklin, or my daughter, or my grandson, or my son, or about one of my darling dogs—Spice or Sugar or Cajun or C.S. or Allspice or Glaze. Or about a great scene I have to shoot that morning, a check I got yesterday, or how wonderful the day will be because my shooting schedule is short enough that Franklin and I can go out to dinner.

On some days I think of the bigger picture: the joyous journey I am on and how amazing it is that this little girl named Deloreese Patricia Early from the slums of Detroit has grown to be sixty-six years old, is still in the prime of her life and has really, really made it. From the slums to the top of a mountain in Bel Air, California! Every day the journey continues to unfold, letting me live the best time I have ever lived: being who I want to be, loving who I want to love, being loved completely and unconditionally in return, having financial security, experiencing professional fulfillment on a daily basis without limitation or discrimination, basking every moment of my life in the magnificence of God's blessings.

This may sound like a dream or a fantasy to you. It may sound like it's too good to be true. Even in that dreamy pre-awake state, I know it's not a dream and that is why it is so wonderful to begin each day as I do: starting with a gentle nudge from my husband and moving to a complete appreciation for all God has bestowed on me in this present time and place.

As some people age they grow nostalgic for yesteryear. Not me. For me, this really is the best of times. Not too bad to be sixty-six and feeling at the top of your form, is it? I am just hitting my stride. Oh, and it gets better and better. I haven't told you the half of it yet.

You may know the part about the hit television series in which I star as an angel named Tess. That's why Franklin and I spend five days out of the week in Salt Lake City, our home away from home, where *Touched by an Angel* is filmed. You may not know that in addition to my work in the field of entertainment, I have another job on the weekends as a minister and teacher at the church in Los Angeles which I founded sixteen years ago.

I don't want you to think that I've always been a spiritually enlightened person greeting my own congregation on Sunday mornings. As you will see, I wasn't always that way at all. I have done a lot of stupid things and repeated some of the same dumb mistakes while life kept kicking my ass until I got it right.

I don't want to give you the impression that getting here was easy. There were no overnight successes, no meteoric rise. My path was one made of small steps, small victories, small miracles.

At the same time, it has been a wonderful journey, full of excitement, laughter, tears, love, losses, and gains. The road was often rough. There were detours and ruts and trenches and plenty of major roadblocks to overcome. It has been dangerous and harrowing. If I have triumphed it is because of my faith and because of those who appeared in my life along the way, those I call my angels.

Long before they became so popular, long before my television series, I believed in angels. They may not literally have wings, but they come in all shapes, sizes, and colors, and hail from a variety of cultural, religious, ethnic, and socioeconomic backgrounds. I believe they are everywhere.

It is written that God said, "I will send my angels to watch over you." In that sense, angels can be anyone in your life sent by God for a reason. They come to protect you, to teach you, to help you, to love you. They come to change your mind and show you the way when you have lost it. They come as messengers. They bring you what you need at the moment that you need it most—sometimes even when you don't recognize your need.

Angels can be your friends, your lovers, your parents, your teachers, your children. An angel can be the employer who hires you and gives you a chance to prove yourself when you lack the necessary experience. An angel can be someone you've never met, someone whose words, talents, or deeds inspire you to be the best you can be. An angel can be someone who sets the wrong example and scares you away from taking the wrong turn.

Some of the lessons angels bring are just the basics, lessons they don't give big banners for: *Stand fast on what you believe. Trust God. Know that all is well. Remember that when life knocks you down, you can always get right back up again.*

These are simple but powerful messages. They can change your life. They did mine.

I have written this book with an emphasis on my angels, with love and gratitude. It is most gratifying to be at my wise young age and be able to look back and acknowledge those who touched and transformed me for the better. As you will see, there were many times when I was too stubborn or blind to realize who my angels were and how important their messages to me were.

By introducing them to you, it is my sincere hope that if there is something you can take away from having read about me and my life, it will be a recognition of some of the angels in your own life, angels you might not have seen as such before. And if you spot them, why not acknowledge what they've done for you or what they mean to you? Thank them. Love them. Bless them.

To quote the Scripture, "Be careful who you turn away from your door; because it might be an angel unaware."

And I also hope that by coming on my journey with me, you may chance to see yourself in a different light and know that you might be that angel unaware to someone else in your life. If you see that opportunity or if you are already acting on it, acknowledge yourself. Thank yourself. Love yourself.

And God Bless You.

part
one

Learning

1931 – 1949

1

The first thing I really remember is being about three years old and walking down our street, Vernor Highway, where I lived and grew up on the East Side of Detroit. I remember my mother had my hand on one side and my father had my hand on the other side and they were swinging me as we walked along.

I remember how tall my father looked, like a tall tree.

I remember my mother laughing in that way she had. Her body would shake and there would be a smile on her face but no sound. Just this wonderful, infectious shaking.

This is my first memory. I remember being soooo happy. It was soooo much fun.

It must have been some time in the late summer or early fall of 1934, or the following spring, and we were out that evening for our weekly treat. Our first stop was going to be the neighborhood deli where

Mama and Daddy would have corned beef sandwiches, Daddy would have a beer with his, and I would have the hot dog covered in chili with relish and an ice cream sundae to follow. It was true magnificence.

Familiar greetings from neighbors and friends, young and old, followed us as we made our way down the sidewalk.

Today Vernor Highway is a modern freeway; sixty-two years ago it was a wide, four-lane street running north-south, one of the city's main thoroughfares. We lived in the middle of the block, on the third floor of a three-story, twelve-unit apartment building next to the Ed-Sol soap factory. Except for one other apartment building across the street from us, not as big as ours, the rest of the homes around us were single-family houses. That made our building, a red brick structure with light cement trim, the tallest and most imposing on the block. It seemed to me, at least, to be the center of the neighborhood. Towards one corner, past the Ed-Sol factory, were a hamburger stand, a pool hall, and a building which housed the doctor's and dentist's offices upstairs above the drugstore. On the other corner were the deli and the movie theater.

This was our neighborhood, at best a twenty-block area which included a school, a hospital, a fire station, and a church that everyone attended. It was a self-contained world, a community where everybody knew everybody, and everybody knew what everybody else was doing most of the time. And, usually, when the weather was warm, like that night in my early memory, everybody was out, waving from their front porches or sitting together in chairs in their front yards or heading off to destinations of their own.

"Evening, Richard," came a friendly male voice from across the street. That was my father's name, Richard. Mr. Richard Early. Richard Thad Early.

"Good evening to you too," Daddy returned the hello in his rich baritone.

"Miss Nellie, Miss Nellie." A woman's voice called to my mother from behind us and we turned to see her hurrying to catch up. It was the woman from down the street whose baby had been sick with fever, for whom Mama had made one of her home remedies from the herbs and roots she grew on our back porch. "Thank you, Miss Nellie, God bless you," our neighbor said, informing us that her child was miraculously fine again.

That was Miss Nellie, my mama, Mrs. Richard Early. It didn't matter whether your ailment was physical, emotional, or spiritual, in our neighborhood everyone knew that my mother could heal whatever it was.

Hearing the good news about our neighbor's baby would have brought a knowing, happy nod from my mother, as if to say she had known that everything would be fine because she had prayed to God about it. That was all there was to it. Mama was a Christian and talked to God all day long, if not in prayer, then in open conversation. With most people, she wasn't a big talker, not unless she had something meaningful to say. The rest of the time, at home on her own or at work, she sort of moaned and hummed as she communed with the Lord throughout the day.

My mother, born Nellie Mitchelle, was a full-blooded Cherokee originally from Dyersberg, Tennessee, not far from Memphis. She liked to say she was four foot twelve inches tall—not five feet, not four-eleven—and she was maybe about that wide. She was soft, cuddly, and jolly in a quiet, inner way. And so beautiful. Mama had silky dark hair that she sat on, it was so long, and I loved when she let me comb it and fashion braids into buns on either side of her head, like a little Dutch girl.

In school, my mother hadn't completed past the sixth grade but her knowledge was of a different nature and she was considered, rightfully so, to be one of the wisest individuals in the community. For me, for Daddy, and for everyone we knew, Mama was psychic, psychiatrist, psychologist, physician, and cooker of the greatest tasting pots in captivity.

Wise as my mother was, she was never boastful about it. She had beautiful dreams and thoughts. And she was a great listener. She had time to listen to all the neighbors' problems and she gave sound advice. Everyone knew that Miss Nellie sided with the truth. No matter what, she could offer a positive reason to carry on, help you see your concern another way, or give you an insight that put you in the other person's shoes.

Mama had this wonderful, distinctive smell that enveloped my childhood and adolescence. The aroma was a mixture of Ponds Cleansing and Cold Cream, vanilla, and spices. Ponds and Ivory soap were her only beauty articles. The vanilla was her cologne and because as a cook she was in the kitchen so much—either at home or in restaurants where she worked—I guess the spices just sort of permeated her skin. There was never a warmer, safer place for me than cuddled up in my mother's loving, aromatic arms.

And as far as fun and excitement were concerned, there was nowhere I would have rather been than going somewhere—anywhere— when my father was along. It was like being out with royalty. In the neighborhood, Daddy was known as King Tut. He was what in those days was referred to as a gay blade (when gay meant fun-filled), a player, who, after providing for all the family's needs, liked to go out to ramble and gamble.

Six foot two inches tall, King Tut was regal in attitude and demeanor, yet he was also a no-nonsense, practical man. And he was so, so handsome. There was a definite strength in his pantherlike walk, a slow, long stride that exuded power. My father may have been a Detroit steelworker, a man who literally poured steel from sunup to sundown, week in and week out for thirty-five years, but for all intents and purposes this man was an aristocrat.

Richard Thad Early had migrated to Detroit with his parents and siblings from rural Arkansas, from somewhere so small it wasn't even a town. He was a naturally gifted storyteller with a special flair for the telling of funny incidents. Great timing and great wit. Daddy knew where the punch line belonged. His regal status was underscored by his role in the community as toastmaster and member of the Masons. Whenever there were introductions or speeches at weddings or anniversaries or christenings, Richard Early was in demand. Some of the toasts he made were funny standard lines he had for the proper occasion. Other times he spoke poignantly and memorably from his heart and the words simply flowed from him spontaneously.

Daddy's clothes were not expensive but he wore them as if they were. Mama kept them immaculately clean and everything was ironed. *Ever-ry-thing.* Undershirts, undershorts. Even his socks. The starch in the shirt had to be just so—no cat faces in the sleeves, but rolled—and the crease in the pants just so. Not because he insisted everything be perfect but because my mother thought it should be for him. Even though there wasn't a lot sent to the cleaners, if any item did not meet with Mrs. Early's approval, it was returned to be redone to her specifications.

Evidently in my parents' case, the way to my father's heart had been through his stomach. It seems my mother was cooking at a particular local restaurant my father patronized. My father went there one evening and noticed this pretty woman working there; once he ate her food, he was hooked for life. You would be too. My mother's cooking wasn't just good. It was unparalleled. She could cook anything. She could cook you this book and even if you knew you were eating a damn book, you'd be asking, "Oh, please, Miss Nellie, please give me another bite!"

Mama had been married two times before. In her first marriage she gave birth to three girls—Nodie, Susan, and Gladys. Through her second marriage she gave birth to Ora Mae and the child she always referred to as "my only son," Rufus David, whom we affectionately called R.D. My brother lived with his father on the other side of town. I didn't meet him until I was six; it was even longer before I met my other sisters, all of whom were grown and living in other cities. My mother didn't talk about her previous marriages or disparage her ex-husbands. All I knew was that she missed her children deeply and prayed for more opportunities to be with them.

After my parents were married a couple of years, Mama thought she had a tumor in her stomach and went to be examined.

"No tumor, Mrs. Early," the doctor told her, "you are seven months pregnant."

That was me, Deloreese Patricia Early, born July 6, 1931. My mother was forty-two at the time of my birth.

After me, Mama and Daddy had no other children. That made me the baby, his baby. I was basically raised as an only child and I loved it.

In both looks and personality, I inherited or learned traits from each of my parents. My coloring was a mixture of theirs, hers light, his dark. Later on, I was blessed to grow tall like Daddy and I, too, could enjoy a party; some of the blessings I got from my mama included the ability to live with myself, peace of mind, and a sense that God is my sufficiency in all things.

So, there we were, the three of us, swinging down Vernor Highway to the delicatessen. The Earlys. Rich, that was what Mama called Daddy, and Babe, he called her, and Ma, as everyone called me from the time I could walk. They gave me that nickname because they said I mothered everybody and everything and that I mimicked, with additions, my mother. Rich, Babe, and Ma.

After our feast at the deli, my stomach so full of chili hot dog and ice cream sundae I thought I might pop, my father walked my mother and me next door to the Arcadia Movie Theater, leaving us there to see our Monday night show, then heading off on his own, maybe to the pool hall or somewhere else in the neighborhood where men liked to congregate.

I grew up at the movies, at my mother's side. We went on Monday nights because the movie changed at midnight and we could see the movies for Sunday, Monday, Tuesday, Wednesday, and Thursday—all for one price. By the time the two double features were over, it was two o'clock in the morning. On Saturday nights we saw the show for Friday and Saturday. We couldn't watch all four pictures on Saturday night because the following day was filled with activities at church.

All those late nights at the movies weren't a problem for me or any of the other children who went with their parents in our neighborhood. We'd all play together in the theater until we got sleepy and it was time to curl up in our mother's arms or on their laps and go to sleep. It was not unlike the way that the TV can be a babysitter nowadays.

We loved all the movies, from the newsreels to the cartoons to the comedies, the musicals, the romances, the cowboy pictures, the action serials with their ten or twelve different installments, the dramas, even the scary movies. We loved all the stars. The women: Bette Davis, Joan Crawford, Barbara Stanwyck, Carmen Miranda, Greer Garson. The men: Tyrone Power, Clark Gable, Robert Taylor, Ronald Colman. There were the Three Stooges, Groucho Marx, Chester Morrison, Johnnie Mack Brown, Gene Autry, Roy Rogers, Lash LaRue. There were the serials' stars: Captain Marvel and Superman. And then there were my favorites: Shirley Temple, Lena Horne, and Ethel Waters—who was the one I really loved the most.

Mama and I were not fond of Greta Garbo. She was too cold, too aloof. We preferred the actors and actresses who were warmer, people we could relate to no matter how different our circumstances.

My mother loved the movies, that was her sin, her only vice. As soon as we left the movie theater, she'd start praying, "Lord, I know I ain't got no business out here this late. I'm working on this movie habit, Lord, I know I shouldn't do it. Forgive me, Lord, and see me safely home." Mama felt it was a very bad thing for a Christian lady like her to be out to two o'clock in the morning at the movies, seeing these stories of worldly pleasures and places. But she had this movie jones and just couldn't help herself. She loved going to those other places, places she could dream about and keep inside her as she lived in the reality of her day to day existence. She prayed all the way home and after she got me settled in bed, she'd go to the living room and say good-night to God, praying one last prayer before she went to sleep, asking for forgiveness. She was serious, very serious.

My mother's praying chair was this big green overstuffed chair with big arms that I loved to sit on but was forbidden to do so. There weren't many discussions about the rules. It was just understood that there was no trespassing on my parents' green chair. After dinner it was my father's newspaper reading chair and during the day and late at night it was her special chair, her praying chair.

Our home was Mama's treasure, and her husband's castle. Their roles were defined to me in black and white. My mother loved my father and there was never a doubt but that he was the head of the house and the law. Period, the end. Likewise, Daddy loved Mama and respected her. And though he was the head of the house, she was the ruler. So it was Mama who called the shots in his castle. And he was exceedingly glad she did.

Our house wasn't fancy but it was comfortable and Mama kept it so immaculate you could eat directly off any surface—including the floor. I didn't know that we were poor. We were doing better than anyone else around us, it seemed. And we were forever helping the other neighbors. My mother always had enough to spare and share. You could get her last anything because she sincerely believed the Lord would always supply our needs.

And being that this was the time of the Depression, something I knew nothing about, there were days when we did have big needs, when money was short and there wasn't anything to eat. At those times, Mama never succumbed to depression or anxiety, she simply talked to the Father. She would sit down in the big green chair, her feet crossed sort of yoga-style, and begin to moan and hum one of the hymns. And she'd speak to the Lord, thanking Him for all He'd done for her and assuring Him that she knew He would never let her down because He had never let her down before.

She and God would work it out. And they always did.

I am not lying or exaggerating. How do I mean that? Well, if she had prayed all night not to let us go hungry, lo and behold, the next morning someone from the neighborhood was at the door saying, "Miss Nellie, my husband bought bread and so did I and it's gonna spoil"—in those days no one had refrigerators or freezers so food went bad quickly—"could you use some of it? I hate to see it go to waste."

For years, I thought she was a witch because she could do things like that. Whatever it was, I knew she could fix, handle, make better anything in the world and that she would always be there for me with love, truth, and understanding.

Mama made God one of the family. He wasn't distant or remote or mysterious. He lived with us, inside us, ever-present. This was a fundamental gift my mother bestowed on me, giving me a personal relationship with God that has sustained me through my life and continues to do so today.

⌒— By sharing her love of the movies with me, Mama gave me another kind of gift.

Like her, at the movies I could go to other places and other worlds so different from my own. These were exotic places like the Riviera, or Mexico, or the Caribbean, places that until then I had only seen on a map. They were warm, tropical places where it was never cold, places I had no idea I would ever go to one day. But I could go to them in the movies. These places gave me pictures in my mind about romance and glamour and about marvelous people who had and did marvelous things. In a few movies I saw where the starlets slept on big round beds covered with pillows and satin, with satin drapes hanging from the walls and over the windows. I just had to have a round bed. When I went home, I cut out a piece of paper into a large circle and put it on my own little twin bed. That was my satin-covered big round bed.

In the movies, women wore thin clothes of shimmering fabrics, gowns that flowed and moved. They wore sparkling jewelry and drank sparkling champagne from sparkling glasses. They had nice things. Pretty things. I didn't have those nice things but through the movies I could. I could be Ethel Waters. I could be Hedy Lamarr or Bette Davis or Joan Crawford.

In fact, from the time I was three, it became a regular event to do the movies of that week for Daddy. I acted out the stories, imitated the different actors, sang their songs. I was funny and snappy like Louise Beavers. I was Shirley Temple dancing with Bill Robinson. I was the beautiful, sophisticated Lena Horne. I'd pop my eyes like Mantan More-land or slink around and be slow and lazy like Willie Best of "Feet Don't Fail Me Now." That living room floor of ours was probably my first stage and my father my first audience.

After work, when Daddy finished his dinner, it was time for him to retire to the living room, sit down in the big green chair, and read the newspaper. I played for a while as he relaxed and then, when he was ready, I began.

Sometimes, so excited to tell him all the scary or funny parts, my words tumbled out of me on top of each other. No matter what I said, if he couldn't understand me, he had only one thing to say: "Who died?"

"Oh, uh, Daddy, w-w-w-wait until I tell, you, uh, oh . . ."

"Who died?" he would interrupt with a stern look until I slowed down, chose and articulated my words carefully and with clear expression, causing him, at last, to grin in approval.

Thanks to my father, I learned the importance of good diction and articulation at an early age and practiced it for many years under his roof. When I later began my singing and acting careers, this would prove to be a most valuable asset. Also, I'm sure it didn't hurt to be exposed to his humor and his storytelling, especially the way his words made pictures in your mind. He used vivid description. You could always see what he was talking about.

I loved making my father laugh and watching his proud face as I performed the movies for him. I loved his eyes, so deep and welcoming, not dark brown, not light brown, but somewhere in between. I loved how they lit up when he saw me, at the end of the day, for instance, when I ran down the steps in our building to meet him as he arrived home from his long hours of work. My father was not overly demonstrative—neither of my parents were—but he always let me know that I was his baby and that he loved me.

Daddy and Mama had very different methods of teaching. His approach was to give me direct instructions or information. He would say it once and then ask, "Do you understand what I just told you?" Before I could answer, Daddy would continue, "Then I expect it to be done immediately."

If it was not done correctly per instructions there was no time for me to explain the circumstances. Mama, on the other hand, had to know every detail of what and how and why. And when she gave me instructions, she could talk for a week. She explained it so many ways, in so much detail, until there was no possibility of a doubtful or wondering look on my face. Mama was actually my first acting coach because I worked so hard to get my face just right to make her stop talking so I could go out and play.

Normally, Mama would work until it was time to go to bed. But on special occasions she was able to join us after dinner in the living room, where she sat quietly on the couch, crocheting while Daddy read the paper, laughing in her soundless way as I reenacted the recent movies we'd seen. She loved to crochet and we had doilies on everything—tables, backs of chairs, the couch, and tiny ones for her "what-not" shelves.

We lived in a railroad flat, which was one long hallway with the various rooms lining it. At one end of the hall was the master bedroom. Next to that, as you opened the front door to the apartment, was the second bedroom, the third bedroom halfway down the hall, and off of that to the left was the bathroom. The living room was at the other end of the hall; off of it was my bedroom and on the other side the kitchen and the back door.

Our home was so cozy and inviting, especially with Miz Nellie's wonderful smelling kitchen, it was at our house that the neighborhood women gathered frequently. When I was around three years old, if they wanted to talk about grown-up lady things which I wasn't supposed to hear, they'd send me for a glass of water.

If one mentioned how thirsty she was, one of the other ladies would say, "Send Ma, she gets the coldest water. It tastes so good."

It was true. After a while, though, Mama began to wonder how that could be. I was too small to reach up into the ice box and she knew the tap water wasn't that cold.

As I said earlier, in those days there were no refrigerators. If there were, neither we nor anyone else in our neighborhood could afford one. Instead, we had this box high atop a wooden cabinet that held fifty pounds of ice which dripped as it melted into a pan underneath that had to be emptied regularly.

So one day when they sent me for a glass of water, Mama followed me and found me getting the cold water out of the toilet bowl. I would flush the toilet and catch the glass full, nice and cold, and take it to whatever very thirsty woman had asked for it.

Well. From then on, they still sent me out of the room. But never again to bring water.

As time went on, I realized that if my mother sent me outside to play so she could have some privacy, I could sneak back and hide in my bedroom which was next to the living room and still be able to hear all the juicy grown-up talk I wasn't supposed to hear.

Using this ruse I was often able to overhear different neighbors coming to Mama for her advice.

One afternoon Miss Janie, a very large friend of my mother, stopped by. Miss Janie weighed three hundred fifty pounds. Despite her girth, she was surprisingly light on her feet, even graceful. When she arrived, I was promptly sent out. Listening from my bedroom, I heard Miss Janie confide in my mother about her husband problems. She was married to a man who cared for her fine, although, it seemed, he wasn't at all romantic. But Miss Janie's soul was so romantic.

"Is he a good provider to you?" Mama asked Miss Janie.

"Yes, he is. He takes good care of me," she admitted, explaining however that he didn't hug her and kiss her the way she wanted him to. "Why can't he kiss me sometimes?" poor Miss Janie complained.

Mama was silent. Then I heard her say softly to Miss Janie, "He's not that kind of man. He loves you in his way. You can't change him and if you love him, you'll have to do it as he is, 'cause that's just who he is."

Miss Janie agreed, thanking Mama, as she resolved to appreciate what she did have, "You're right, Miss Nellie. I have to remember that. He loves me in his way."

My mother genuinely cared for people. And she would keep your secrets. She was not a gossip. She abhorred gossiping. You could talk to her about anything but there were some things she would not talk to you about: her children problems or her husband problems. Family was personal and I mean *perrr-sonnn-allll!*

Because everyone confided in Mama, I usually got an earful from my spy post in my bedroom. That was wonderful unless Mama found out. Naturally, she always did. She always found out whatever I did that I wasn't supposed to have done. I don't know how. It was scary. I thought she could read minds or see through walls. It was that psychic thing.

Oh, and she was psychic in other ways. Over the years she'd often give me warnings, for example, that she had a bad feeling about me riding the bus that day—and then, sure enough, I wouldn't ride it and the bus would end up in an accident. As I told you earlier, I was convinced she had to be a witch.

When I got into trouble, a lot of the time it was my own mouth that did it. Say I had hidden and eavesdropped when Miss Janie was confiding her secrets to Mama and had managed to get away with it, somehow the next day right as my mother was trying to make a point with me, I would blurt out something along the lines of: "That wasn't what you said to Miss Janie yesterday!"

Even if my Mama didn't have ESP, it was not easy to get away with anything in a neighborhood like ours where everybody was aware that I was the child of Richard and Nellie Early. Everybody had direct permission from my mother to stop me from doing anything they thought was wrong. Mama didn't allow anyone else to touch me but she gave everybody the authority to speak to me and, if necessary, escort me home to her. This later became a pain in my lower posterior, especially in my teen years when it seemed the entire neighborhood was following my courtships and reporting back to my mother.

But the bottom line was that these adults were my extended family. I knew they all loved me a lot and that my well-being was really their chief concern.

In this family of grown-ups was a cast of loving and interesting characters. At the top of that list was the woman who lived right across the hall from us, someone I considered my real sister—even if we weren't blood related. Her name was Louise Hatcher, a very attractive woman, about thirty-five or so. Very flamboyant. Her husband was the head baker at one of the largest bakeries in Detroit. In our neighborhood, that kind of a job for a Negro (as we were called then) was a biggie.

Louise had such pretty things. Clothes, makeup, jewelry. And she let me play with some of those things too. Though she made me mind, Louise wasn't as strict as Mama. She treated me as her favorite baby sister—not like my other sisters who lived far away and I wouldn't meet for many years—and Louise was like a daughter to Mama too.

This is what I mean by God sending angels to give you what you need. My mother missed her older daughters fiercely and, just as I needed and yearned for a sister to love, Mama needed someone who appreciated her like Louise, whom she could look after and care for as she would have her own daughters if she could have. Louise was that angel for Mama and me.

Louise's husband, Jimmy, was nice and loved her very much. But he was not very exciting and Louise had this torrid love affair going on with Jack, a married man who lived down the street. They wrote love notes to each other and had me deliver them—with a quarter for each delivery. Because I was so small, no one in the neighborhood suspected that I was the go-between. I thought their relationship was so romantic. Just like in the movies Mama and I saw.

Louise was my diversion from the humdrum. She seemed always to be involved in some daring, magnificent situation.

Then there was Annie Mack from down the street who was *the* character of the neighborhood. Didn't matter what the occasion, Annie Mack would arrive in formal wear, along with hat, gloves, shoes, and pocketbook—outfitted in ensembles like nothing we nor anybody else had ever seen. She designed her own wardrobe based on ideas from high-fashion magazines. But by the time her sewing lady had finished and she put it on, the end result always looked a little strange. Annie didn't care. She saw herself as absolutely beautiful. And, really, on the inside, she was one of the most beautiful, giving, concerned, sweet ladies you could meet. She adored Mama and was always giving me nice things, including her hand-me-downs. Once Mama took off the garland of roses or the marabou collar, the dresses were usually just nice, straight Simplicity patterns that eventually worked fine for me.

Jacquline Baylock was close to my age and my nearest playmate. Her family lived on the third floor of our building also, at the other end of the porch. Jacquline's mother, Mrs. Baylock, was a real live lady barber which was very unusual for a woman in those times. We never knew exactly what Mr. Baylock did for a living. But they had "good money," my father used to say. In other words, they had more than us and maybe more than anybody else in the building.

That was hard for me to believe because my daddy was such a good provider. It was my father who taught me to appreciate the value of a hard-earned dollar, an appreciation I have never lost. Together he and Mama, his "helpmeet," did everything they could to make ends meet. And they did—with even enough left over to put a little away into the "rainy day" can. Living as we did, we never knew when that rainy day was coming.

Rainy day or not, my father never, ever missed a day of work in his adult life. He worked sick or well, drunk or sober.

Daddy liked his nip a whole lot. He started every day off at four-thirty in the morning with three fingers of Calvert's Reserve—or Four Roses or some similar whiskey—mixed with three teaspoons of sugar. He drank that drink every morning not to get drunk but for the medicinal benefit. It gave him energy.

Then Mama fixed him a full breakfast, a meal the size most people eat at night: biscuits, eggs, ham, pork chops, rice (Daddy loved rice). Afterwards, she poured him this big cup of coffee and one for herself and the two of them sat together, talking quietly.

If I was awake I could hear them since my bedroom was between the kitchen and living room.

Whenever my father brought up a concern to my mother, something that might take a few days for him to fully get off his chest, Mama would inevitably reassure him. If it was a money problem or a personality conflict at work, no matter what, she had familiar words to say: "Rich, I don't know how God will make a way out but I know He will." She knew God would fix it because she had been praying and her prayers were always answered.

This was utter nonsense to Daddy. He had familiar words, too: "Babe, now you know, if you want your prayers answered you got to get up off your knees and hustle." He said that so much Mama embroidered it on a sampler and made it into a wall hanging he hung above his bed.

One of the ways Daddy made extra money was with his Friday night poker games. Unfortunately, he had a habit of losing whatever he'd won that night by making some outrageous bet at the end of a game. Being the *house* was about the only way Daddy would actually make money from poker. That was fun for me because the game was held in the living room so, as usual, I could listen and peep from my bedroom.

As toastmaster of the games, my father might begin with a few toasts and introductions which were followed by great laughter and then, as the cards were being dealt, great seriousness. Everything became very still. Then from someone: A sigh of tension from one player. Then nervous laughter from another. Then others chimed in with a joke or a compliment or a boast or bluff.

When Daddy made one of his wild bets, I could tell how much he loved the excitement. I could hear it in his voice. He would holler loud and talk gambler trash and he would seem so happy or sad as the cards went—all of it that I heard and imagined through my bedroom door.

On other Fridays after work when the games weren't at our house, Daddy began his weekend with a long bath. He trimmed his fingernails, soaked his feet, and trimmed his toenails that were so thick you could hear them as they hit against the walls or the dresser or the trunk in his room. After powdering himself head to toe, he dressed to the nines: white shirt, his best suit and tie, and his dress-up shoes.

The tie had to have just the right crick in it—hooked at the bottom of the knot just a little to the right. He spent forever getting that crick. Then he spent even longer with the cock of his hat. The brim had to be broken just right—a little to the left.

When he was satisfied, Daddy walked through the apartment in his King Tut long-legged slow panther walk so Mama and me could admire him. And finally he would leave and be gone until Sunday afternoon after church.

The church in our neighborhood that everybody attended was the Olivet Baptist Church. My mother and I had lots to do there all Sunday long. There was Sunday school and church service, and serving the food for after the service, and then gospel singing practice, and the meeting of the Baptist Young People's Union.

I loved every minute of it. More than anything, church was getting-together time. The families could socialize and us kids could run and play and sing. I really liked the singing part.

By the time Mama and I arrived home from church we knew Daddy would be showing up soon. Sure enough, round about three o'clock, we'd see him making it across the vacant lot on Montcalm Street to the back gate of our building.

This was the same man who had left so immaculately clean and coiffed on Friday night. Now, the weekend over, his hat that was cocked just right was gone (it was always returned by Tuesday after work), the un-cricked tie was now across his shoulder, his pants twisted, coat all falling off almost down his back.

Here comes Daddy, leaning on the wind, happy and cussing this character he always talks to when he's drunk, this character who is some-times friend and sometimes frightening enemy. So, Mama and me, we run downstairs to get him. Sometimes he lets us, sometimes not. But one way or another we get him upstairs where Mama can sponge him down and put him to bed.

In a few hours it would be four-thirty Monday morning and my fa-ther would wake up, eat his breakfast, and leave to start a new week's work at Detroit Steel Products.

As you surely must realize by now, in a neighborhood like ours, everybody knew what my father was up to his nights away from us. And I am also sure that my mother, who was anything but a fool, was proba-bly the first to know but would not let it disturb her one iota.

During those times when I was eavesdropping from in my bedroom, it was interesting to overhear some misguided lady with the audacity to make a comment to Mama about it. Every now and then some "well-intentioned" alleged friend would; especially if Daddy had really had a sensational weekend—beat up somebody or got beaten or been seen with what the nice ladies called "some chippy."

So the minute a remark was made, even the most well-intentioned remark, Mama would turn and speak very quietly, in an icy voice: "You do not know my husband and so you couldn't understand him or what he does . . ." By this point Mama would be standing over her "friend's" chair with her hand under the woman's armpit. Before the woman knew what was happening she was on her way out the back door.

I loved that rush act. It got so the other women would warn anyone who started in by saying, "No need to try to help her, Miss Nellie won't thank you for it," which was *absotively posolutely* correct.

⌒⎯ Let me say here, in the event you haven't observed this yet about me as a small child, that I've always been an "all or nothing" kind of person. That was the situation when I was three years old and was pronounced gravely ill with rheumatic fever.

This was over sixty years ago. Without all the medical advances that have been made since then, a bout with rheumatic fever was a very scary thing. Rheumatic fever is an infection that first attacks the joints. In its most severe form it affects the heart and can do permanent damage. The symptoms tend to recur and these recurring attacks tend to weaken the heart. The doctors told my mother that I had the worst case possible. They were very pessimistic. The illness would damage my circulatory system, they said, and I would never walk again.

Mama wouldn't hear of it. There was no way she was going to accept their prognosis.

You should know by now what she did. Yes—you are right—she talked to the Father.

She told me that I was going to be well soon and that the illness was not coming back. You know why? Because she had prayed and God was taking care of it.

Then my mother proceeded to become the next Sister Kenny, the woman who found a treatment for polio while Jonas Salk discovered the cure. Mama had read about Sister Elizabeth Kenny in the newspaper and, as a loyal listener to Kate Smith's radio show, had heard Kate Smith interview Sister Kenny about her treatment that used a combination of hot and cold compresses.

My mother was Sister Kenny all over me. And as she tended my body, she also tended my spirit. Each day she wrapped my legs first with hot, then cold towels, massaging my legs as she told me how God made legs in the first place. As she changed the towels and continued the massage, together we thanked God that my legs were perfect. And soon, they were and I have never had a problem with them since.

My mother always allowed me to see her faith working. She said God would take care of me and He did.

After that, I was rarely sick. If I ever threatened to come down with something, Mama made sure to mix me up one of her home remedies. She was an herbologist, a bona fide expert in the use of herbs and roots and in the knowledge of their medicinal benefits. She would make hot drinks of the herbs, or poultices, or hang whatever it was around my neck. To this day I can't stand to wear a necklace because of all those years she was forever hanging some strange-smelling root around my throat.

When I got to be a teenager, Mama tried her best to teach me herbology and I would not have anything to do with it. To me it was Mammy-made. I was a modern high-schooler and didn't want to learn all that antiquated mumbo-jumbo. Fifty years later I'm going to every herbologist in the world, spending an arm and a leg to find cures she made back then.

See what I mean about doing dumb stuff?

Similarly, my mother was a remarkable seamstress. I never appreciated it. I wanted to wear store-bought dresses like I saw in the magazines and like the other girls had. Of course, here I am later in life, spending a fortune for a dressmaker so I don't have to buy clothes from the store.

Dumb again.

Except for herbology, which my mother learned from her upbringing, there was little else I can remember hearing about Cherokee beliefs and customs. One superstition she did maintain was the idea that having your photograph taken would steal your soul.

As a result, there are hardly any pictures of Mama in existence. The one I keep and cherish was taken by surprise as she came around the corner. She didn't like that at all. Even so, the expression on her beautiful face in the photograph is one of pure serenity.

⌒— I see my mother's face in my mind today and I can smell the aroma of Ponds Cold Cream, vanilla, and spices. I see my father's face, his deep eyes, his regal walk. These were my first two angels whom God sent to give me exactly what I needed to make it in a world that was not at all easy.

I am so blessed to have entered the world through my mother and to have spent my formative years in her love and tenderness and tutoring in the basic principles of my life. I am so blessed to have received from my father and mother the groundwork which gave me the strength to weather the life situations and challenges I've had to face on the road out of the slums to the top of the mountain, where I now reside in the greatest of comfort.

I don't suspect my parents envisioned where I would come to. That wasn't important. The important principle they taught me was to live successfully where I was, not to strive for another better day to be happier but to make the best of the present.

My parents were the angels who taught me the lessons of self-reliance and belief in self. At the same time they taught me that God would be there to help with whatever I couldn't handle on my own.

That is called faith. I learned it from a father who was practical and a mother who dreamed. I learned it looking at a man who had nothing but who provided everything. I learned it listening to a woman telling me, "God will find a way out." I couldn't argue with success.

Despite what happened next, an abiding faith was instilled in me forever. Faith would bring me through the road ahead, never flagging. If my faith ever failed me, I probably would be dead by now.

I learned to really believe—and you can add a thousand more

reallys—that the Lord loves me and wants only the best for me. That is an absolute. I made mistakes and I will again. I know I may step out of the light and go off and make the biggest mess in the world. But I always know that I can step back into the light.

I have known that since I was Babe's and Rich's little girl.

2

During the time I was still bedridden and recovering from rheumatic fever, another angel appeared in my life. Her name was Bernice White. A beautiful young lady in her early twenties—feminine, pretty, bright, and a most loving human being—Bernice and her husband moved into one of the apartments downstairs in our building.

Bernice loved me from the moment she set eyes on me and was happy to come look out after me whenever Mama had to go work in the restaurant. Bernice had fun entertaining me during my recuperation. Unbeknownst to me at the time, she was actually teaching me by inventing all sorts of educational games. These were games that taught me to count, games that taught me my letters, games that taught me to spell. She was such a good teacher and made learning so much fun for me that by the time I fully recovered from the rheumatic fever and got up out of bed, I could recite my alphabet and say my numbers to one hundred.

Whenever we went out in the neighborhood Bernice was like my agent, encouraging other adults, "Oh, you should hear Ma do her alphabet. You should hear her count." They had no trouble getting me to do it because whenever I did they seemed to find me so amazing and they would tell me how smart and cute I was. I really liked that. So did Bernice.

I really liked doing anything with Bernice. She was as lovely as all the women in the movie magazines, almost like a young Lena Horne—or a Halle Berry of today. And she was what they called "common law married" to this *hunk*. (Back then in the state of Michigan, six months of cohabitation was enough for a common-law marriage.) Gorgeous! Not much good but gorgeous. How gorgeous was he? He was the most attractive man in the neighborhood. Young like Bernice, he was cool—nothing ever excited him—and he had *savoir faire*. As a four-year-old child, I certainly didn't know what *savoir faire* meant but he had it. He was the first man I saw who was unafraid to show his affections to his woman where others could see it. He was forever lovin' up Bernice. I thought that was wonderful.

Bernice loved children, it was obvious; he, on the other hand, didn't want children. "I'm young and have life to live," he was glad to point out, "and I can't be tied down to feeding and clothing no child."

As usual, God really knew what He was doing when He put Bernice in my life, as well as putting me in hers. She needed a child she could love and teach. I needed someone young like her to show me that learning was a wonderful, exciting experience. What a gift that was to me at my early age, at a time before I began school and encountered all the many obstacles to learning I would face. Not surprisingly, I went on to become an avid reader as a child and teen, my nose always buried in some book or another. Bernice helped give that hunger to me and a good hunger it was. "That Ma," Mama used to say, "she eats books."

Bernice arrived at our house one morning when I was about four and a half and announced, "Listen Ma, this morning I'm taking you to go see the principal at Bishop Grade School. We have an appointment."

She dressed me up in my best dress and my best shoes and the two of us walked over to the school. In the principal's office, I was introduced to the principal and the kindergarten teacher. Then Bernice had me do my letters and numbers for them. Afterwards, the principal and the kindergarten teacher conferred briefly.

The kindergarten teacher explained that I was much more advanced than the children in her class and that I belonged in the first grade.

"How old did you say Deloreese is?" the principal asked Bernice.

"She's five years old," Bernice answered, smiling her prettiest, proudest smile.

"All right," said the principal. "She'll start next week in the first grade." I was to start in One-A, as opposed to One-B, which was how they split the grades up in those days according to the level of the students.

That was how I skipped kindergarten and began school at the age of four and a half in the first grade.

From that day on, Mama began to impress upon me the importance of having an education. None of my older sisters had graduated from high school and Mama felt responsible because—through no fault of her own—she hadn't been able to raise them and give them the chance. And so, to make up for it, it became my mother's major goal in life to see me graduate from high school.

Bishop Grade School was close enough to our house that I was able to walk home each day for lunch. While we ate together, Mama and I listened to the midday radio shows we both loved. *Kate Smith* was first, followed by *Our Gal Sunday* and then *Helen Trent*. Like the movies, the radio was another way for us to dream and travel to other places. And there were more exciting things to hear on the radio in the evenings after Daddy came home from work and the three of us would gather to listen together once dinner was over and he finished his paper reading.

Like the movies, the radio shows were a regular topic of discussion in the neighborhood—whether it was to fuss about the *awful* thing that had happened on a soap opera or laugh about a joke on a comedy or try to solve one of the cliffhanger mysteries on the detective shows. Then there were the times when Joe Louis was going to fight and everybody, I mean *ever-ry-body,* got together and prayed before we listened to the radio broadcast. When Joe Louis came on, the world stopped. Traffic on the streets came to a dead halt. Inside homes, at the pool hall or the bar, not a word was spoken until the fight was over. Nothing else mattered. This happened in our neighborhood and everywhere in black neighborhoods (we were called Negroes then) wherever radios reached. In my childhood days, no one came close to Joe Louis. He was an inspiration to a generation of black men and women, boys and girls. He was *the* hero, a black man that the world respected in a time when so few black people were given respect by the world. All of us, consciously or not, had our hopes and dreams tied to his accomplishments. When he won, he won for us. He won not only a boxing match, but freedom, fairness, equality, justice, dignity.

The radio was also where everyone kept up-to-date on the popular music of the time. However, of the secular music I heard on the radio (the standard fare of the thirties and forties) not much stands out in my mind except for Kate Smith who had a strong, belting voice that impressed me. Other than her, my musical roots came directly from the church. My first songs were the hymns and the gospel songs which included, most memorably: "Near the Cross," "Yes Jesus Loves Me," "His Eye Is on the Sparrow," "The Old Ship of Zion," and "Swing Low, Sweet Chariot."

When the choir leader at Olivet Baptist Church discovered that, small as I was, I could carry a tune, keep tempo, and remember all the words, I was made a soloist with the choir. By the time I was six, they started having me sing solos at the end of the service, right before they passed the collection plate. In a way they were using me—but for a good cause. They did the same whenever our choir was singing on the radio and listeners were being invited to come to the Olivet Baptist Church. The idea was to have my young voice singing over the airwaves to show what a fun place our church was for children.

Singing on the radio was a big deal and all the neighbors were proud that their very own Deloreese Early was beginning life as a prodigy. I didn't know what that meant but when someone said it I thought it sounded good and was happy to be it. Then, one hot afternoon when I was over at Jacquline Baylock's, my friend at the other end of the porch, I got an idea.

"Let's do a concert!" I proposed. Jacquline was taking piano lessons and I wanted to play piano, so I spent a lot of time at her house watching her play and singing along to whatever her lessons were at the time.

"A concert?" she asked, looking nervous already.

"You play, I sing," said I, the young entrepreneur. "We can invite everybody in the building and charge admission. Twenty-five cents a person."

Jacquline was hesitant. I was insistent.

Finally, she agreed and we decided upon three songs. We did two of her lessons, "Barcarole" and "La Ploma," and I wanted to do "What a Friend We Have in Jesus."

On the following Sunday after church, a large group from the neighborhood and our building came up to the Baylocks' for the concert. The turnout was tremendous: our parents, my big sister Louise from across the hall, sporting a new flamboyant hat for the occasion, Louise's nice husband Jimmy the head baker, Louise's sister Allie Mae with her hips slinging as usual, a smiling, proud Bernice and her gorgeous husband, 350-pound Miss Janie walking so light on her feet with her unromantic but good-hearted husband, and Annie Mack from down the street wearing one of her newest and quite amusing fashion creations. There was Mr. Jones, the building janitor, who was a mean man but paid his admission, and his wife Mrs. Jones (who put up with her surly husband as best she could until she had to say something which caused him to beat her). Completing the crowd were a smattering of other adults and their children.

Our first two songs went over big, and the finale, "What a Friend We Have in Jesus," brought down the house. We were a hit! When we counted our earnings, we were ecstatic to find we had made $4.25 each.

My first financial success. Jacquline and I raced to the corner drugstore for ice cream and a stash of candy. Were we ever happy? Yes-sir-ree.

It wasn't really about the money. For me, it was about doing something I loved to do and giving enjoyment to all these people I loved at the same time. We had great prestige after the concert. *Ever-ry-one* talked about us for weeks to come. My first taste of celebrity!

This singing thing was for me. After that, I discovered a wondrous place to practice, develop, and experiment with my voice. It was in our bathroom, singing out the window where there was a skylight shared by all six bathrooms in the apartments on our side of the building, alongside another skylight that was for all six apartment bathrooms on the other side of the building. Somehow, I discovered one day that by singing in the skylight, my voice would travel, bouncing around in that shaft which went from basement to roof, doing amazing things. Things like reverberation and amplification. No, I didn't know what those words were. What I knew was that if I sang in this skylight, my voice was big and ringing and I loved the way I sounded.

Cleaning the bathroom was the chore Daddy had chosen for me in return for my allowance. Once I found out about the skylight, it wasn't a chore to me at all. In fact, every day when I got home from school, I'd do my homework first and save doing the bathroom for afterwards so I could take my time, cleaning and singing for as long as I liked. Our bathroom became my place to play after school.

After a while, tiring of my limited repertoire of church songs, I decided to become a troubador, making up songs and singing about the goings-on in the building and neighborhood:

> *Oh, Mr. Jones beat Mrs. Jones last night, I could hear it through the wall of my bedroom . . .*
> *Well, Louise saw Jack last week and they hugged and kissed and had a Coca-Cola at the drugstore.*
> *Miz Butler had some candy and she wouldn't give me none of it.*

*A whole lotta candy. I never did like Miz Butler anyway. She's a mean
old lady, a mean old lady . . .*

Day after day as I sharpened my songwriting skills and my vocal
cords, my voice was being reverberated and amplified right into all the
other bathrooms—the Joneses', Louise's, the Butlers', and everybody
else's.

Apparently, those concerts of mine weren't as popular as the one I
performed with Jacquline. It got to the point where the neighbors
wanted to put me out of the building. Eventually, my mother's only re-
course was to board up our skylight.

⌒— "Deloreese Patricia Early," Mama began one morning, not long
after my sixth birthday, "time to get baptized. We put it off long enough
now."

The prospect of being baptized scared me to no end. Because I was
afraid of water, I hadn't learned how to swim. I wanted to be a Christian but I didn't want to drown to do it. There was no changing my mind.
I knew this baptizing thing was gonna kill me for sure.

Nevertheless, Mama laid down the law. After speaking to Reverend
Bruce, our minister at Olivet Baptist Church, my fate was sealed.

Reverend Bruce was a Baptist preacher, a Baptist preacher in every
sense of the word. For those of you unfamiliar with ministers of the
Baptist faith, that meant, for one thing, that he was very theatrical in his
presentation and that he strove to stir reaction in the audience. The more
the congregation responded, the more he fed off of it. He sang his sermons in a musical meter, his voice rising and falling dramatically. Reverend Bruce was all that. He was energetic and powerful. And, most of
all, whatever the platform of the Baptist Church was, regardless of
whether he felt it was right or wrong, or was indifferent, that was what
he abided by. There was no attempt to adjust or examine the platform

according to the concerns of the people and the actual circumstances of their lives.

In short, by the time the day and place of my baptism arrived, Reverend Bruce was ready and able to perform the duties of his cloth. Or, so he thought, until he encountered one terrified six-year-old Deloreese Early.

It's funny now but it was the scariest thing in my life at the time.

The water in the baptismal pool came up to Reverend Bruce's waist. I was barely taller than his knee. I knew there was no way I wasn't going to drown.

When he finally carried me out into the water, me kicking and screaming and splashing, he tried to reason with me. "I won't let you fall, just hold on to me."

"I know you're gonna drown me!" I screamed and screamed.

"Don't you want to be a Christian and give your life to God?"

"Yes, I do, but you might drop me and I will drown!" I kept screaming.

He prayed, he begged, he cajoled, he pleaded.

I screamed and screamed.

In the middle of a huge, long scream, I saw Mama come to the side of the baptismal pool and give me one of those looks I knew that said: *If you keep embarrassing me, if he doesn't drown you, I will kill you personally myself!* And as she looked that look dead in my eye, she said to me in no uncertain terms, "Get baptized or get out of there!"

While I was looking at my mother, Reverend Bruce dunked me.

I was wet, cold, and shaking all over. But I was baptized.

In honor of my baptism, my father gave me my first set of wheels: a red tricycle with white markings on the side and two white saddlebags that went across the back.

It was on my red tricycle, every Saturday morning from the beginning of spring to the end of fall, that I accompanied Daddy, riding along at his side, as he picked up the numbers along his route.

In the late thirties and forties, there was a strong distinction between the black neighborhoods on the East and West Sides of Detroit. Heads of households on the West Side had the better jobs—doctors, lawyers, factory foremen, government workers—and could afford a more comfortable lifestyle than the families on the East Side, where we lived. The people on the East Side were more often in unskilled labor—factory workers, domestic help, etc. On the West Side, folks were moving up and getting ahead; they were known as the strivers. On the East Side, where poverty and hardship were all around us, we were the survivors.

Black Bottom was the roughest East Side neighborhood of all. It was the red light district, south of Gratiot Street, which could have well been a railroad track to us since anything south of it had the same significance as "the other side of the tracks." North of Gratiot was our black neighborhood. So right across the street from my world, another really dangerous world began.

Anything could be gotten in Black Bottom. Whatever it was—*do you hear me?*—whatever it was that was illegal you could get it with no trouble at all in Black Bottom. Drugs, prostitution, thieves, murderers, pimps, the numbers. You name it.

Everybody played the numbers. It was illegal but everybody played the numbers. *Ever-ry-body.* Like the legal lotteries of today, hitting the numbers was a chance to come into some money you didn't have. You got five dollars for a penny. You could win a down payment on a house in the West Side. You could buy that car that you didn't own. It was the Dream.

Picking up the numbers every Saturday was one of the ways my father made extra money. My tricycle was a numbers-picking-up machine. Daddy put the numbers slips he collected in one of my saddle bags while I put "the goods" that I collected in the other saddle bag.

Our first major stop was the corner drugstore, where the owner, Mr. Bernstein, would give me candy or a spoonful of ice cream if my school pictures were good. Mr. Steinberg at the grocery store would give me a bag of potato chips to sing "Jesus Loves Me"—my big hit at that time. At the next stops, I might be given a bag of popcorn or a piece of chewing gum or a fresh-baked cookie. Or more candy.

I lived for Saturdays when my father came to pick me up—back from wherever he went on his weekends. What could be more wonderful than to spend most of the day with Daddy, ride my tricycle, eat ice cream, and collect candy enough for the whole week?

It was a while before Mama found out about my candy stash. She knew about the numbers and Daddy, but when she finally deduced that her Rich and her Ma were picking up the policy slips with the little red tricycle, she just *went off.* She talked to Daddy and put an immediate stop to it.

How Mama found out, I will never know. I told you she was psychic.

After my excitement with Daddy came to an end, everything went back to normal. I sang with the choir at church, went to school, and lived as the rest of the people in our lives, old and young, everyone working to make ends meet and trying as best they could to hold on to some kind of existence.

Yet another way that my parents supplemented our income was by renting out one of the rooms in our apartment. My favorite tenants were Nelson and Belle Evans, an attractive couple, who lived with us several years when I was young. Every few months or so, when things were getting really boring in the neighborhood, Nelson and Belle had this ritual they went through which tended to provide a lot of excitement for everyone.

Most of the time, the Evanses got on splendidly and lovingly. Nelson was a nice, good, kind man, and an excellent provider. And, as a couple, they went on to have a long and prosperous marriage. But every once in a while, Belle had this deep-rooted, driving need for Nelson to beat her. It seemed as if she just had to have this whuppin'. Like an itch she couldn't scratch. Until she had it.

Nelson worked as a Pullman porter on the night train that went to Chicago and back, a route that kept him away two or three days at a time. Usually, when he arrived home, Belle would welcome him in with sweet words, set a gorgeous table with her own best linens, and serve him a wonderful meal made of some of the finest cuts of meat which Nelson had acquired from the train (where all the food was packed and individually wrapped) and brought home to put in the ice box.

During the Depression, Nelson had kept himself alive by eating navy beans and Silver Cup bread. A bowl of beans and a slice of this white bread, that was his meal twice a day. That was it. After that time was over, if there was anything in the world he hated, it was navy beans and Silver Cup bread. He also did not like to be told to kiss his wife's ass. Nor did he like to be called out of his name, which would have been any demeaning name that could be called, like "motherfucker" or "son of a bitch."

Whenever Belle was ready to get this whuppin' she needed, the first indication was that before Nelson got home she'd take one of Mama's restaurant-sized pots and start boiling up navy beans. Next, she'd take all those fine steaks and pork chops and whatnot from the ice box, and carry them all out to the incinerator in the back yard, pour kerosene over them, and burn them up. It smelled like barbecue in the neighborhood but we all knew it was just Belle Evans needing her whuppin'.

Then Nelson would arrive home, opening up the front door as usual, saying to Belle, "How you doin', honey?"

She'd say, "Kiss my ass."

"Now, c'mon, Belle," he'd say calmly, "don't talk to me like that."

She'd say, "Kiss my ass."

Nelson would take his shower, get settled in, and then come to the table where he would find no cloth on the table, no napkins, nothing. Just this pot of navy beans and a loaf of Silver Cup bread.

He'd say, "You know I don't want this, Belle."

And Belle would begin to cuss him out of his name, calling him, "You motherfucker, you son of a bitch! I told you to kiss my ass, motherfucker . . ." And so on.

That did the trick. At that point, Nelson would pick Belle up, bring her through the living room, and take her into their bedroom. We could hear him bouncing Belle off the wall. It was so audible that all through the building everybody would look up at each other at their dinner tables and, in between mouthfuls, they'd say, "Nelson's beating Belle." And everybody knew that after the whuppin' was done, the neighborhood would be well entertained by the lovemaking which would follow.

Nelson would leave the next day, get on the train and go back to Chicago and when he returned home again, Belle would have cooked him some incredible repast with grilled steaks and baked cakes, all served up on a lace tablecloth. She would be just fine.

And the rest of the neighborhood would go back to waiting for the next diversion.

⌒⎯ Early one summer day when I was about six, something magical happened. After hearing Mama talk so often about "her only son," he materialized in the flesh.

My brother, Rufus David, was eight years old and I adored him from the moment I first saw him that day his father, John Daniels, brought him to live with us—after showing up unannounced at our front door.

As I said earlier, I never knew what had happened in my mother's earlier marriages. But what I eventually observed with both of her ex-husbands—Wiley (the father of Nodie, Susan, and Gladys) and John (the father of Ora Mae and Rufus)—was that both men were forever trying to get Mama to come back. One of John's ploys was to seem considerate by allowing "her only son" to come live with her.

"Nellie," John began as he pushed Rufus into the hallway, "he needs to know his mama. I wanna do what's best for Rufus."

Of course, my mother was overjoyed to have her son living with her. And Daddy immediately accepted Rufus into the family. My father, like so many men, always wanted a son and he had no problem with Rufus being that son. After John Daniel had dropped Rufus off with the clothes on his back and nothing else, Daddy took it upon himself to dress him and teach him and spend time going places with him whenever possible.

As for me, Rufus (R.D. we usually called him) was the handsomest, cleverest, and most loving person that I had ever known who was my size.

R.D. looked like both Mama and his father, who was a nice-looking, slender man. My brother had a healthy, ruddy complexion, a color similar to mine, and, at eight, was lanky and tall for his age. He was ingenious. With everything. Later on, as he grew into manhood, he proved to have a knack for fixing things and a great eye for interior design. He became such a whiz with sound he could build a hi-fi from spare parts. As a child, Rufus held a wealth of information for things I knew nothing about and as we went through the neighborhood, he made me see everything in ways I hadn't before.

R.D. showed me animals that lived in back yards, insects that lived under rocks. He took me up to the Eastern Market, a nearby early-morning farmers' market, and pointed out all the various kinds of fresh produce that farmers came to sell. We went over to the Woolworth's and sat on the tall round stools and spun around. We ordered ice cream sundaes and ate every last lick. On a really daring escapade, we boosted from the store. He showed me how we could sneak candy into our pockets and run away and hide. It was thrilling—the fear of being caught followed by the joy of getting away with it!

We turned the back yard into the Wild West and played cowboys and Indians. We staged wars and a lot of times I won and beat him at his own game. Once, after school, I tied him up in a tree and left him there for three hours.

Naturally, when Mama found out I was the culprit, there was hell to pay. So after I got a whuppin' for that, I snuck up to his bed late at night and hit him upside the head.

In case you hadn't noticed, my mother was the disciplinarian in the household. She was strict and kind. She was the mother and we were the children and that was that. Period, the end. She was not to be messed with and we were to respect that—*or else*. And *or else* was an ironing cord folded a couple of times or a switch from the tree outside in the back yard. You prayed for it to be the switch because the ironing cord was a monster.

Mama wasn't abusive about it. She used force only when she felt it was necessary, sometimes by storing up our transgressions and address-ing them at a later date. I'd think she had actually forgotten something I had done wrong—how I had talked back to her or how I had gone across the street when she said I couldn't or how I had taken R.D.'s shoes and hidden them. Then the hammer would drop and, with a whack or two, depending on the extent of my wrongdoing, she would refresh my mem-ory about each error of my ways. I used to say, "Whip me now," to which Mama would reply, "In due time."

I will never be able to tell you how much I hated "In due time"!!!

Oh, R.D. had a way with Mama that was masterful. If, for example, we had stolen some candy and she asked if we had done it, I would an-swer truthfully. I knew I would get into trouble but nowhere near as bad as if I lied about it and she found out. But when Mama asked R.D. if we had stolen the candy, instead of lying, my brother simply looked at her with big innocent eyes and asked her in response, "Mama, do you think I would do that?" He could charm her into forgetting her question.

R.D. was magic to me. He turned the ordinary into the extraordi-nary. He rounded out the family to an ideal foursome. He was my mother's joy and my father's pride. At the end of the day, when it was time for Daddy to come home, now there was a daughter and a son to dash down the three flights of stairs to meet him.

But after three months had gone by, John Daniel appeared at the door one afternoon not long before the dinner hour. Daddy hadn't got-ten home yet.

"I'm taking my boy back," Rufus's father stated. "Now, you can come with us, Nellie, but whether you do or don't, I am taking Rufus with me." This was all part of his ploy to get Mama back, using his eight-year-old son like that.

I watched helplessly as my mother packed every bit of the clothes and toys that R.D. had acquired over the summer, crying all the while. R.D.'s father took all the things from Mama, grabbed R.D. by the arm, and took him away.

I will never forget my father's face when Mama told him, through her tears, what had happened once he got home. Daddy was heartbroken. We were all crushed for a long time.

My adventures were over and I missed R.D. terribly.

The following summer—which seems an eternity when you're seven years old—John reappeared with Rufus. As we came to find out, he had pawned all the clothes and things R.D. had taken with him. There stood R.D., again, with only the clothes he was wearing. John said, "Nellie, I was wrong to take this boy back. I thought about it and I want you to have him. He needs his Mama, he's been crying for you all."

With that, John left and R.D. stayed.

We went right back to being the family we had been before. Once more my father embraced R.D. as the son he always wanted.

R.D. had been back living with us for another three months when John again showed up at the front door. He told my mother he had come to take R.D. back. At first, Mama refused so John threatened her with severe physical harm unless she turned the boy over to him. Whatever the words were that he said to her, I don't remember. All I remember was that my mother was crying. This man was hurting her enough already and when he reached to hit her, I ran into the kitchen and grabbed a knife bigger than I was. I ran back to the hallway and tried to stab John.

Mama wrested the knife from out of my grip, saying to John in a composed but intense voice, "I will not allow you to disrupt this home again nor take advantage of my husband." She called R.D. inside from the back yard and told him he would have to leave with his father. This time, she packed only his toothbrush and a pair of pajamas into a brown paper bag.

John was furious that she didn't give him all the things R.D. had gotten during this second stay: toys and clothes that he would have liked to sell or pawn like the last time.

R.D. never learned the real reason Mama packed so little for him this time. He grew up believing John's version: that his own mother put him out with just a brown paper bag. That lie followed him into his adulthood. "I never got any breaks," he complained as he got older, "even my own mama put me out with just a brown paper bag." It played heavily into the insecurity from which he suffered as an adult.

Several years passed until we saw R.D. again. Once he was old enough to catch the streetcar by himself, he started slipping off and coming to see us on Saturdays. He adored Mama and she felt the same way about him. "Rufus David," she'd say whenever he was sad that he couldn't spend more time with her, "you're my only son and I am proud of you and I know that as you become a man, God will give us more time together." It was her prayer and she knew it would be answered, so she waited patiently, peacefully for that time.

Some of our happiest days with R.D. came in his teens when he was able to come spend a long weekend with us for Thanksgiving. Thanksgiving at the Earlys was a much-loved and eagerly anticipated celebration. Mama cooked for three days beforehand while R.D. and I went crazy smelling those tantalizing smells wafting through the house. No matter how hard the times were, together my mother and father saw to it that our Thanksgiving table was laden with a feast fit for royalty and enough to feed an army.

That meal was so sumptuous and amazing, family members with whom we were not close or who lived in other cities would bridge their distance or their differences and beat a path to our door. As a result, Thanksgivings were the rare occasions upon which I got to meet the relatives on either side of the family. Most of them were on the Early side. On the Mitchelle side, Mama had no living parents or siblings and her favorite aunt Clara lived in Tennessee and was too old to come see us on the bus. However, every now and then, some of my mother's nephews and nieces, my cousins, showed up for a visit.

On Daddy's side of the family there were three sisters and two brothers, all of whom, except one, were living in Detroit. But you wouldn't have known it for as often as we saw them, which was seldom. No one ever came out and said it but the problem was that they didn't like Mama. They were just jealous of how pretty and wise and beloved by everyone in the neighborhood she was. Aunt Kate was the most hateful. Some years earlier Kate's leg had been broken and the doctors had done a poor job setting it, leaving her bowlegged in that leg. She was angry about breaking her leg in the first place and she stayed angry all those years. Everything about her was angry and nasty. But do you think she would miss Mama's cooking on Thanksgiving Day? No-sir-ree.

Daddy's brother, my uncle Marcelus, was off in his own world anyway. I think it was some other world like England. Marcelus was highly educated, the most educated member of the Early family, and he had a well-paid job with the government. Very proper, my uncle seemed to fancy himself as some kind of British lord. Whenever we saw him on Thanksgiving, he arrived cane in hand, in full British attire—knickers, woolen sweaters with suede patches on the elbows, the works. After he left, R.D. and I liked to imitate him and make each other laugh. Nobody would have ever said it or even hinted at it but Marcelus was probably a gay blade of his own sort (when gay stopped meaning fun-filled). Nothing wrong with it, the topic just wasn't talked about back in those days.

My aunt Capitolia, Daddy's younger sister, was actually very sweet. And Cappy, as we called her, loved her big brother Richard. He was her pride and joy which made Aunt Cappy, if not close to Mother, then at least respectful to her.

Then there was Daddy's other brother, Uncle Willie, a minister who lived in Kalamazoo, who made the annual pilgrimage to our house for Mama's Thanksgiving cooking. Since he had the longest trip to make, Uncle Willie was usually the last to arrive and by then the house was full of people and Mama was starting to put the food out.

One Thanksgiving I remember when R.D. was able to come for dinner, the bounty that came from Mama's kitchen seemed even more bountiful than ever. There was a big golden brown turkey, a platter of fried chicken, a pork roast, a beef roast, mashed potatoes, greens, macaroni and cheese, string beans, candied yams, stuffing for the bird, gravies, and, of course, the rice that Daddy loved. For dessert there were

pies and cakes, most notably sweet potato pie and three flavors of cake—
plain for me (my favorite), coconut for R.D. (his favorite) and chocolate
cake for Daddy (his favorite).

Uncle Willie, forever bound and determined to convert my father,
came in that day, late as usual, in no hurry.

"Hey, Willie," Daddy said, ushering him in, hoping to speed him up
to the table. "How ya' doin'?"

"Oh, brother," Uncle Willie came back, talking in his slow preacher's
voice, munching out every syllable, "I'm doin' all right in Jesus. Are you
with Jesus?"

My father didn't want to hear that and didn't respond. "Let's go,
Willie, time to eat." And being gracious about it, Daddy asked him if he
wouldn't mind saying the blessing once he got to the table.

Well. Uncle Willie didn't just bless the food, he went on ad infini-
tum. First he stood from his chair and began, "Oh, Lord," and then
paused. "Oh, wonderful Savior." Another pause. "Oh, blessed God." A
long pause.

By then R.D. and I were looking at each other hopefully, thinking
maybe Uncle Willie was going to give us a break and let us eat before the
food cooled off.

"Oh, holy Jesus," Uncle Willie started again. "It is so marvelous that
we woke this morning without the death cloth on our faces. We woke up
in our sound minds. We can see today. We can hear today, Father. We can
walk and talk today, Father. Oh blessed Father . . ." And then he went on
and the food that was hot and steaming was getting cold and Daddy was
getting madder by the second. Mama was clearing her throat and
Marcelus was nudging Willie to sit down and Cappy was gesturing the
same. Everybody sitting at the table was looking at each other, knowing
that if Uncle Willie didn't stop there was a point with Daddy that he was
going to reach and Daddy was going to say exactly what he said, finally:
"Sit the fuck down and let's eat!"

It was the same every year. Every year Uncle Willie left with hurt feelings because Daddy cussed him out. And every year Uncle Willie would push him to that point on purpose.

That year, I recall, when it was the first time we'd seen R.D. for quite a while, it was up to my father to make a toast after the meal, like every year. His toast was always short and touching and he inevitably said something humorous about how lucky the family was to have a man of Uncle Willie's piety at the table. That year, after doing his best to make Willie feel better, Daddy toasted all of his family, saying at last how especially happy he was for that day to have a son under his roof.

It was his way of saying that love wasn't conditional on the amount of time shared. This too was another thing I was to learn about angels who come along the way. Sometimes, they are not meant to travel the whole distance at your side. Sometimes they walk with you as angels only for that leg of your journey. R.D. was put in my life at a certain time as that big brother I'd been longing for. He taught me how to invent excitement when there was none. He protected me in certain situations and, through our playing and our fighting, he taught me to defend myself and hold my own and how to be tough when necessary. Remember, I had no qualms about pulling a knife on a grown man who was threatening my mother.

For that particular time in childhood, I was blessed with R.D. as my angel. That was enough. Although circumstances beyond my or my parents' control prevented him from continuing in that role over the next years, later in life, at a much different juncture, R.D. and his wife, Delores, would serve as angels by helping bring another and most important angel to me.

What is said is true: God works in mysterious, magnificent ways.

⌒ The Dozens is a game the kids used to play in school to see how much they could insult your mother. If you wanted to play, you had to top the remark by insulting their mother even worse. I didn't play the

Dozens. Far as I was concerned, nobody was gonna say nothin' about my mama and live. Luckily for them, nobody had ever tried. That was, until about 1940, when I was nine years old and in the fifth grade.

At school that year there were two big bully girls named Thelma Jackson and Marlene Foster who were going around intimidating the other girls. We were all afraid of them. I was much smaller than either of them and I was no fool. My approach was to avoid them. But the more I did, the more determined they were to do me in.

Thelma and Marlene walked up to me in the hall one day with taunting smiles. Marlene shot one of those *watch-me-now* looks over at her protector Thelma as she took a step in my direction. And Marlene said to me, "I hate to talk about your mama, she's a good old soul, she's got a spring-back pussy and a rubber asshole."

I went C-R-A-Z-Y and grabbed Marlene by her hair, wrapped it around my hand, dragged her down the hall and outside onto the school grounds, and around and around that school yard, dragging her by her hair with my fingers up to her scalp. Thelma, so scared she couldn't move, only stood by and watched. They got a teacher who tried to pull Marlene away from me and Marlene fell and I dragged both of them until I was tired.

I just went crazy. It's a wonder they didn't send me to jail. But they did expel me.

Mama went just as crazy on me. Yes—you are right—with the ironing cord. Every time I tried to explain that I was only defending her, Mama cut me off, saying, "I did not send you to school to fight, I sent you to learn."

My behind was bruised but my reputation was in cement. After that incident, nobody ever messed with me at school. Not that year, or the next year, or the year after that. My reputation followed me from grade school to high school all the way to graduation.

Although not as life-threatening as schools are today, when I was growing up the schools on the east side of Detroit were extremely tough. You had to learn to stand your ground. If you wanted an education, you had to fight. So having a reputation wasn't about being cool. It was about survival.

One day when I was twelve years old, Mama announced that she and I were going to take a bus to Gary, Indiana. Sensational! After all this time, I was finally going to meet my three older sisters—an event I had been dreaming about for years. And Mama was going to see her three oldest children, whom she'd been praying to see again. It was the most exciting thing that had ever happened to me. My first trip out of the neighborhood. Super-sensational!

On the bus to Gary, Mama and I were so excited talking about all the fun we were going to have, I really didn't notice the changing scenery of the world outside the Detroit city limits. We talked about how we were going to be staying at my sister Nodie's house and how my sisters Gladys and Susan were coming down from Chicago to meet us at Nodie's too. It was going to be one big happy family reunion—for all of two weeks— and I wished I could have driven the bus myself to get us there faster.

Mama had been deprived of the chance to mother her older girls into adulthood. Their father, Wiley, had kept them away from Mama much in the way that John had kept R.D. away; he was punishing her by withholding her daughters unless she gave in and went back to him. And so, as I understand it now, they resented me for having Mama all to my-self. But at the time it wasn't so easy to understand.

Over the first few days of the visit, instead of doting on me like my angel sisters Louise and Bernice, my supposed real sisters kept saying to me: "You think you're so cute, don't you?" I didn't think it, I knew it. So they didn't faze me. I was twelve years old, a pudgy thing, round like Mama, with legs that looked like sticks, but I was still confident in who I was. Also, my hair was long like Mama's and I wore it in braids and threw it around all the time, 'cause I loved it so much.

Then they'd say: "You think you're so smart, don't you?" I didn't think it, I knew it. So that didn't faze me either. Eating all those books as I did, I was constantly spouting out some new information I'd recently read or expounding on ideas I found interesting.

My sisters weren't interested in those ideas. They couldn't relate to a sheltered girl of twelve who seemed to know the world through books. They knew the world their way. Each of my three older sisters had been pregnant by the age of fifteen. My sister Gladys was a stunningly pretty prostitute, one of the most sought-after in Chicago. She was a natural beauty who had no idea how beautiful she was. Beautiful figure, beautiful face, beautiful hair. She had big brown eyes you could swim in and a cute turned-up little nose. *Beeea-uu-ti-ful.* My sister Susan, also a prostitute, also attractive, had the claim to fame of being a *high yellow*—which meant she was light-skinned and her hair wasn't nappy and, in some cases, she could pass for white. In that day and time, the ability to *pass* was often helpful, allowing her to go places and do things from which other Negroes were barred. Nodie, who had been a prostitute too, was a stocky, well-built big woman. Nodie had a hardness about her face but if you looked at her eyes sometimes you could see the human in her trying to push its way through. It was there even though she never really let it out.

The one person who felt like family to me was Nodie's husband, who was a foreman at a steel mill in Gary and whose name was, fittingly, Clemon Forman. A big man, he was over six feet tall and weighed about 250 pounds. I dubbed him the *Fat Man* in honor of a character by that name on a radio show and the name stuck to Clemon for the rest of his life.

By the end of the first week of our visit, Fat Man and I had become buddies. He took me on rides after work and on any errands he had to run for Nodie. On the nights when everyone was hanging out in the living room, Fat Man would sit on the couch and have me sing for him, after which I'd run and jump on his lap and he'd squeeze me and tell me how wonderful I was.

One night, halfway through our visit, I was singing for the Fat Man, Mama was in the kitchen cooking dinner, and Nodie, Susan, and Gladys were drinking, hollering at their kids for being underfoot, and being seemingly oblivious to me. I finished my song and ran to Fat Man for my squeeze. All of sudden, Nodie grabbed me from the back and threw me down on the floor. "You little bitch," she said, "you leave my husband alone."

Mama heard me fall and came running into the living room, asking, "Are you all right, Ma?"

Nodie said to my mother, "This little bitch has been all over my husband since she's been here and I want it stopped."

Before Mama could say anything, Fat Man spoke to Nodie, saying, "You're drunk. This is just a child. And a part of my family. If you think it's anything else, you must not think much of me as a man . . ."

"Are you taking up for this little bitch?" Nodie shouted.

My mother silenced the room. "That's it," Mama said. She took my hand and began to lead me out of the room. In case there was any doubt, she turned back to Nodie: "She is not gonna be here for you to call her out of her name. She's going home with me. I won't stay here for you to call her a bitch. Not one more minute than I have to." And then Mama raised her hand and pronounced, "It is written." That was her allusion to the Scripture and that meant she had nothing more to say. She turned once more, marched us out of the room and started packing.

Susan and Gladys tried to calm Nodie down and, at the same time, convince Mama to stay. She wouldn't hear a word of it. After calling the bus station and finding out there was a night bus in an hour, we were soon on it, on our way home.

I could count the times on one hand that I ever saw Mama truly angry. She never really cussed. She didn't even say "shit." Her version, when she was upset, was to say "shhhh" and cut it off fast with "t" at the end. Shhhh-t. On those two or three times I remember her in a rage, her phrase was, "Piss, puke and corruption." When she said that, baby, she would clear the house. Daddy and me knew to split. And fast. *Piss, puke and corruption.* That was sho' 'nuff cussin' for Mama.

She was that mad the night we left Gary. Needless to say, Fat Man never said, did, or thought anything Nodie implied. Mama knew and I knew that I was a twelve-year-old Christian child and I sure didn't think of him as anything but my big brother Fat Man.

I came home never wanting to see any of them again. They did not care for me much and I cared for them less.

After all our happy expectation, all Nodie had for me was hate. But there was, as there usually is if you look for it, a silver lining. Although I didn't realize it consciously, a little part of me grew up after that visit. From earliest childhood I had written a script in my head about the way it would be one day when my so-called real family was united. Now it was time to forget that script and write a new one, a script full of my dreams of finding my place in the world. In writing that new script, it was finally clear to me that being blood related didn't necessarily make for one big happy family. I knew from then on that the real family I sought was the family I would make, a family made up of love, starting with my parents, my brother too, and all the angels I already knew who were part of this extended family I was creating and those other angels I would meet along the way.

So, as it is written: *Seek and ye shall find.*

Not very long after we got home from Gary, I met another one of my angels, an angel whom God was sending to me as a minister and teacher—just at the time I most needed him.

Some years earlier a new church had opened in our neighborhood. It was called the Church of Our Faith and was said to be interracial and interdenominational. I doubt people in my neighborhood knew what those words meant and if they did, the concepts would have still been unheard of. Blacks, whites, Baptists, Presbyterians, Methodists, Episcopalians, you name it—all worshipping under one roof? That was unusual.

Church of Our Faith was a block and a half from us, at the edge of

Black Bottom. A large church, they had bought the building from a white congregation who had moved out, along with most of the whites who were moving, once Negro families started moving up and into our neighborhood from Black Bottom.

My curiosity was aroused because all the kids who went to Church of Our Faith were always talking about the fun classes they could take there after school and the fun church field trips they went on. Plus, I heard their choir was something exceptional. For the longest time, I had wanted to go over there so badly but Mama went to Olivet Baptist Church and that's where I sang in the choir and on the radio and I was going to go where she went. Period, the end.

Then, I started to ask questions at church you weren't supposed to ask. Not just at Olivet, but whenever we went to other churches to sing or attend their services. Before long, I was put out of nearly every church I visited or was taken in front of their board for a reprimand. Still, I had these burning questions that no one seemed to answer, questions about the gospel of sin and damnation I was hearing and about how I was nothing and about how I couldn't do this or do that and how I couldn't go here or go there.

How can I be nothing if I am made in the image and likeness of God? If I can't do this and I can't do that, why did God make those things? And what does going here or going there have to do with who I am as a person in God's eyes?

These were questions that didn't have easy answers. But rather than say that, the church authorities responded by telling me I was fresh and fast.

It was at that point, when I was twelve going on thirteen, in the spring of 1944, I finally got up my nerve to go over and attend a service at the Church of Our Faith.

Listening to the two ministers there, Reverend Barnes and Reverend Travis, was the spiritual drink of water I had been thirsting for. They were different. Instead of pronouncing that we were nothingness of all nothingness and were doomed to burn in hell because God was watching and knew what we were doing that was wrong (since no matter what we did, it was wrong), Reverend Barnes and Reverend Travis spoke about how loving God was, how we were like Him, and how He would provide for us, care for us, and protect us. Reverend Barnes, a doctor of theology, was an energetic, articulate man in his early forties and the senior minister. Reverend Travis was ten years younger, tall, thin, warm, and he conveyed a feeling of joy not just about worship but about life. Their approach was progressive. Rather than lecturing and preaching, they were teaching.

At Olivet, Mama had always sat right in the front row and had trained me from birth to do the same. So, of course, when I went the first time to Church of Our Faith, I went directly to the front row in front of the choir.

The wonderful thing about gospel music is that everybody knows the same hymns and songs. It is the attitude with which they are sung that will vary from choir to choir and church to church. Having sung all the years at Olivet, I knew all the songs well, so when the Church of Our Faith choir began to sing, I too began to sing. I was singing as hard as they were.

With that first song, we got it goin' and it went over big.

Detroit's spirit of competition applied not only to the big three auto makers—each trying to outdo the others with the shiniest, biggest, baddest cars coming off their lines—but to almost every area of life. That included a great competitive spirit between choirs and it was all over town that at Church of Our Faith they were really bad (superb!). And they were, but by the second song, I got over so good I was feeling like—they ain't s-o-o-o-o-o bad.

After the service, a couple of people I knew in the choir introduced me to the choir director.

"God bless you," he said. He told me he thought I was wonderful. I thought so too and his saying it made me feel right at home.

"Do you belong to the church?" he asked.

I told him I didn't.

The choir director explained that he'd love to have me in the choir if I ever decided to join. "We could use a lyric soprano like you," he added.

The very next Sunday I joined Church of Our Faith. Singing with that choir was heaven, pure heaven! It was music, it was socializing, it was excitement, it was belonging, it was being respected, and it meant a whole lot of loving care. It made such a positive change in me that after going there for a few weeks, when I broke down and told Mama I had joined, she acquiesced without reservation. It didn't matter to her where I served God; what mattered was that I did. So she was happy.

Dr. Barnes and Reverend Travis, being as innovative as they were for their time, understood that young people didn't have the foggiest idea about most things that were talked about in a Sunday service. They recognized that children wiggled and wriggled and got noisy or sleepy and kept their parents from enjoying the service. And so they organized a Young People's Church—not just in name but in actuality.

It was housed on the basement level of the church. We had our own offices, our own Sunday services, and our own choir. After starting as a soloist, thanks to everything I had learned singing at Olivet Baptist Church, I soon was chosen to be the Directress of the Youth Choir.

Though there was other adult supervision, Reverend Travis was our advisor and our adult leader. Handsome as well as young, he talked and listened to us, played with us, and planned fun activities for us around the clock. There were those fun field trips I had heard about, outings and adventures and concerts for the choir. After school there were classes in cooking and sewing for the girls, woodwork shop for the boys, arts and crafts for everybody. We were constantly making things to give to our mothers and fathers for the various holidays. The church provided us with an after-school hangout. We were kept so involved, doing delightful things, that there was no time to be out on the streets getting into trouble.

Reverend Travis was probably the first male authority figure in my life, other than my father, whom I felt I could trust. And there were some things I could talk to Reverend Travis about that I couldn't with Daddy.

The guidance I received from my father was of a different sort. I remember once when Mama had gone to the grocery store that I was getting dressed to go out in a dress that zipped in the back. Having zipped it as far as I could, I skipped to the living room and asked my father if he would help me zip the dress.

"What would you do if I were not here?" he asked.

"But you are here."

"Yes," my father said, looking up from his newspaper, "but they'll be a time when you need to zip this dress and I won't be here. Now, there must be some way you can zip it."

It wasn't mean or cold. What he was saying was that I had to learn to be self-sufficient. So I went back to my room and tugged and stretched and pulled until I got that zipper up by myself. It made me very happy to have handled it on my own.

That was Daddy's unique style of teaching. Often with few words. Of course, I knew he loved me. Still, on a day-to-day basis, there wasn't a lot of conversation between us about the concerns of being a twelve-year-old female adolescent.

Reverend Travis, on the other hand, was better equipped talking to teenagers. All of us in the Young People's Church loved him and he had enough love and time to give back to each of us, making each person feel special. As my angel, Reverend Travis did not bring me the message that I was more special than the next person. At the same time, he did a lot for my self-esteem. He stood up for me when I asked the questions you weren't supposed to ask, trying to help answer them or admitting there weren't answers. He respected my mind and my talent. His message was that I was special and it wasn't just something I thought. It was true, he let me know, and it was all right to feel that way. This was knowledge that God wanted me to know at that very time and He put Reverend Travis in my path to help me accept it. This was knowledge that would, in turn, help propel me to the next place where another angel was already waiting in the wings, an angel who would impart those next truths I needed to learn.

That angel's name was Mahalia Jackson.

3

There's a myth a lot of people believe about success. Some people have the idea that an angel looking like Ed McMahon walks up to you on the street, hands you a check for millions of dollars and announces you can leave the slums because you're a Big Star now.

Well, that may happen. In my case, it did not. Warner Brothers never sent a limousine to my house to pick me up and take me to makeup for my role in *Gone with the Wind*.

What happened to me was slightly less spectacular—at least, in the short run. It was an opportunity I was given, an experience which would ultimately shape my life and my career. A door was opened and I was able to walk through it. You might call it a stroke of luck or a fluke or an instance of being in the right place at the right time. I prefer to call it God sending an angel. Either way, it happened when I had just turned thirteen, at the end of July, 1944, in the heat of a Detroit summer.

All the major gospel singers came through Church of Our Faith when they came to Detroit. Among them were The Soul Stirrers, The Mighty Clouds of Joy, The Pilgrim Travelers, The Spirit of Memphis, The Clara Ward Singers, Beatrice Brown and her Inspirational Singers, Willie Mae Ford Smith, Thomas Dorsey, Roberta Martin and the Martin Singers, The Caravans, the original Five Blind Boys, Beatrice Brown and Her Son, James Cleveland, Wynona Carr, Robert Anderson, Eugene Smith, and at least a host of others. But the most celebrated of all to grace our church was Mahalia Jackson who, with her rich soulful contralto voice, was moving into her peak as the singer soon to be called "The Queen of Gospel."

That day in July the Church of Our Faith was packed to overflowing to hear Mahalia and her group sing. There was no air conditioning in those years and everyone, dressed in their Sunday finery, was fanning themselves with the hand fans that the funeral home gave out.

As the directress of the Young People's Choir, I was especially excited that we were going to be singing background for Mahalia and that I was going to be singing the first song of the concert, "Christ Is All." Not noticing the heat or the density of the crowd, I began softly, yet strong and certain, and built from there. When I hit my high note—"Christ is 'Aw-aw-all'"—I could feel the energy in the room rising.

I *tore* it down. And the choir was with me all the way. Then Mahalia was introduced and before she began she praised us with deep sincerity, saying that we were the best young people's choir she had ever heard. Nobody could touch us, she said.

The heat in the room rose higher still with the spirit as Mahalia started to sing. The tambourines were playing, everyone clapping, the four members of her group swaying as they sang, and our choir singing too, everyone caught up in the joy of singing praise to the Lord. We were so caught up in it that when the lead soprano with Mahalia's group collapsed, we all assumed that because she was a large young woman—close to three hundred pounds, if not over—and because the spirit was high, she had fallen under the spirit. She was that heavy. And it was that hot.

But when they revived her from her faint, she was unable to continue so she was taken into Reverend Barnes's office. Meanwhile the concert continued and unbeknownst to Mahalia (or to me) a doctor from the audience went to examine the woman, whereupon he discovered she was six months pregnant. She was so large, there had been no indication of her pregnancy.

There were six weeks remaining on Mahalia's tour and the next leg of it included engagements in the South. The lady's husband, along on this leg of the tour, was at her side when the doctor announced the happy news. But the husband was adamant in not wanting his pregnant wife traveling on a bus in the South. In the 1940s, the South was not the greatest place for Negroes to be in poor health or to need medical attention. Many famous and not so famous blacks had been denied hospital service and had died because of the lack of help. One of our greater losses was legendary blues singer Bessie Smith who died in 1937 after being injured in a car accident in Memphis. Although it was never admitted, it was long said—and we believed it—that she had been turned away from all the area hospitals because of the color of her skin.

After the program was over, Mahalia went back to Reverend Barnes's office to see how her lead soprano was faring and was informed of the situation. This was a problem—she needed a replacement. And, because she was leaving on Tuesday, two days later, she needed a replacement fast. Reverend Travis came up with a possible solution, recommending the soloist and directress of the Young People's Choir, thirteen-year-old Deloreese Early, a lyric soprano—contingent, of course, on parental permission. Mahalia got a chance to hear me sing again that afternoon in a radio broadcast our choir performed and she agreed I was the perfect choice.

Now the challenge was going to be to convince my mother. When Reverend Travis offered to go and speak to her, Mahalia decided to come as well. That was when, after we finished the afternoon program, finally, the Reverend came and tapped me on the shoulder, quietly telling me what had transpired.

The evening air had begun to cool the heat of the day, while the sun was setting slowly in the sky. Reverend Travis and Mahalia walked the four blocks to our apartment building, me tagging behind them, praying all the way, promising God a long list of good things I was going to do if He made Mama let me go, and promising an even longer list of the bad things I would never do again as long as I lived.

Plee-aaaa-seee, God, make Mama let me go!

Up the three flights of stairs we climbed.

Mama met us at the door. "Good evening, Reverend Travis, I'm always glad to see you," she said, even though her eyes let me know she assumed at once that I had done something so wrong that the preacher had to bring me out of the church home to her. She appeared to brace herself, preparing for the worst.

But the first words from Reverend Travis were, "Mrs. Early, it's my honor to introduce you to Miss Mahalia Jackson."

"I am the one being honored," my mother insisted, greatly pleased and impressed. She was very much a Mahalia fan, as was most of the Christian society of that day. Now she thought whatever it was I had done, it had offended Miss Jackson. Mama started looking at me with those looks that could cut rock.

The Reverend told her what had happened.

My mother listened politely.

Seeing neither enthusiasm nor disapproval, Mahalia spoke up, saying, "Mrs. Early, I assure you, I will take personal good care of your daughter and see to it nothing happens to her. You can depend on that."

"And," the Reverend added, "it will be a great learning experience for Deloreese."

The two went on to say that I would be making money to help out at home, as well as being able to help me get my books and school clothes for the fall.

I looked down at my shoes. We couldn't afford new ones so when they became worn out on the soles, I lined them with cardboard or newspaper. In the summer it wasn't so bad, but in the winter the newspaper was always getting wet and I had to take extra newspaper with me everywhere to replace my lining.

They had made a strong case for me going. But still Mama was impassive.

Reverend Travis explained, "Miss Jackson does need to know your decision as soon as possible. She will be singing on Wednesday in Richmond, Virginia, and would need for Deloreese to leave on Tuesday night."

"I understand," Mama nodded. She said she would pray over it and sleep on it that night, letting them know her decision on Monday morning.

She proceeded to do just that. And I proceeded to go crazy all night, barely sleeping at all, waiting for the answer.

It's now four-thirty the next morning and I creep hesitantly and anxiously into the kitchen where Mama is fixing Daddy's breakfast and lunch. Saying nothing, trying not to look overly hopeful or desperate, I make the coffee, set the table, and mix up Daddy's morning drink of whiskey and sugar, washing whatever dish or utensil Mama uses as soon as she's done.

My mother says nothing. Not even, "What are you doing up at this time of morning?"

My father comes in for his breakfast. We feed him, first his drink, then a plate of pork chops, eggs, biscuits, and grits. Then he drinks his coffee.

I wait.

As Mama fixes his lunch, also full, I wash each dish or utensil after she's finished.

I wait.

Daddy kisses us both good-bye and leaves for work. Then we clean up what's left to clean. Mama gets herself a cup of coffee and pours me a glass of milk.

After what seemed an eternity, she indicated that we should sit down at the table and finally she spoke, saying, "We have to talk. And you should know God is gonna be talking right along with us."

I nodded nervously. Didn't sound good.

Mama took a drink of coffee and continued. "I prayed about you doing this and even though I didn't think you should go, I asked the Father to tell me if it wasn't right. He didn't."

I exhaled a sigh of relief. If God didn't tell her it was wrong, that was a positive sign.

Mama went on, "I know this can be good for you. All I need is your honest word that you will do the best you can, 'cause you'll be doing it in the name of Jesus, and your honest word that you will remember who you are—a Christian and a young lady."

I promised and hugged and kissed her. I thanked God and everybody in the Bible, Reverend Travis, Reverend Barnes, and Miss Mahalia Jackson. Then I promised some more and I hugged her some more.

Mama waited as I danced around the kitchen with my thanks and my promises until I quieted long enough for her to say—and I will never forget it if I live to be a thousand—"We don't need all of that, all we need is your honest word. And, remember, you won't be just giving it to me. You will be giving it to God, too."

"I give you my honest word," I said simply. "I'll do my best."

Mama took me in her arms and prayed, telling me she would be praying for me until God brought me home safe and sound.

⟋⎯ Here, at the age of thirteen, I had heard enough about how blacks were treated in the South to know it could be a frightening place. We knew about lynchings. We knew about black people getting woken up in their beds and dragged outside and hung from a tree. We knew about black families being burned up and shot to death.

We knew about unspeakable things happening, things like what would happen some years later to a boy named Emmet Till, who in 1954 was beaten to death for looking at a white lady. She took offense at the way he looked at her and a group of men got together to beat this boy to death. A person has to be on a real mission of hate to beat the life out of another human being.

When I set off on tour with Mahalia, those were the kinds of things we had heard about the South.

But that kind of hate didn't just occur in the South.

The year before, in 1943, I experienced firsthand what it was like during two nights of violence that rocked my city. The event was recapped in *The Chronicle of America* as follows:

> *As America fights a racist Hitler in Europe, racial hatred has set off riots at home . . . The worst violence erupted June 20 in Detroit, where 300,000 Southern whites and blacks have migrated to work in the war plants. In two days, 35 were killed, 600 wounded and thousands held. Thurgood Marshall of the National Association for the Advancement of Colored People said Detroit's police used "persuasion" on white rioters but "ultimate force . . . revolvers, riot guns and machine guns" on Negroes . . .*

The police *talked* to the white rioters, they just *killed* the black ones. Of the thirty-five killed, one death was that of my cousin, Junior, whom four white boys held down under water and drowned at Belle Isle Park, a mile from where we lived. It could have been R.D. It could have been me. We grieved for Junior's death and for the losses of other families we knew.

It was shocking—not because there were some white folks who did crazy things like that, we already knew that. It was shocking because they were doing it to Junior, to little children killed by white police because stray machine-gun fire aimed at rioters caught them; it was shocking that it was here in our neighborhood. But that was the way the world was, our experiences taught us, and there wasn't much we could do to change it. Try to change it and you died, we had learned.

As I got older, I came to understand that from the time of slavery, the white slave master did all he could to separate the family. He set you on your own as a single individual, without roots or ties to others; you were taught not to trust each other. That was the real weapon of the slave master, a weapon not abolished with the abolition of slavery. It meant that I couldn't put myself in the line of fire and count on you as another black person to help me because the idea was to save yourself, not to save everybody. Self-preservation is the first law of nature. So, you might say, "All right, let's fight this oppression, I'll stand up with you," only to get in the heart of battle and back out and leave me. That doesn't make you a bad person; it just means you don't want to die for me.

This is why, when the Reverend Martin Luther King, Jr., began, some twenty years later, to call out for a different way, he had such a hard time at first getting others to fight alongside him. No one had ever seen it work before. We needed him, one of God's great angel messengers to us all, to teach us.

In the meantime, segregation continued to thrive, especially in the South. And, as we headed into the night, en route to our first stop, Richmond, Virginia, Mahalia began to school me, as did the other singers in the car, cautioning how important it was to "stay in your place."

That didn't make sense to me. I wasn't planning on going out to riot. After all, on a day-to-day basis in my neighborhood, I could go where I wanted, do what I wanted, say what I wanted. Everybody knew me and was nice to me, white and black.

In entrusting me to Mahalia's care, my mother must have certainly warned her to stand ready in case I decided to say whatever I wanted to say out of my mouth, which I was known to do. Mahalia's job was to put a hand or a foot in it, if need be, to keep us all from being killed.

But for every word of warning she had spoken, the first time we stopped for food, I was the first to jump out of the car. Mahalia shouted my name and said, "Wait for me," stopping me just in time from running into the wrong door. She took me around the back to the colored window. The food was good but the idea of the colored window was hard to digest. At the next stop, where we found out there was no colored bath-room, I had to pee so bad I almost wet myself until she told me to go and find a bush to pee behind.

Getting the drift of what everybody was talking about, I never felt comfortable during our other engagements in any of the Southern states we were in which included Virginia, Georgia and Arkansas. When we were in public, afraid of doing or saying the wrong thing, I didn't speak much. That was a new experience.

Mildred said not to worry. She was the kind, attractive, younger woman who was with Mahalia, was for Mahalia's side, and for whatever Mahalia said. That was how we understood it: if Mahalia said it, that was all that needed to be said. Mildred, also a fantastic piano player, told me, "You stay right up under Mahalia and you'll be fine."

I did do that but I wasn't happy about it. In my teenage reasoning this tour business wasn't what I had in mind. From what I knew, Mahalia Jackson was an important person which, by extension of my being in her group, made me one too. And, according to the movies, when you were important, things were done for you and fixed for you. Once I got out there, it was nothin' like that. At all.

Out the window went my ideas about how exciting it was to be spending six weeks out of my mother's house to go on tour with Mahalia Jackson, meeting and partying with glamorous, glittery people. Even if that had been available to me, it wouldn't have happened. My mother knew exactly what she was doing when she looked Mahalia Jackson in the eye and said, "My girl is a good girl. I wouldn't let her go with just any-one. But I trust you and I'm gonna let her go with you. I expect you to bring her back to me as she is."

Well, Mahalia took every word Mama had said into her heart, her mind, her body, and her soul. She turned out to be twice as tough as my mama. *Where are you going? What are you doing? Why are you wearing that?* Things even Mama let me do on my own, Mahalia had to know about.

Because of that, little did I appreciate how much she was teaching me in other areas, how much I was learning just being in her presence.

The part of those six weeks that did live up to my expectations was the music. The singing was wonderful. The songs Mahalia did were the same gospel songs I knew and had been singing for years but they were done Mahalia's way. She said, "If you choose a song because you like it, then respect it. You don't have to fix it." Her way, therefore, was a straightforward type of singing, with her own phrasing and a New Orleans flavoring. Just straight ahead. Simplicity abounded. The harmonies and rhythms were gorgeous. All along the tour, the crowds were sensational. Mahalia was in full throttle and magnificent.

The last engagement of that trip was in Chicago—the highlight I had been waiting for. Chicago, the big city, big churches, big stores, and the excitement of appearing with a big-time singer in her own back yard. Chicago was Mahalia's town. Though she had grown up in New Orleans, she'd lived in Chicago since her teens and was respected there above all other gospel singers, long before the world knew and accepted her for the power she was.

Great! This was going to be my chance to show what I could do, in Mahalia's town.

As a native of New Orleans, Mahalia had grown up on the cuisine there and she loved, best of all, to cook and eat gumbo. She put everything into it—shrimp, andouille sausages, chicken, fish, okra, vegetables—*ever-ry-thing* but the kitchen sink. This I recall in vivid detail as I was staying at her house with her in Chicago. I was sleeping in a bedroom above the kitchen and fumes from the all-day gumbo cooking came directly into the room. My two shirts, two blouses, my dress-up shoes, and my robe for performing, all smelled like gumbo the entire time I stayed there. Forever after, I hated gumbo and to this day can't stand the smell of it.

None of the gumbo concerns could dampen my excitement for the grand culmination of the tour there in Chicago—a Sunday afternoon tent revival that ended in a mammoth program. The tent had been raised in a spacious field in the neighborhood, chairs set up, and a platform erected for the preacher and the choir. People in that neighborhood, along with members of other Chicago churches, all came together to sing praises and hear someone special. This Sunday it was to be Mahalia And Me. In my mind that was the group: Mahalia And Me. The other three singers were just for background and Mildred for accompaniment.

When Mahalia called on me to start the program, I confidently began to walk the sawdust cover of the tent floor and do my thing, singing with all my might. Responses came from all around me. "Amen!" said one man as I sang. A woman shouted, "Hallelujah!" Another said, "Amen." More shouts followed. The rest of the people clapped their hands in rhythm and stomped their feet.

I must be hot tonight, I thought as I came to the end of the last chorus, let's see what Mahalia does after this. Everyone was applauding wildly, asking for more, but that was it, my big solo. I had no other number. Thinking fast, I let the music play and grabbed onto another chorus which really roused the people. I turned it out and tore it down. With cheering of "Sing, child," and "Praise the Lord" ringing out around me, I sat down smug as can be, knowing there was not a thing Mahalia could do about it.

She joined in with the rest of the people. As one woman called, "To God be the glory!" Mahalia added her own "Sing, child," and someone else shouted, "Hallelujah."

When the crowd quieted down, not completely (her timing was impeccable), Mahalia remained seated and began to moan. No song in particular, only whatever changes Mildred was playing on the piano. No words, just moanin' low and deep, until she broke out into "Precious 'Lawd,' " the words flowing from her as purely as the moans and hums which came before them.

Mahalia sang the entire song seated. It wasn't even as if she was singing for others; rather, it seemed she was speaking directly and only to God. The audience responded with a reverence and awe, as if they knew they were in the midst of a private conversation such that it was a personal experience for each one of them.

I have never been stupid and I realized something that evening in a Chicago tent revival. It dawned on me that there was a different kind of feeling others got from Mahalia than from me. Mine was an enjoyment based on a more surface, rhythmic, cute thing; hers was a deep spiritual experience for everyone involved.

It was hard to fathom—how did she do it? After I had done my big number, as cute and effective as I was—what was it she had that I didn't? I was younger and surely better-looking. Besides, my voice was as good. In fact, in my mind, it was somewhat better than hers because I could do more curlicues and more slides and hit higher notes. How could she do this?

Oh, isn't it interesting how youth can often miss the point entirely?

The point I was to eventually discover after two more summers of touring with Mahalia and studying her closely was that she was coming from the inside and I was coming from the outside. She was worshipping God and I was showing off.

Until I grasped that, the question of what her secret was continued to plague me. I went home from that first tour, determined to somehow obtain that quality or craftsmanship or whatever the name of it was.

"Reverend Travis," I asked during one of our talks, after I'd gotten back into the routine of school and church activities, "what do you think it is Mahalia has that other singers don't?"

After a pause, he said, "With Mahalia, it's all about God."

Hmmmm. What did that have to with your voice?

I asked my mother and her answer was similar: "When Mahalia sings, you can feel the God in her."

Hmmmm. What did that have to do with your voice?

It remained a nagging issue. Whenever I sang, I watched people to see if I could do what Mahalia did. Something was still different.

I resolved to uncover her secret. The next summer, on tour with her again, I began to watch her very closely. I noticed that whenever we were in the car on our way to a program, the rest of us were laughing and singing but she was silent. She didn't even seem to be with us.

After a week of observing this, I asked her about it. "Why are you like that when we're on our way to a program?"

"How do you mean?" Mahalia asked.

"You don't seem friendly like you do the rest of the time. You seem mad or far away or something."

"I am far away," she said. "I am in the presence of God. I am letting God fill me with his presence."

My old questions arose. How did she do that? How could I do that?

Then I began to see that before our concerts when we prayed together, afterwards Mahalia took time to go to a corner or quiet space and pray to herself. She closed her eyes and prayed alone. Until this was complete for her, we didn't go on, no matter what the time was or what the crowd felt. That was her secret. That was how she did it. And never once in all the times I saw her did she fail to sweep the place clean, no matter how simple the song. Or maybe because of the simplicity. No flurries. No acting. Just Mahalia and God. The people knew it. They felt it. They hungered for it and she gave it to them. You didn't just hear some singing with Mahalia. You had a God-filled experience.

It was starting to make sense to me.

The other major lesson I got that summer from Mahalia was a business lesson. She taught me her equivalent of "no tickee no laundry."

Because there had been a few engagements where the promoter didn't pay before the concert and then when we finished singing was suddenly nowhere to be found, Mahalia adopted a policy of *Money First or No Program.* The first time it happened, there was a full audience with people paying to stand in the back. When the promoter said he couldn't pay her until after the concert, she chose not to go on at all. Another time, before everyone got into place and began to sing, she went up to the stage and asked the audience, "All of you paid to get in here, didn't you?"

The crowd called out, yes, they had paid.

"Well, you better get your money back because I am not singing. The man in the back that took your money says he doesn't have enough to pay me. Even with all you people in here. I hate to disappoint but I'm sure you understand that I've got to pay these children who came here to sing with me and get them back home and be able to give them something to eat."

After the uproar that ensued, she added, "God bless you and I hope I get a chance to sing for you one day."

The people went crazy and stampeded the area where they had paid to get in. Somehow, the next thing we knew, the money magically appeared. And Mahalia went on and sang, as magnificent as ever.

I saw that happen more than a few times. She made honest men out of a lot of promoters.

When I went home after my second summer with Mahalia, I thought I had learned a great deal. But nothing would compare to the lesson which came a year later, a point in the future to me which seemed another lifetime away.

⟶ Stick a pin right here.

This is the story of how I fell in love, madly in love, with an angel in disguise. I saw him for the first time at the Big Top, our corner hamburger stand next door to the drugstore and the pool hall where all the hustlers hung out. In that very first split-second of seeing him, everything in me just stopped. It's a wonder I didn't die. *Ever-ry-thing* stopped.

His name was Seabourn Brooks and to the rest of the neighborhood he was a pimp. To me, he was the most hypnotic dream of a human male person I had ever seen. Before he even said a word, I saw him turn and look at me, the movement of his body like dancing. There was a sense of constant and catlike motion about him, but no hurry whatsoever. There was such grace in the way he turned and looked at me. His skin was a similar light brown to mine but warmer somehow. His eyes were light brown, almost yellow. And he looked at me like I was the most beautiful dream of a female person he had ever seen, like I was Ava Gardner and Ethel Waters rolled into one. As if everything in him had stopped too.

Hold that image for a moment while I set the stage. I'm fourteen years old and although I'm just beginning to stretch out, I'm still a little pudgy thing. I have a cute face, cute hair, and, it's true, the other boys around are starting to discover me. But I'm no glamour girl. Even so, Seabourn Brooks looks at me for the first time and seems to be just taken away by me, by this little pudgy thing.

The power of that moment could not have descended on me at a more impressionable time. All kinds of changes were going on in my life, including a new school where I had started the eleventh grade. I had followed the example of my best friend, Matilda Maddox, after she used her aunt's address to transfer to Northeastern High School the year before. Being for middle- to upper-class whites, it was a better learning facility and better funded.

Mama suggested I use Aunt Georgia's address and also transfer. And so it was arranged for me to attend Northeastern.

As a minority of two black teenagers in an all-white school, Matilda and I were harassed in many ways. Ways that when you described them to others, you sounded absurd—as though you provoked the problem. Subtle, insidious ways. Say you're in study hall doing homework and you leave to go to the bathroom; when you return your work is gone, no one knows where it is, and you have to start all over. Homework assignments were given to us with more pages to do than others and they had to be turned in quicker. In choosing our course work, we were steered to the domestic art classes—cooking and sewing. As if training for the outside world in any real professions wasn't needed.

Through all this, Matilda was my saving grace—always there with a look-on-the-bright-side word of comfort. A year older than me, she was a big sister, a friend, and a mother all rolled into the body of an adolescent.

Because of my reputation that had followed me from the time I beat up Marlene Foster back in grade school, nobody threatened us physically, nor did anyone call us names outright. Still, there were the remarks and innuendoes that cut to the bone. But together, Matilda and I kept our heads up and persevered.

One big disappointment about Northeastern was that I was not allowed to attend music class because I did not have the proper prerequisites. I had transferred from Miller High School, the public facility for Negroes that was in Black Bottom, where the only music class had been a very basic one. In fact, it was the only class I ever really enjoyed as a teenager. The music teacher, Mrs. Wagstaff, a very feisty white-haired little lady, taught me some fundamentals of music theory and harmony, along with a bit of reading music. She even used my voice to demonstrate scales or various sounds. Though it was unfortunate that I never had other opportunities to receive more of a formal music education, I was happy to have had Mrs. Wagstaff to give me the little music training I did have.

Besides the changes at school, I was starting to feel my physiological changes. Mama knew it and, fearing I'd get pregnant, ruin my life, and never break out of the slums, she meant to hold them in check. Her decree was: "No dating until after your sixteenth birthday." That wasn't going to be until after I graduated!

There was no talking to Daddy about it either. His decree was: "You will do as your mother says."

God had spoken in the Early household.

So, of course, sneaking came into play.

It was in this state of flux—the school problems, the awakening of my sexual urges, together with a new rebelliousness at home—that I met Seabourn Brooks.

At the Big Top, the corner hamburger stand. Tall, handsome, *sex-xxx-yy,* witty, charming, with a sly smile—not sly like a fox but sly as in a confident, knowing smile that came on slow and spread wide, a smile that knocked me down. Emotionally, I had only just come out of comic books only to go straight into love stories. In love with love, poetry, romance, I had been storing up all this fourteen-year-old passion to put on one person. And there he was. Not only the kind of man you dream of, he was my dream come true.

I was on my way home and had stopped in at the Big Top to buy myself a Coke. He was in there with an entourage, a regular group of men who hung out. Seabourn Brooks had to have been the youngest pimp in the neighborhood. He was in his twenties while the others were in their thirties and forties. And yet, I could tell he seemed to be respected and even admired by them.

After I ordered the Coke at the counter, Seabourn cocked his head and spoke his first words to me: "Hey, Junior. What are you doing in here? You get your Coke and get on outta here. Next time you want a Coke get it from the drugstore. It's right next door." He pointed in the direction of the drugstore as if I didn't know.

Everybody was quiet, looking at me. The way he talked to me was like he thought he owned me. That got my attention.

Hand on my hip, Coke in my hand, I turned back to him and said, "I'll get my soda wherever I want. You don't even know me, much less own me."

Everybody laughed. And so did he.

"The drugstore," he repeated with a commanding look that thrilled me. "I don't want to see you in here again."

Everybody at the Big Top went, "Oooooh."

Brooks, that's what he was called in the neighborhood, gave me his look again, the one that said, *Get outta here and get out now.*

He turned away, saying something else under his breath, out the side of his mouth, a funny commentary of some sort on our interaction. Whatever it was, everybody at the Big Top fell out.

I found that one mannerism of his so enchanting I began to do it myself. Still do it to this day, as a matter of fact.

Everything about Seabourn Brooks was enchanting.

Weeks went by before I saw him again. Every day when I got off the streetcar coming home from school, I'd look for him. Soon, I began to ask some of his friends from the Big Top or the pool hall about him, sopping up whatever crumbs of information I could.

One day when the streetcar stopped, the door opened and there he was, smiling his knowing smile, his yellow-brown eyes sparkling. As he helped me off the car, he asked, "What do you want? Why are you always looking for me?"

"I wasn't looking for you," I said, cool and calm while my heart went pitta-pat. "I just wondered where you were and were you all right."

"You *were* looking for me. That is your first and last lie to me." He stared hard and then, in a softer voice, said, "You never have to lie to me. I'm so glad you were worried about me. I missed you too. Go on home now."

I cannot at all describe the feelings inside me. He *missed* me. He was *waiting* for me. He *talked* to me in front of everybody on the corner.

I strutted and floated up East Vernor Highway that day for all the world to see.

Over the next weeks and months our courtship unfolded. I found out, bit by bit, that Brooks had six working women, two of them real beauties. Four were prostitutes, the other two were boosters (thieves). These women absolutely adored Brooks, each trying to out-produce the other for his attention. Their reward? Some private time with him.

His women had the prettiest clothes and shoes I had ever seen and they were dressed differently every time I saw them, with beautiful makeup on and their hair always fixed so nice. I thought they were wonderful. They thought of me as a child that Seabourn liked to play with, and what made Seabourn happy made them happy.

Seabourn Brooks was forbidden fruit, but what seemed to me wonderful tasting fruit. A pimp to the neighborhood, the police, and the rest of the underworld in which he lived, he was my all and all, and they just didn't know or understand him.

Days, weeks, and months would go by in between getting to see him. Then one day, I'd walk by the corner and there he'd be—a vision for my senses, smiling his sly smile, talking and laughing with his regular group. With an air of nonchalance, as if on my way to do something else, I'd walk past him and whisper, "Got something to tell you." Or, "I got an 'A' on my English paper. Don't you want to see it?"

Seabourn would tell his friends, "I gotta talk to Junior a minute," and he'd walk with me a ways, the two of us talking about whatever latest news I had.

After a while, he took to walking me all the way home, asking questions as we walked along, always listening with great interest to my answers. Like I really knew what I was talking about. And most times I did because of eating up all the books I did, which I now ate more than ever so I could be smart for him.

He praised me for being smart, for my sense of humor, for my insights, for the way I described people I knew and the funny things they did. Seabourn was one of the first people in whom I confided about my interest in becoming a psychiatrist one day. Most people in the neighborhood had no real idea what that was but Seabourn did. And when he asked me questions about the science of psychology that I couldn't answer, the very next day I was at the library, checking out a stack of books on the subject. The next time I saw Seabourn, I spent my whole walk home pontificating on psychology as the study of human nature and human behavior. Whenever we talked, I felt a closeness to him I'd never felt with anyone and I believe to this moment he felt that closeness, too.

Here was an instance of Seabourn acting as God's angel, bringing me the message that I didn't have to be like or look like his other women to be beautiful to him. He seemed to like me because I was different, because I was me—a powerful lesson that many young girls don't always have a chance to learn.

Brooks made me feel like the woman I knew I could be (whatever that was at the time) and yet our exchanges were made up of nothing more than looks and implication and sweet innuendo. He respected my age and inexperience which, I might add, drove me crazy because I didn't want him to consider my age and I didn't want to be inexperienced any longer. I wanted to experience *him*.

Fall turned to winter and winter turned to spring. Soon it was summer again. The days were long and hot and lazy. And with my romance, innocent as it was, I was having a ball! So when it was time to leave again on tour with Mahalia, it was mostly with a heavy heart.

Besides the separation from Brooks, this third year was without the excitement of the other trips. It was old stuff now. I thought I had learned all there was to learn from her. Well, I was wrong. And that summer would prove to be a true Learn Humility lesson.

Towards the end of the tour, we arrived at a location outside of Richmond, Virginia, where we were scheduled to sing. It was a church in the middle of a field. We saw no houses, buildings, cars, or people in any direction. But by seven o'clock that night the church was full to overflowing. People came out of nowhere on mules, in wagons, some of them coming as far as five or ten miles on foot.

After we commenced the program and had sung a couple of songs, it was my turn to sing. I started with all guns blasting. When I got to my high note I hit it and held it. But then, from somewhere and somebody else, I heard a note higher than mine, clear and powerful.

Undaunted, I hit a higher note and held it, staying on it with an endless breath as I walked down the aisle trying to see who was singing. When I got to the back row, I saw a girl with pickaninny braids, dressed in coveralls and a farm shirt. She smiled at me and hit a higher note.

I went up again, almost choking on the note. And she smiled and hit a higher note and slurred that note to a still higher note which I couldn't even reach.

Ooooh. I am mad now. Back to my seat with the group I go. *Emmm-barrr-assed.* Who did that country bumpkin think she was?

When the program was finished, Mahalia went to talk to the girl and her mother. Seeing that, I stormed out to the car. While the rest of the group mingled amongst the crowd, meeting and greeting them as we usually did after a concert, I sat in the car and sulked.

Not for long. Soon I heard Mahalia saying, "There you are, De-loreese," as she opened the car door, preparing to say something to me.

Arms folded, I looked the other way. Whatever she had to say, I didn't want to hear her. She was a traitor for talking to that girl who embarrassed me.

"That was something, wasn't it?" Mahalia said simply.

"Not to me!"

"Ain't it grand, the way God has of bringing up talent in the strangest places?"

I jutted my chin out, and looked up at her, asking, "I guess now you want her, right?"

"What makes you think that?"

"Well, she sang a higher note than I did."

"It's not about how high you sing. It's about feeling the presence of God." She paused, waiting for me to soften. When I didn't, Mahalia continued, "The Bible says if we keep our peace the rocks will cry out. You just heard another one of His rocks cry out."

I knew she was right but I couldn't let down. I said nothing.

That was when Mahalia said, sternly and directly, "Deloreese, you've got to get over your Miss Wonderful thing and just be who you are, doing what the God in you says do. You are not in competition. You're in God's service. And neither your voice nor my voice are the only voices God has." She took another pause, smiling now a little bit, telling me that I would do and feel and sing a lot better if only I could realize that. "Just be glad that He called you but always remember you are not the only one He called. So don't get beside yourself or you'll always be caught short like tonight. Now get out of this car and come in here and meet and congratulate this child. It will mean a lot to her, coming from you."

I followed Mahalia back inside, going over to the girl on my own and introducing myself. Sweet and in awe of me, asking me all kinds of questions about how I sang so well and had so much confidence, she didn't even know what a powerhouse she was.

The lesson I learned that night was one which God had sent Mahalia as my angel to teach me. Her words and variations of them echoed throughout my life, helping me on many levels: "You're not in competition, you're in God's service; you're not the only one who can do it, there is someone who can do it different and maybe even better."

I have remembered that. It helped me when I began my career and it helps me today. I don't need to compete because if you want Della

Reese, you have to come to me; I have all the Della Reese available that there is. When I began singing secular music, admiring and listening to some of the top artists who inspired me, I realized I couldn't sing like Dinah Washington, Sarah Vaughan, Ella Fitzgerald, or Nat King Cole. But they could not sing like me.

Good, bad, or indifferent, what I had was my own. My uniqueness. The power that came from that lesson allowed me to go forward and do what I do as a singer, and later as an actress, spokesperson, and teacher—all without fear, intimidation, apprehension or competition. I am what I am. And nobody else can be the same I am that I am.

There was another angel who came along the way to help Mahalia make me aware not to show off but to show the God in me working through me to me. And wherever that girl with the braids and coveralls is today I thank her for being there that night.

My gratitude to Mahalia Jackson has grown over the years for really giving me a foundation in the art of communication. What she taught, mostly by example, was not only about singing gospel music but about pop, jazz, blues, Broadway, classical, you name it. It's about filling yourself with the spirit of whatever you're singing about, of really going to that place and letting listeners go with you. The art of communication would become more and more important as I journeyed on.

When I was fifteen years old and counting the minutes until I got back home to Seabourn Brooks and all my friends in the neighborhood, I wasn't able to appreciate how much Mahalia had done for me. That happens. Sometimes your angels do their work without your knowing it, and too soon they're gone so that by the time you realize what they've done, it's too late.

Mahalia Jackson died in 1972 but as God would have it, I got a chance to talk to her again a few years before she left. In the late sixties, over two decades after I had been under her wing, she and I were both doing *The Ed Sullivan Show* on the same evening. It was the first time we had seen one another in all those years. Here we were, sharing a dressing room together—my perfect opportunity to tell her how much I had learned from her, how grateful I was, and how much I respected her. "You know," I said, holding back my tears, "I didn't realize how much you taught me until I started becoming successful and reporters would ask me questions about music or singing and as I answered, I listened to myself and I heard you, everything you said to me twenty years ago."

Mahalia smiled, nodding as if she understood but saying nothing.

Then my tears began. "I hope you can forgive me," I said, unable to stop from crying at this point. "I wish I could have thanked you at the time."

In her own Mahalia style—straightforward—she forgave me. "It was all part of God's plan," she said. "I'm glad He used me to teach you." She took a beat as she fought her own tears, before adding, "Deloreese, I'm telling you now what I have told the world already. Of all the gospel singers I have sponsored or taught, you are the only one who has ever given me credit. You have thanked me the best way anyone could."

That was a marvelous day. In that backstage dressing room, we became real friends. We hugged and we both cried and she told me she loved me and had always been proud of me.

After that, Mahalia Jackson went out and *tore* down the *Sullivan* show. And I didn't do too badly myself.

"Quit school?" Seabourn looked at me like I had spoken a blasphemy.

It was early in the year of 1947. High-school graduation was now in sight but it all seemed so pointless to me.

Over my senior year, my relationship with Seabourn Brooks had progressed to the extent that, by now, when he walked me home, we would stand downstairs in the hall and talk close together for as long as was humanly bearable.

By now everyone in the neighborhood referred to me as Brooks's girl. "Don't talk to her, she's Brooks's girl," they'd say, inferring all kinds of things. That was heaven to me. But as God and I both know, Seabourn was a gentleman through and through even though I made it pretty torrid in that hallway with almost kisses and the smoldering looks that passed between us, looks of *I want you, because I need you so much, because*

I've got to have you; you're too young; I'm old enough to feel this way; I have to go now; wait; go on upstairs; wait; no; see you later.

My mother and father didn't know about our hallway meetings. But they made sure to let me know I shouldn't be talking to Seabourn Brooks anywhere. That was ridiculous to me. After all, Daddy was King Tut, and he knew Brooks from the pool hall; but he didn't want his princess, his baby, his star, having anything to do with this man because he knew him very well. The worst part was how Mama belittled him and yet everything Brooks said to me was something she could have said. If she was bugging me about something, he was the first to say, "She's just doing this because she loves you and because she only wants the best for you. Now you don't understand that because you're a little girl. Your mama is wise and she is really right. You have to listen to her."

When Seabourn wanted to tell me something I needed to hear, I was always Junior to him. Even as I did start to stretch out and become a little less pudgy and saw some progress in the chest area. On the topic of school, he sounded exactly like her, saying, "Junior, you have got to graduate. To get ahead in this world, you have got to get your education. You want to end up like me? Look at me. I was too fast and too smart to graduate and now this is the life I'm in, out here on the street. That what you want?"

Earlier in the year my math teacher, Mr. Tucker, and I had been seriously locking horns. I was a class cut-up; Tucker was a tyrant. I told Seabourn about it, saying that if Mr. Tucker failed me I wouldn't graduate and I didn't care. Seabourn calmly suggested, "There's got to be another math teacher in that school. If not, I'll go and talk to Tucker." And that's what he did. Problem solved. Period, the end.

Then one winter's day downstairs in the hallway, Mr. Jones, the apartment building janitor, spotted Seabourn and me immersed in close conversation. Mr. Jones was the kind of guy you would cast to play Ebenezer Scrooge. You can probably imagine what he did. Yes—you are right—Mr. Jones went and told Mama about finding us in the hallway.

My mother was *livvv-idd.* She blasted Seabourn, telling me what a lowdown dirty nothing he was, and that I was never to see him again.

Too mad to cry, I told her, "He may be a nothing but he's done nothing!"

She repeated herself that I was never to see him again. Under penalty of certain death.

The next time I saw Seabourn at the corner, I told him what had happened, how much of a drag school was, and that I was gonna quit and leave home.

"Quit school?" he repeated. "You're not gonna quit school. No woman of mine is a quitter." He followed with a lecture on the need for a high-school education. As we talked, he walked me only halfway home. Seabourn had those long, lanky legs and that slow stride. He stopped not far from our building and with a smile coming on, he said, "You know how proud I'll be when you graduate? I'll be so proud I'm gonna surprise you in a big way."

"How's that?"

After I graduated, he said, he was going to go and talk to Mama and Daddy and ask for permission to see me and date me. With that, he turned and walked back down the street.

I stood on the sidewalk watching him move into the distance in that dancelike prowl of his, my mind preserving that moving picture of him for posterity. Watching until he disappeared from sight, I turned the other way and headed on home.

I guess I knew the part about talking to Mama and Daddy would never happen but I hoped anyway.

A short time later, Seabourn started walking me all the way home again and our stolen hallway conversations resumed. One late afternoon, the last possible person I expected to see walked in on us as we were talking downstairs. It was Daddy, home earlier than usual from work. He calmly sent me upstairs so that he and Brooks could have a man-to-man talk, leaving me never to know what was said that day.

What I did know was that Seabourn Brooks stopped walking me

home. From then on, our communication was limited to looking at each other in passing with our *I'm Dying for You* looks. We kept our distance. Or, rather, he kept his distance.

In this time, as I pined away, Matilda and my other friends were starting to make plans for the Senior Prom. At home, my prom dress became a topic of discussion. It cost something like thirty-nine dollars, an exorbitant price, and Daddy didn't have the money for it. Louise was trying to get me one on loan but had been unsuccessful. Then, my "grandfather" Mr. Hopkins (he was a good-hearted man, but not my mother's father) suggested that Aunt Georgia—the wealthy aunt whom we never saw—could buy me my dress. Mama talked to Georgia and arranged for me to go see her to get the money.

Mama gave me the bus fare and I made the trek over to East Grand Boulevard and Brush where Aunt Georgia's building was. My mother only gave me the one-way fare as Georgia had agreed to give me money for the bus home. As soon as I got to Aunt Georgia's, she wanted me to go to the kitchen and wash her dishes. No sooner had I finished that, than she wanted me to go sweep out her living room. When I finished sweeping, she wanted me to go make up her bed.

By now I have had it. I say to myself—*Unhh, unhh. I ain't gonna do that.* I'm ready to go home now.

"Deloreese, did you hear me? I said, I want you to go make up the bed now."

Trying to be respectful, I said, "Aunt Georgia, Mr. Hopkins said you were gonna give me money for my prom dress—"

"Money for your prom dress? Well, I need new refrigerators in my tenants' apartments. For the money you want, that would be a down payment on a new refrigerator."

"Why did you have me come up here, if you weren't gonna give me money for the prom?"

"Oh, don't you talk to me like that!" she warned. Then she said, "You'll get over not going to the prom . . ."

"Forget about it," I interrupted. And before she could say another word, I grabbed my coat and left, not knowing how I was going to get home without the bus fare. Well. I started walking. I walked. And walked. And walked. I ended up walking all the way home from Brush to Vernor Highway. Let me give you an idea of how far that was. When I left Aunt Georgia's it was a clear, moderately cold day. As I walked, with no boots or galoshes or scarf, it began to snow. By the time I got home, I was a snowman. Completely covered with snow. Mama gasped when she saw me. And when I told her what had happened, she went straight to the phone, called Aunt Georgia, and that was the last we ever heard of her.

At the time, there was no apparent lesson to see. But as I look back at a mean-spirited person like Georgia, I wonder if God doesn't put people like her in our lives on purpose, just to show us how not to be.

In the case of the elusive prom dress, my angels turned out to be a whole mess of people who loved me and pitched in money together so I could buy it. Louise organized it all, probably putting in more than anyone, along with Daddy and the rest of my extended family in the building and the neighborhood. Georgia was dead wrong—I didn't have to get over not going to the prom.

Whether I would ever get over being forbidden to talk to Seabourn was another issue altogether. Then I stopped seeing him around. Weeks and weeks went by. Winter became spring and graduation was fast approaching. Still no sight of Seabourn. Little did I understand that he was trying to protect me by not coming around. For reasons I didn't know, and not because of me, he had started using more drugs.

Alcohol, marijuana, cocaine, heroin—these were substances that were around my neighborhood for a long time. When poverty and hardship prevailed and life was something you wanted to escape, sometimes getting really high on a Friday night was the only way to feel good. Even if it was just to buy a pint and drink it alone. Some people could do drugs the way you have a glass of punch at a party. Others became addicts. Brooks had become a heroin addict.

Winos and junkies had been dying all over the neighborhood. After weeks of not seeing Seabourn, I decided to just go by his house—an act which was absolutely forbidden.

One of his girls answered the door and hollered to him that I was there. She gestured for me to follow her into the living room where I saw Seabourn on the couch like I had never seen him—harsh and loud and uncouth.

"Now you know, now get out of here, Junior. I've told you, you have no business here."

I stood, frozen in place.

"Get out now!" he screamed at me. "Right now!" Standing up, he started toward me, scaring me so bad I ran to the door. For a moment, I looked back and saw Seabourn falling over a coffee table. Turning away again, I ran out the door and all the way home and up the three flights of stairs and into my room where I suffered as no one has ever suffered before or since.

Cut to: The day before graduation, a jail cell at the police station where I am being held.

Let me explain. That day was known as Skip Day, a tradition wherein all the seniors were allowed to skip school that day.

When I told Mama about it, she wasn't buying any. "No," she said, "I'm not sending you to school to skip. I'm sending you to learn and if there is no one there but you, you're still going to school."

Now, you should know I was not going to be in school alone. And so, even though I wasn't in the mood to party, a group of us skipped together and went over to Robert Wilburn's house. Robert had to climb in the bathroom window to let us in because his father had forgotten to leave the key in the mailbox. Unbeknownst to us, a neighbor across the street saw only a pair of legs going into the window. Not knowing it was Robert, she called the police. By the time the police busted in on us, we had beer and cigarettes and music playing, along with some necking that was going on.

The police hauled us all off to jail. Once everything was cleared up—an innocent mistake—they informed us that all we had to do was tell our mothers' and fathers' names. Our parents would then be contacted so they could come get us.

I was never giving them the name of my mother because there was nothing the police could do to me as bad as she would do. So, everybody else went home and I, as noted, was taken to a cell.

There was a cot and a toilet in the cell. When I walked to the window and looked out through the bars, all I could see was the nearby dome of a building and pigeons everywhere. There were so many pigeons. Somehow the sight of them spurred me to tears. I began to cry, silently praying. It was more of a plea than a prayer. *Please, God, I promise if You could get me out of this without Mama finding out, I will never disobey her another minute of my life, forever and ever . . .* And so on. I pleaded and promised until finally, three hours later, a guard came to let me out.

I followed him down the hall and there, standing in it, was my stone-faced mother who said to me: "I have six children and I have never had to come to the jailhouse to get any one of them before now."

And then she was completely silent as we walked home. It hurt worse than if she had beat me.

That night, I was to sing with our glee club, of which I was a member and soloist. After dressing for the event, I was coming through the living room on my way out. Mama was sitting in the big green chair, her praying chair, and looked up at me to ask, "You're not ashamed to stand up there and sing just coming out of jail? How would they feel about your voice if they knew you were a jailbird?"

That hurt too. But I went ahead to the event and sang as scheduled, in great pain.

The next night was graduation. This was the moment I had heard about all my life; the great goal had been reached. But with my various problems weighing on my heart, the pleasure for me was not what I had expected.

Daddy couldn't get off work to attend the graduation ceremony. But

Mama was there, beaming with pride. This was her dream come true, more so than mine. One of her children had finished high school. She felt she had finally been able to give me what hard circumstances prevented her from giving her other children.

As they called my name and I walked onto the stage to receive my diploma, I looked down to see my mother and smiled at her with thanks. And there, beyond her, in the back of the auditorium stood Seabourn, tall and proud. He saluted me and threw me a kiss. And then he was gone.

After almost two years at Wayne State University, I found that I wasn't impressed at all with college. Nobody from my neighborhood was there and the other students, mainly from the upwardly mobile West Side black families, seemed to look down on me. In retrospect, I know that wasn't true. It was my sheer fear, like a defensive wall, that drove them away. Not a good way to make friends and influence people.

My desire to become a psychiatrist dissolved fast when I found out I had eight years of medical school ahead of me. Somehow I'd thought you could just take a class or two and then get out and start fixing people's minds.

Daddy helped to make me feel I didn't need college by pointing out how hard he and Mama were working to send me to Wayne for a degree "they" (the ruling white powers of the world) weren't going to let me use anyway. "You're seventeen years old," he reminded me one night as he read his paper. "You're a woman, and you need to get on with your life. Settle down, find a husband, save some money. Do what your mama did." Daddy believed and instructed me to believe that I needed a man to be complete. He also believed a college degree was a liability in finding a husband. "Don't no man want a woman like that. A man want a woman to love him and take care of him. Nobody should teach him. A man should teach a woman." He looked back down at his paper and back up again, saying, "Don't be too smart to have a husband." To him it was like they used to say in our neighborhood—"Don't be too hip to be happy."

But Daddy's advice was moot. Mama insisted I stay at Wayne. And so I went, hating it every step of the way.

In the meantime, I was branching out from singing with the church choir to also singing with some local professional choirs, including a new one called the Original Hutchins Gospel Trumpeteers. My social life wasn't terrible either. At seventeen, I was taller, slimmer, and cuter than I'd been only a few years before. There were plenty of boys hovering around, making themselves available to me. There was the boy who took me out to dinners, the boy who took me dancing, and the boy who took me to the movies. There were the boys who hit on me and flirted with me. I didn't care about any of them. Of course, human nature the way it is, my not caring made me seem that much more exciting to them.

The one I cared about was Seabourn. He was still my main love and the one, I was sure, destined to be my partner in life. He had been in Cleveland all this time, getting himself straightened out. When some of the problems he had with the law blew over, he was coming back. And until then, I could have fun with the other boys but nothing more.

One Saturday in March of 1949, on an afternoon a few hours before it was time to go rehearse with the new group, my mother called me into the living room. She was sitting in her big chair, her green praying chair, and I sat down at her feet as she began to talk to me in a way she very rarely did. In a personal, meaningful way. Mama, smelling as always of Ponds cold cream, vanilla, and spices, told me how proud she was of me and how much she loved my going to college and what a fine young lady I had turned out to be. She told me she knew what the neighbors were saying about how fast I was because of all the boys I dated. My mother looked at me thoughtfully, asking if I planned to marry any of them.

I said, "No."

She put her hand down on my shoulder. "You're a young girl," she said, "and you have the right to date anybody you want. But when you take a man to God and tell God you want to be married for life, you will have to give these other fellows up and be true to him, do you understand?" I nodded and Mama continued, "Marriage is sacred in the eyes of God. Remember that."

I said I would. I knew I would because once I married Seabourn, I could be true to him with no sweat.

My mother and I talked for the longest time. She told me a lot of things that she'd never told me before, nothing dramatic or revealing, just little details of the inner life of Nellie Early, of those beautiful dreams and thoughts of hers. And then we did something we almost never did: we played.

We went into the kitchen where she took out some mayonnaise, chopped up a piece of lettuce and a tomato, and put them in a bowl. And we ate from that bowl together, laughing and soppin' in that bowl. It was wonderful. And as I left for my rehearsal that night, it struck me how good I was feeling and how loved I knew I was.

I hitched a ride to rehearsal with Marie Waters and her husband, George Waters, both of whom were slated to be angels in my life further down the road. At that stage, I had just met them since joining the Original Hutchins Gospel Trumpeteers and I appreciated getting the ride since rehearsal was all the way out on Eight Mile Road in a rural area.

After rehearsal, I began to feel funny. My head hurt almost like a migraine and, for no apparent reason, I felt weepy. Unable to hold back my tears, I just began to bawl uncontrollably as the pain in my head worsened. I had no idea why but I was possessed of the need to get home. "I've got to get going," I kept telling Marie and George. "I really need to go home." They were socializing with the other group members and made it clear they weren't ready to go home. Finally, at eleven P.M., I announced that I was going to catch a bus. Hurrying to get my coat and hat, I started out the door.

Because Eight Mile Road was far out in the country, the buses were very unpredictable, showing up when and if they did. Being mindful of that, Marie and George refused to let me go on the bus, saying it wasn't safe. Unhappy about having to leave, neither of the Waterses said a word to me in the car as they took me home, dropped me off, and drove away.

Mama had always had premonitions of things and in my seventeen years I had found there were times when I had them also. That night I was having a horrible premonition except I didn't know what it was. Only that something was wrong. I ran upstairs. When I reached the third floor, Louise, my longtime angel sister from across the hall, opened her door and took me into her apartment.

"What's the matter?" I asked.

"How did you know?" she asked.

"I don't know, but what is it?"

Louise put her arms around me, explaining, "Your mama left the movies early tonight and on the way home, she must have fallen down on the steps. I found her and got your daddy and he called the ambulance." She told me that he was with Mama at the hospital and that I was to wait with her until he returned.

It sounded as if she had broken her arm or leg. Or maybe sprained something. But at three A.M. when I saw Daddy through Louise's window as he walked down the street to the front door, I knew it was bad. Where he usually stood tall, he was bent over; where his stride was always brisk and rhythmic, he was walking real slow. From the top of the stairs, I watched him climbing, becoming weaker and slower with every step— as if he had programmed himself with just enough energy to get home and it was draining fast. I went down to the second floor and met him there at the top of the steps. My father literally fell into my arms, telling me, "Mama is real sick, baby, real sick. She's had a cerebral hemorrhage, sort of a stroke."

Jimmy, Louise's husband, and I helped Daddy up the stairs and into his bed. My father and I sat on the bed together, not talking at all, and he held me until I went to sleep. When I woke up in the morning, I was alone.

In a matter of minutes, I left for the hospital, which was in close walking distance. Because it was a county hospital, there weren't enough rooms and beds to handle the patient load so there were gurneys in the hall. I found Mama on one of them. She was unconscious but I held her and told her I loved her. As I looked at her, she stirred somewhat and after a bit, her cheeks seemed rosier and there was a faint smile on her lips. This allowed me to begin to feel that everything was going to be fine. Mama was going to be all right.

I walked back home, singing, and praising God aloud that my mama was going to be all right. At home, I made myself busy, getting out the broom and sweeping and thinking about making everything nice and tidy for Mama when she got home. Louise stopped over to see how I was and Aunt Capitolia, Daddy's sister, arrived to stay with me until he got home from work.

"Mama's going to be all right, I know," I told them, describing how well she looked, sweeping the dirt out the front door. As I leaned down to sweep it into the dustpan, I saw my grandfather, Mr. Hopkins, coming up the stairs crying. He saw me and said, "You po' child, yo' Mama is gone on home."

He was wrong, I told him, very annoyed. "I just saw her and she had rosy cheeks and she smiled at me and she couldn't be dead." To prove it, I went to the phone and called the hospital to ask about her. I was told by a nurse that my mother was doing as well as could be expected.

In a fit, I turned on Mr. Hopkins, calling him a senile old man, and a liar and a fool.

Then Daddy walked in the door. He didn't have to say anything. Now I knew she was dead for sure.

I went in my room and locked my door and cried for two days and two nights. Family and friends, practically everyone in the neighborhood came up to the apartment, all trying to be of help. They tried to feed me, I wouldn't eat. They tried to talk to me, I wouldn't listen. My father told everyone, "Leave her alone, she has to find her own way."

I was dead inside. Destroyed completely. I only came out of my bedroom to go to the bathroom. Before I went, I listened first to hear if anyone was in the living room, which I had to cross to get to the bathroom. On one of my bathroom trips, my father came down the hall and stopped me. "I know how bad you feel," Daddy said. "But I feel worse. I've lost my wife and my baby just when I needed her most. I feel so all alone now."

I ran to my father's arms, vowing to be all he needed me to be. As I wiped my tears, Daddy looked at me and saw that my hair had a gray streak in it that wasn't there before. In three days, a thick strand had gone completely gray.

"Don't worry anymore," he said to me, almost as though he was speaking to music, in a song that wrapped around me and lingered in my ears, "we're gonna be all right. We're gonna miss her, but wherever she is, she's watching over us."

The entire neighborhood, and then some, came out for the funeral of Nellie Early. Because Mama loved and cared for everyone, she was so beloved by everyone. All of her children were there at her graveside: my sisters—Nodie, Susan, Gladys, and Ora Mae—and, of course, R.D., who lived in Detroit.

R.D. and I, as close as ever, consoled each other as best we could. Ora Mae, like my other three older sisters, was never overly fond of me. Like the others, she was envious of the time I had spent with Mama. Plus, she hated that Rufus and I were so close.

But despite the old resentments, it seemed for the time being that our common grief brought all of us together. At least, it seemed that way.

After the funeral, a group of us went over to a speakeasy on Hastings for a drink. A lot of the neighbors were there, as well as one of the young men I was dating. After a couple of drinks, he asked me to come outside with him, saying he had something to tell me.

We walked down Hastings in the cool March night air. "Just found out something you need to know," he began with a serious tone. "Your mama is not dead."

I looked at him incredulously.

"That was your grandmother. Gladys is your real mother."

Stunned, I shot back at him, "You and whoever said that are a god-damn liar. I don't even know Gladys. Whenever I called for Mama, it was always Nellie who came and Nellie is and always will be my mother."

I never spoke to that boy again.

Daddy was too drunk when he came home that night to talk to me about it. But the next morning, he told me that Gladys had a mean pimp who took all of her money and she had him believing I was her daughter and she was paying my mother to keep me. Gladys lied to keep some of the money for herself that she made when she tricked at night, the same amount of money that her pimp thought she was paying Mama. "Don't worry," my father said, in his reassuring deep voice, "I'm your daddy and Babe is your mama. You are the daughter of Richard and Nellie Early."

Gladys's lie continued to follow me for the rest of my life. Well-meaning and not-so-well-meaning individuals over the years were always bringing up to me who they had heard my real mother was.

No sooner had the incident about Gladys died down, but that very day Nodie approached Daddy about taking me back to Gary so that I could work for her while she and Fat Man would try to put me through college. Two things I would have rather died than do.

"No," I told my father as he debated Nodie's offer, begging him to let me stay at home. Daddy told Nodie my place was with him.

"Very well," Nodie said and proceeded to box up and pack all of my mother's belongings. These were Mama's cherished items that she had collected through thirty-two years of marriage. Linens, silverware, glasses, clothes, knickknacks, even small pieces of furniture. She left Daddy a pot, a skillet, plates for two, silverware for two, and two sets of bath and bed linens. Nodie took pictures from the wall and personal photographs. She took all the doilies and tablecloths my mother had crocheted all those years. Just *ever-ry-thing.* She packed it all up and took it back to Gary.

The most infuriating part was that Daddy had told everyone to take whatever they wanted. Everyone else had selected a small token, some memento, and Nodie took all the rest. In the middle of her pillage, I asked Daddy to stop her but he said it was her mother's stuff and she could have it if she needed it. I never forgave Nodie for that.

Put your pause button on right here for a minute. Let me say a word or two about forgiveness from my older, wiser perspective. Forgiveness is a powerful act, a freeing, liberating act. It took me a long time to learn that forgiveness didn't mean trying to convince myself that what Nodie did wasn't wrong. She was wrong. She was mean and selfish. It hurt me even more that she did it to my father, a man who gave and contributed to Nodie's own well-being continuously, as well as to the rest of his wife's children—whether they were his or not.

My idea of forgiveness is letting go of resentment that does not serve your better interest, ridding yourself of negative thoughts. All they do is make you miserable. Believe me, you can fret and fume all you want, but whoever it was that wronged you is not suffering from your anguish whatsoever. My attitude is, why should someone undeserving occupy space in my mind rent-free?

It was many years before I knew how to kick those unwanted tenants out. But in a way it was Nodie, someone so hard to forgive, who helped me begin to understand. For that one lesson, who knows? Maybe she too was a kind of angel in disguise.

I left Wayne State University—which pleased me greatly—to take care of our home and of my father. Through March, April, and then May, we did fine. On Memorial Day, May 30th, with picnics and fun planned, I get up early to begin the food preparation and there in the kitchen I see this woman standing over the stove, cooking.

"What are you doing in my mother's kitchen?" I ask.

"Ask your father," the woman says.

Storming into his room, I ask, "What is that woman doing in my mama's kitchen?"

Daddy says, "Making my breakfast."

"My mama is not cold in her grave and you got this woman in her kitchen?"

"Your mama is dead and she is not coming back. I gotta go on living and I need someone to help me."

I say, "If she stays, I am leaving!"

He says, "I will really miss you."

That was it. Louise dragged me over to her place to change my mind and when she couldn't, she went and talked to Daddy, siding with him in the end, anyway. Soon all our neighbors and friends, Reverend Travis, Reverend Barnes, Miss Janie, Annie Mack, everybody, were all descending on the apartment trying to convince me not to go.

Hindsight is so marvelous. Today I fully realize that my father was so helpless without my mother, he could not function. She had taken such good care of him he really didn't know how to boil water. He was right, he did need someone to look after him.

But on May 30, 1949, all I could see was that my father had chosen this woman (in my mama's kitchen) over me.

I had thirteen cents to my name. I packed my belongings in a steamer trunk and although everybody was still telling me not to go, I was determined to leave and I did. Thirteen cents and a steamer trunk. Without help, I couldn't even get it down the stairs from the third floor. So I called the cab stand down the street and asked for Ollie Aikens, one of my would-be suitors who had been hitting on me, and asked him to come pick me up.

Ollie was a short, round young man with an Oriental cast to his eyes. He looked like a Buddha. When I called him, he said, "Have you made up your mind to be with me? And me alone?"

"Yes," I said, without feeling.

Ollie came and picked me up in his cab, hauled my trunk downstairs and put it in the backseat. As he drove slowly down Vernor Highway, I looked out the window at the place that had been my home for seventeen years.

Deep down, I knew this was it. I knew I had just left home for good.

Where I was going, I did not know. Everything ahead of me looked dark and uncertain.

I felt very lost and alone. But, of course, I wasn't. My angels were traveling with me, their lessons and their love filling me with everything I needed to move ahead. Onward and upward.

At the front of the pack was my mama, whispering in my ear, reminding me of God's love and protection, letting me know I was not at all lost and not at all alone.

Singing

1949 – 1961

~

5

My prospects for making it out of the slums were looking small to nil right about now. I was a seventeen-year-old girl with a cumbersome steamer trunk and thirteen cents to my name. For seventeen years I had been sheltered in the safe harbor of my parents' love. Now, I had neither Mama nor Daddy to warn me about the world that lay beyond the neighborhood which had reared me, the only world I knew.

I had no marketable skills. No job training. No formal music background. No acting classes. No show business connections.

All I had—or so I *thought*—was this young man, Ollie Aikens, who was behind the wheel of his cab, trying to reassure me as I wept profusely about a mama who was dead and a daddy from whose house I had just left for good.

"You made the right decision to be with me, girl," Ollie was saying, smiling his Buddha-like smile, as he drove west to the next neighborhood over. It was no more than ten blocks from Vernor Highway but when Ollie stopped the car in front of his mother's house, where I would be staying with him, it could have been Mars for all I knew.

For all I knew, Ollie was right as he promised, "You know, I'll stand up for you. Everybody else don't care for you like I do. You can count on me, Deloreese. You stay with me now, I'll take care a' you and whatever you need."

What I did not know was the imminent peril I was in. If anyone could have used an angel at that very moment in time and place it was me.

And—yes, you are right—God sent me one. Had He not, the fork in the road I had just taken would have certainly proven to be my undoing.

My angel was Ollie's mother, Mrs. Aikens, a nice Christian woman who was to quickly school me in a few things that Mama didn't live long enough to teach me. First off, Mrs. Aikens explained, I wouldn't be able to get around with that trunk, so we went through it together and she took me to a shop where I was able to sell it and some of the unnecessary items I was hauling in it. Now I had some money. Not a lot, but more than thirteen cents. Now, I had thirty-two dollars and thirteen cents.

During the next days while Ollie went to work, I stayed in with his mother, cooking for her and helping her clean the house. As I did, I sang hymns and gospel songs that were of comfort to me and familiar to Mrs. Aikens, too, songs that made her clap her hands and shout. We became very close in no time.

Over the first week, Ollie would come home each evening and sit down to a large dinner I had prepared, telling me how good the food was and what a good wife I was going to make for him. Then he would have sex with me, roll over, and go to sleep.

When I closed my eyes, it was still Seabourn I saw in my dreams but with everything that had happened I could feel those dreams fading fast. Even so, it comforted me to dream of the day we would finally get to make love. See, where I come from, sex was never a bad thing. It was a wonderful thing. The only problem was the potential of getting pregnant. Otherwise, in a neighborhood like mine where nobody had much money, sex was the biggest, best entertainment we had going. It was not looked down on. It was a natural thing, what I call a normal mean, a way of life. That's what you did, you grew up and had sex.

All of that said, I knew already that there was a difference between sex and making love. I knew what Ollie and I were doing was sex. And being that he said he loved me, was taking good care of me and was going to marry me, I accepted the situation and resolved to make the most of it.

After ten days went by, I went to the kitchen early one morning for a cup of tea. There, already up and waiting for me, was Mrs. Aikens. The expression on her face was one of alarm. She wasted no time telling me, "You've got to get out of here. This is not a place for you."

My look of confusion prompted Mrs. Aikens to break down and tell me about Ann, Ollie's woman. That she was a whore for Ollie, and very dangerous. And if Ollie wanted to keep me, Ann would demand that Ollie turn me out too.

"Turn me out?" I repeated, as if she couldn't be serious.

Mrs. Aikens was dead serious. "You are a good Christian child," she said, "and this is not the life for you. You can sing and make a good living and not end up on the street. You been to school. You can get a job until your singing comes through."

"But Ollie never talked to me about Ann or any of that," I insisted. "He loves me and wants to marry me."

"Well, child, you may not know it but you don't want to or need to marry him. He's my son and I love him but I know him for what he is—no good."

Mrs. Aikens led me out of the kitchen and began to pack for me, telling me as she hurried, "Get dressed. I know somewhere you can stay for the time being."

Within the hour she took me to stay at Mrs. McBride's, a friend of hers, who lived another four blocks west, and who had a room to rent for seven dollars a week. Mrs. McBride made me pay an initial payment of two weeks' rent out of my $32.13. Mrs. Aikens watched me count out the money, thanked Mrs. McBride for allowing me to be a tenant, and before telling me good-bye, said, "Now you've got to find a job and don't spend your money unless you have to. You keep on trusting God, He won't let you down." She gave me a brief hug and then she left.

As I understand it these many years later, Ollie had run his game before and he would run it again. The idea was to pamper me that first week and then by the next week, put his plan into action. Mrs. Aikens got me out of there in the nick of time. I knew her for less than two weeks in June of 1949 and never saw her again after that day. But that made her no less an angel than if she had physically swooped down on wings and picked me up to save me from being plowed over by a Mack truck. It was not only the situation with Ollie from which Mrs. Aikens protected me; in those ten days she also reminded me to keep my eyes open, to place my trust in God and not in the predators on the streets. In addition, she brought me the message that my singing could really take me somewhere, a belief I didn't even grasp yet. And finally, Mrs. Aikens helped me complete the rapid transition from adolescence to adulthood into which I had been thrust by Mama's death.

It hit me as I watched her leave that day from Mrs. McBride's house: I was grown now and, for the first time in my life, I was really on my own.

Mrs. McBride had two daughters very near my age who looked up to me as a woman of the world. So I liked them. On the other hand, Mrs. McBride thought I would spoil them with my worldliness and wanted them to have nothing to do with me.

This did not concern me. I had a more pressing matter on my mind: finding a job. There were many skills I did not have but when an opening came up for driving a produce truck, one skill I did happen to have was the ability to drive. Just as important I had a driver's license. Although we had never owned a car, after high school, Matilda Maddox's boyfriend used to take Matilda and me out for driving lessons in his large stick-shift Dynaflow Buick. Luckily, I had the license and the guts to learn how to handle the gears in the truck so I got the job. My route was to drive the truck from the farms outside of Toledo, Ohio, delivering the goods to the Eastern Market, not far from my old neighborhood. I would leave Sunday evening and be back at the market by 4:00 A.M., leaving again on Tuesday evening and returning once more by 4:00 A.M. the next morning. And so on for the rest of the week. It was a hundred dollars a week and payday was every two weeks. I can still remember picking up my first pay, the first time I'd ever had two hundred dollars of my own. That independent feeling I got looking at my own hard-earned money was definitely a powerful one.

In the meantime, I was hired to direct two choirs, one in River Rouge, a Detroit suburb, and one in Ecourse, Michigan, another community not too far away. The choir directing jobs each paid twenty-five dollars a month.

It felt good being self-sufficient, earning a decent living, and knowing I could take care of myself. But deep down there was a large void in my life. It was the lack of a family, a family I was yearning and praying for whether I knew it or not.

Well. God didn't make me yearn and pray for long.

⚬——— Get out your pins and stick a few more here. This is where a few special angels were about to alight in my life, the first of which was the very sister I had always wanted. It was Marie Waters, who, together with her husband George, had given me the ride home that night when my mother was dying. Over the course of rehearsing sporadically with the Original Hutchins Gospel Trumpeteers, we had not seen each other since that night until one evening that summer when rehearsal was held at the Waterses' house. Upon hearing of my situation, the tall, attractive Marie—as much like Lucille Ball as you'd ever want to be—made the decision then and there to take me under her wing. "Why don't you move out of that room you're paying seven dollars a week for and move in here with us for free?"

Their place was out in River Rouge, a small three-room apartment that Marie's father had built above his house, alongside a second apartment upstairs he built for Marie's sister and her family. There was hardly enough room in the Waterses' place for Marie, George, and their growing teenage son, Porgy (as we called him); not to mention that Emory Radford, the pianist for the group, was staying there already.

I told Marie how much I appreciated the offer but that I couldn't impose.

"There is no imposing," she replied, insisting along with George that I move in immediately. Their attitude? The more the merrier!

They were right, too. The five of us in this small upstairs apartment, we had a ball. Laughs, love, fun, food, and songs all day long. There were dinners we'd all help make together and nights watching Marie's little TV—so small you could barely make out the images—while we laughed and screamed away. Especially roller derby. That fierce roller skating was a favorite of Marie's.

With fewer expenses, before long I was able to stop driving the produce truck and concentrate on my choir directing and singing. Included in this, of course, was the growing reputation of the Original Hutchins Gospel Trumpeteers. Besides the exceptional piano playing of Emory Radford, the group included Morris McGee, the lead singer, his wife, Priscilla, George, Marie, and myself. We worked on our arrangements during every spare moment, sometimes building up from George's strong bass, putting Morris on top of that between the bass and Priscilla's alto or second alto, then Marie's clear contralto on top of that, leaving me to alternate between soprano and tenor on top of Marie. Or, we might build down starting with my soprano—all depending on the song and the feeling we wanted to achieve.

Marie belonged to the New Liberty Baptist Church, a storefront church on the East Side, where she played piano for the choir. In addition to some fantastic singing over there, the church boasted a young, charismatic, *very* attractive minister, the Reverend E. A. Rundless. In his early thirties, the Reverend had a superb voice himself. In fact, he had been one of the original Soul Stirrers, one of the most popular quartets at the time; when he was called to the ministry, the great Sam Cooke replaced him in the group.

The first time I visited New Liberty with Marie, I was asked to sing and the church *went up.* It didn't take much more than that, and a look at Reverend Rundless, to get me to stay.

I was introduced that Sunday to the lovely, gracious Mrs. Earnestine Rundless. Unaware that she was slated to become a most important angel to me, I have to admit, I was slightly less than overjoyed to discover that there was a Mrs. Rundless.

I don't know what you'd call him now but in those days, the Reverend was what we called a *fox.* A natural born fox. The kind you'd love to have run around in your henhouse. A short while later, I thought I'd struck gold when I found myself sitting next to him in a car on a cross-country trip.

The Original Hutchins Gospel Trumpeteers had been invited to perform for the National Baptist Convention in Los Angeles but when we arrived after a long bus trip nobody knew anything about us, including who was going to pay us or where our hotel accommodations were. As it turned out, Reverend Rundless was attending the convention and saw to it that we were taken care of. When it was time to return to Detroit, he offered to take some of us back in the car with him. Morris decided that he would send Priscilla and Marie back on the bus and that he, George, Emory, and I would ride with the Reverend.

Of course, riding up in the front with him and the other three men in back, sometimes asleep, I meant to really get to know the Reverend. In the biblical sense and in every other sense. But the moral of the story is that not all temptations or flirtations should neccessarily be acted on. In this case, had things gotten out of hand, I would have missed out on knowing one of my most significant angels.

The Reverend was certainly flattered and probably interested too.

As heated-up as it got in that front seat, though, somehow he had the wherewithal to stop it before anything really happened, telling me, "I can't do this. It's not right. There's my wife . . ."

"Your wife?" I interrupted, playing around, whispering low, "I ain't interested in your wife. Forget her. I can help you forget. I got something to make you feel good."

"I know," he laughed. "But you'll have to wait and get to know Earnestine. You two are gonna be such good friends."

And he was *absotively, posolutely* correct. The next time I went to New Liberty Baptist Church, Earnestine and I got to talking after the service and after ten minutes a magnificent, lifelong friendship was born.

New Liberty soon became a real home to me—socially, mentally, spiritually, and lovingly. And soon Earnestine, who was only in her mid-twenties at that time, became my mentor—which she remains to this day. Beautiful inside and out, sweet, caring, and wise, she was everything you would imagine an angel to be. Through her, the way she lived, the way she dressed, the way she spoke, and the way she treated others, I gained my first exposure to the elegant side of life. Earnestine had taste, style, and class. You could see her touch all around her. There were napkins to match the tablecloth. Lovely china and glasses for everyday use. Thick carpets, beautiful furniture, lacy curtains, walls with mirrors covering them. Earnestine wore pretty, tailored clothes with everything matching—hats, bags, gloves, shoes. *Ever-ry-thing.* And she was so kind to everyone in both deed and word, and not in an ostentatious, showy way. She genuinely cared about others.

One of the lessons Earnestine helped reinforce in me was that the way you present yourself to the world can often be a reflection of how you see yourself. So careless dress or careless speech can signal you don't think very highly of yourself.

Earnestine taught me many things Mama tried to teach me but was unable to, perhaps because angels only bring lessons you are ready to learn at that given time. For me, the time was ripe to learn from Earnestine things such as how to behave socially, how to dress, how to present myself to the world. She taught me by the example of her own life, demonstrating how to be a lady, how to be successful as a woman and wife, how to keep a loving husband happy, and how to wear his love beautifully.

"Deloreese," Earnestine asked one evening when I was over visiting at the Rundlesses in their home which was above the church, "would you mind going downstairs with me? I have some announcements to make to the choir."

Happy to go along, I followed her downstairs. Finding the choir still practicing its last song, Earnestine began to sing with them in her wonderful, rich, warm voice, and I began to background her—but with a different background from the one that the choir was singing.

Earnestine and I were doing something different from the standard gospel style of the time. Normally the pattern was to have a lead singer with a choir or background group singing a three- or four-part harmony. When there were two lead singers, one would sing the line while the other sang the same background as the rest of the choir. Then they would trade, and the other lead would sing the line while the first lead sang the same background with the rest of the choir.

That night, going against the standard mode, Earnestine was our lead, and I was the second lead, singing at the same time on that line, using different rhythmic patterns and expressions from hers, still with the choir singing the three- or four-part harmony as background. So Earnestine might begin: *"I love the Lord, I hear his cry . . ."* And I would echo just behind her, modulating up a third: *"I love the Lord, I hear his cry . . ."* As the choir would chime: *"Hmmmmm . . ."*

That was the beginning of a new style of gospel singing, one which had not been done until we hit upon it.

The song we were singing that night was a rhythm song and we began to walk and sing. Earnestine got to feelin' good, I got to feelin' good, and the choir was workin' out. Hearing this joyful noise unto the

Lord, the Reverend Rundless stepped out of his office and soon he got to feelin' good.

When we stopped singing, he applauded and said, "I want that song for Sunday morning. And, Deloreese, I want you to come and sing it with Earnestine just like you did it tonight."

After that Sunday service I became the choir director for New Liberty and let my two other choir directorships go. A short while later, when the Reverend started delivering Sunday afternoon radio sermons, Earnestine and I decided to put together a group to sing on the broadcast. Since he called his show "Moments of Meditation," we called ourselves The Meditation Singers. In addition to myself, Earnestine, Marie, and George, our group included De Lillian Mitchell who sang tenor, Early Moore, a baritone, and Emory Radford on piano and organ.

Developing our new style of singing with two leads, Earnestine and I got to the point where I was able to sing almost in her breath. That would have been very difficult for someone else, but as close as we were, I could anticipate her changes, sing with her slurs, even slur under her slurs.

Meanwhile, those radio broadcasts were a springboard to concert bookings and dates all over Detroit, Pontiac, Chicago, Cleveland, Buffalo, Toledo, Pittsburgh, Richmond, Lynchburg, and anywhere else we could go to and still get back home for those who needed to be at work Monday morning.

The Meditation Singers fast became a force to be reckoned with. Singing with our distinctive rhythmic style, we were eventually recognized as one of the most influential groups in the gospel scene, going on to be named to the Gospel Singers Hall of Fame. This was a great time to be a part of the developing world of Gospel. Detroit itself was having a heyday.

As a matter of fact, one of the names just starting out back then was a teenage Aretha Franklin, whose father, the Reverend C. L. Franklin, was young and attractive like Reverend Rundless. He and Reverend Rundless often took turns bringing their respective congregations to each other's churches, which was how I first heard Aretha—a definite musical talent even then.

⟨⟩ Dreams die hard. Especially young dreams. During this period, one of my dreams that had never died was Seabourn Brooks. Finally, over a year after Mama's death and my departure from the old neighborhood, Seabourn returned to Detroit, many of his problems behind him.

Seeing him again after all this time and all the events that had transpired did nothing to diminish my old desires. And when I told him I was no longer inexperienced Junior anymore, he no longer had a reason to postpone what I'd long been dreaming of. Well? Well. It was wonderful. More wonderful than anything I had even dreamt it would be.

What they say is true: Some things are really worth waiting for.

Then again, they also say that you can't go back to yesterday. My dreams may not have changed but I had. I realized, at last, what I had probably always known, that our ultimate paths weren't meant to run together; Seabourn knew it too. And so we parted once again, not without sadness or love.

In the meantime, while I was very wary about trusting any man who had not earned my trust, there were several young men I dated in the church. Not that I cared much for any of them. But it was fun to go out to eat after the service. And it was equally fun to see them vying to be the one to take me.

One Sunday after church as we were socializing outside, I was introduced to a very handsome, nicely dressed, well-spoken young man. He looked like a honey-colored Zachary Scott. *Cuuuuute.*

His name was Vermont Adolphus Bond Taliaferro. I thought that was pompous and probably a lie.

After the introduction was made, my sister Marie rushed over to me to tell me something. "They say he's the cousin of the football player," she whispered.

Hummmph. That didn't impress me because I didn't like football to begin with. Mr. Vermont Taliaferro was cute, though, I had to admit.

As was our custom on Sunday evenings after the day's church activities were done, a group of us went out to dinner that night and someone invited Vermont to come along. At the restaurant, he sat directly across the table from me and couldn't seem to keep his eyes off me. And yet, he never said a word.

In the car on the way home, Marie, Earnestine, and Emory were teasing me about this Mr. Vermont Adolphus Bond Taliaferro and how he was acting.

"C'mon, Del," laughed Emory, "tell us what's goin' on with you two."

There was nothing and I wasn't going to dignify the question with a response. So I said nothing.

"Oooooh," said Marie, "there is something goin' on."

Even Earnestine prodded, gently, saying, "Deloreese, you can tell us. He's a charming young man."

"I don't even know him," I insisted. "That's all there is to it."

They didn't believe me. They believed me less the following Sunday when Vermont came again to church and to dinner and, again, stared and never said a word. It happened the same way the next Sunday.

Then, on the third Sunday, as The Meditation Singers were preparing to leave for Pontiac to perform a program there, I spoke to Vermont, asking why he just stared at me all the time.

"I don't mean to," he said politely, "but I can't help myself. You're so lovely."

Me lovely? What jive, I thought. No one had ever said that to me. They said, "You cute." Or, "Nice buns." But, lovely? I was not even prepared to believe I could be lovely, although it made me feel so wonderful when he said it.

Vermont came that afternoon to Pontiac and after the program was over, he suggested that, on the way home, we visit his friend's hunting lodge.

It was a very nice lodge outside of Pontiac. It may not have been the Rockefellers' hunting lodge, but it was still luxurious to me. Certainly, none of the young men I dated had ever taken me to a place like that. There was a fire in a large stone fireplace, big picture windows through which we could look out over beautiful grounds, and a night sky filled with shooting stars. The setting was intoxicating, the music was excellent, and Vermont courted me royally. He fixed my drinks, we danced, he held me close. He was a gentleman and a prince.

As the music played and I felt his body warmly pressing against mine, over two years of defenses that I had built up since living on my own began to melt away.

When the night drew to an end, he asked, "Would you object if I kissed you?" A gentleman through and through.

I didn't object at all. That night he and I became an item. And every time we saw each other after that, he proved over and over to be the most tender man I had ever met. The most considerate, the most attentive, and the most affectionate. In the time we were going together there was not once that he came to see me without presents or flowers. Doors were opened, seats pulled out, concerns expressed: "Are you warm enough?" "Would you like my coat?" "Where would you like to go?" "What would you like to do?"

Vermont Taliaferro swept me off my feet with kindness and sincerity. After going together for six months, he asked me to marry him. There was no hesitation in my response. Everybody approved of him, Reverend Rundless, Earnestine, Marie, George, the church, and me most of all. Of course, I said yes. Yes, yes, yes.

We planned a simple wedding to be held at New Liberty on a Sunday after church services, with Reverend Rundless officiating. The one wish I had always had for my wedding was that my father would give me away. And so, after all this time, I went to see Daddy.

Even though I hadn't seen him since the day I rode away in Ollie Aikens's cab, I had checked up on my father. I knew that shortly after I'd left, while I kept moving towards the West Side, Daddy had moved into a smaller place in the old neighborhood, a little further east. A place more suitably sized and priced for a working man without a family. Besides, with Mama gone and Nodie having taken all her things, our old home on Vernor Highway was never the same again anyway. Since that day when I had seen that woman cooking in my mother's kitchen, there had been other women in his life, I assumed; after all, he needed someone to cook and look after him. But Daddy never remarried.

When I found where he lived, I could see he lived alone. After I knocked on the door, there was a moment before he opened it that a thousand questions ran through my mind about how he was going to react, how he might have changed, what he was going to say. My heart beat hard as the door was opened and I saw my father, tall and proud in his carriage, no different than he had ever been, standing there in the doorway, his eyes lit up with more happiness than could ever be expressed in words. As he saw me, he began to cry, and he pulled me into his arms and held me there tight, telling me, "I am so glad you've come home. I missed you."

Crying too, I held on to him just as tight.

We spent the rest of the day together, something we hadn't done since those Saturdays we spent when I was a child riding alongside him on my red tricycle. When I told him all that I had done and everything that I had been through, Daddy told me, "Del, I am so proud that you made it out there and that you were not ensnared by the street. And your mama would have been so proud too."

That was all that was needed to be said. No blame nor self-reproach. Just how much we missed each other and how good it was that we were both doing all right.

Then, at last, after I told him about Vermont, I said, "Daddy, we're getting married next week and I want you to give me away. Will you?"

"It's been so long since I've been in a church they may not let me in," my father said.

I said, "It's okay, Daddy. I know the minister and I'm sure you can get in."

Well, I got my wish and that next Sunday, surrounded by family and friends, I became Mrs. Vermont Adolphus Bond Taliaferro.

When the wedding was over, as we were standing outside the church, greeting loved ones and accepting good wishes, Vermont leaned into my ear and asked, "Do you have enough money for cab fare home?"

"No," I told him. I had spent all of my money on my wedding dress and on the flowers.

By the time Vermont could explain to me that he didn't have any money on him, everyone else had gone home. There we were in our wedding attire, stranded in front of the church on the East Side with the room that we were renting many blocks west of there. As much as I didn't like it, I ran upstairs to Earnestine to borrow cab fare.

Riding home in the cab, Vermont could not have been more embarrassed. "I swear to you," he promised, "that will never happen again."

To prove it, he went out the next day and got himself not one but two jobs—a day shift at Ford and a night shift at Chrysler.

We started off our married life rooming in another family's house, as was the custom for many newlyweds in those days. True to his word, Vermont was a wonderful provider, very conscientiously feathering our nest with necessary and creature comforts. It was quite the love nest too. He was the first real lover I ever knew, fully committed, fully present. For the first time I didn't just have sex, I was making love. And being made love to, wholeheartedly. We experimented in ways I had never even heard of, Vermont guiding me ever so gently along the way.

I was in love. In love with Vermont and in love with love. I loved the loving, the nesting, and the taking care of my man the way I'd always planned one day when only the right one came along, living life out of *Better Homes and Gardens.*

When he returned from his shift at Ford around two-thirty in the afternoon, my focus was serving him his lunch, spending time with him, and then cooking dinner while he slept. After he ate, I'd serve him dinner and then see him off in time for him to make it to his eleven o'clock night shift at Chrysler. I cooked from Mama's recipes, recipes from *Bet-*

ter Homes, from *House Beautiful,* from Betty Crocker, from Earnestine, from those I found in the newspaper and from anywhere else I ran across them.

After six months, Vermont's hard work yielded a down payment on a house for us on the West Side. This was It. This was the Dream. This was the upward and onward my mama had dreamt of and told me was possible. A short while later, Vermont surprised me one afternoon by giving me my very own car, the first car I had ever had, a brand new shiny sea-green Buick. A month after that came a fur coat, my first fur coat I had ever had. A month later there was the first diamond ring I had ever had. Next came the first diamond earrings I had ever had. My wallet was full of money, the first money I had ever had that someone else gave to me. And for the first time ever, I had charge accounts at all the fine department stores in town. J. L. Hudson's, Winkleman's, Crowley's.

It should have been perfect. But it wasn't. And the reason that it wasn't was that something happened to Vermont. Evidently, when the man said, "I now pronounce you man and wife," to Vermont that meant he owned me. And the better we did, the nicer I thought things were going with us, the happier I thought we were, the more possessive he became. I didn't know it right away. I didn't see it coming. But, looking back, there were subtle hints that I should have heeded.

There was, for example, the beautiful new freezer he bought me. They had a plan that if you bought it with a certain amount down, it would come full of food. You could order all the cuts of meat you wanted and all the different frozen vegetables and side dishes you wanted. So when Vermont presented me with this new freezer, fully stocked, his comment was, "Now you won't have to spend as much time at the grocery store."

He bought me a big new TV, telling me, "Now you won't need to go out to the show so much."

These were thoughtful gifts, I thought, not realizing at first that they were being given with the incentive of keeping me from going anywhere without him. For Vermont, the more I stayed around the house,

My mother, Nellie Michel, taught me about God, cooking, and how to live with myself, and how to love my husband.

ABOVE RIGHT: My father, Richard Thaddeus Early, was bigger than life to me, and taught me diction and how to tell a funny story.

How snug Deloreese Patricia Early felt, leaving eighth grade on her way to high school (I had no idea what wonders life would hold for me).

Can you find a very young Deloreese Patricia Early in this photo of the Original Hutchins Gospel Trumpeteers? (Second from right.)

The happiest day in my mother's life was when I graduated from Northeastern High School. She had prayed she would see one of her children do so before she died.

Daddy Braggs was the first to build an entire show around me and place my name up on a marquee. He was one of the best showmen I ever knew. Our professional relationship lasted longer than our personal one.

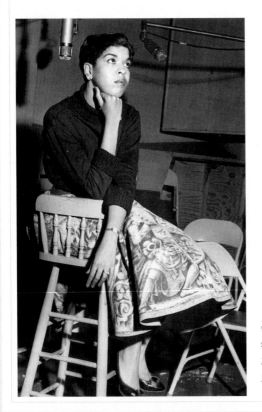

In my first New York City recording studio, where dreams did come true.

Photo by David Jackson, property of Johnson Publishing Co., Inc. All rights reserved

TOP: *A twenty-five-year-old* Della Reese on the road, with nothing to do between shows but read and sleep. *Photo by David Jackson, property of Johnson Publishing Co., Inc. All rights reserved*

ABOVE: *This was my hit-record-making* machine: Hugo and Luigi (A&R men for RCA); me, pretending to read a chart; and my manager, Lee Magid.

One of the twenty-one appearances I made on Ed Sullivan's show. Never was there a greater champion for me. *Used by permission of CBS and Solar Entertainment*

With a dress like this, all the movement is from the knees up. But it was a sensation during its day. *Photo by Moneta Sleet, Jr., property of Johnson Publishing Co., Inc. All rights reserved*

WELCOME
CHICAGO'S MOST COMPLETE WEEKLY

AMERICA'S
RECORDING
FAVORITE

DELLA
REESE

AT THE

SCOTCH
MIST

DELLA REESE

Chicago was a good town for singers. Places like the Scotch Mist, Mr. Kelly's, the London House, the Cloisters, and the Sutherland Hotel were great for perfecting your craft and showing off new gowns. Here I am on the cover of *Chicago Welcome* magazine.

While I was working at the Cloisters on Sunset Strip, one of my biggest thrills was the night Shirley MacLaine, Sammy Davis, Jr., and Dinah Washington dropped in to see me perform. As you can see, they loved me. *Photo by Jules Davis*

My favorite photograph.

The Mike Douglas Show introduced me to cohosting on television. Here, Mike had invited my greatest heroine, Ethel Waters. One day I will perform in a film about her life. *Photo property of* The Mike Douglas Show

The stars were out this night. I was sitting next to Sidney Poitier, who was talking to Johnny Mathis, and Nat and Marie Cole were across from me. Hot diggity dog! *Photo by Jules Davis*

Twenty years separate these two Dellas, but the music is still as sweet. *Photo by Jules Davis, used by permission of the Las Vegas News Bureau*

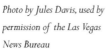

Photo by Jules Davis, used by permission of the Las Vegas News Bureau

A reunion of the Meditation Singers. We were the first to sing gospel in a Las Vegas lounge. (*Left to right*) Earnestine Rundless, Laura Lee Rundless, Marie Waters, DeLilian Price, and me, singing lead. *Photo by Moneta Sleet, Jr., property of Johnson Publishing Co., Inc. All rights reserved*

Three former Idlewild, Michigan, performers: Jackie Wilson, me, and George Kirby on Daddy Braggs's television show in Chicago. Braggs was one of the greatest impresarios of the '50s. Had he been white, he would have ranked with the best Broadway producers.

How did two gospel singers wind up singing in Las Vegas? Me from the Meditation Singers and Lou Rawls from the Soul Stirrers. I guess it was simply ordained. (Smile)

Carmen McRae and I started a dress shop called Cardella's. Our dreams were big, but the profits weren't. This told us not to give up our night jobs. *Photo by Paul Slaughter*

The Last Minstrel Show should have made it to Broadway but was killed by the racial sensitivities of that period. Here I am with Clebert Ford (*left*) and Howard Roberts. *Photo by Roger Greenawalt, property of Hunt / Pucci Associates, Inc.*

On the right, sitting next to my sister-in-law, is Dorothy "Butter" Smith. She was smooth as butter and taught me how to survive with street smarts.

My handsome brother, Rufus Daniels, and his beautiful wife, Delores. Delores was more of a sister than sister-in-law to me. We grew up together.

Dumpsey kept me sane traveling with me on the road, until the state authorities demanded I place her in school in California. This picture was taken backstage at New York's Basin Street East. *Photo by Reputable Service Co.*

the better. And so, he bought me silky lingerie, in order, he said, that I could be more comfortable lounging at home.

The shoe was getting ready to drop. It finally got to the point that his possessiveness, building slowly but surely, set the stage for what happened next on his job.

There was this guy that Vermont knew from work who had hit on me and whom I had refused. It was nothing. I didn't care to look at another man, much less flirt with one. Not to mention that he was supposed to be a friend of my husband's. As I would later piece it together, one day at work this friend said to Vermont, "Man, you is a trick. Workin' so hard for that woman, boastin' how fine she is. When she is probably out fuckin' around every day and night 'cause she knows where you are and knows how to time you."

That afternoon, knowing nothing of this conversation, I ran to the door to meet Vermont as he arrived home. The first thing he did, he hit me so hard he knocked me up the stairs.

I lay there. I didn't know what was wrong and I sure didn't know what to do.

He circled around me and stalked me through the house, questioning me about who I had been with and why I was cheating on him, demanding to know how I could do that when he was trying as hard as he could to do right by me.

"Vermont, what do you mean . . ." I tried to stand up. WHACK, he hit me down again.

"I don't know what you're talking about," I tried to tell him. WHACK, WHACK, WHACK, he beat me harder.

I cried, I begged, I pleaded for him to stop.

Nothing I said made any difference, except to make him even angrier. The angrier he got, the more he beat me. He beat me up so bad that when he finally took a breath and stopped to have a look at me, he broke down in sobs and fell on his knees. "Forgive me, baby, please forgive me," he begged tearfully. "It's just that I love you so much, it just that the thought of you with someone else makes me so crazy. I know it's not true, I swear I know you would never do that. But all the way home on the bus I kept thinking of the idea of you cheating and it ate away at me and I couldn't control how mad it made me." Vermont promised on his knees, through his tears, that he would never touch me again—as long as I didn't leave him, which I was already packing to do.

I believed him. And I forgave him. Ashamed of himself and grateful for my forgiveness, Vermont had flowers sent to the house and bought me a wristwatch that had a diamond band on it. He cared for my wounds and cooked my food and stayed home from work until I was better.

He erased any doubt from my mind and I believed with my heart that he just made a mistake, one he would never repeat again.

That was my mistake, a big one.

It got worse. Much worse. It got so bad that if I went to the store, he would accuse me of sleeping with the clerk. If I went to the bank, I had slept with the teller. And every time I went to church, I had been sleeping around with my so-called Christian friends.

Every time I got ready to pack and leave him, I could hear Mama's voice, her words echoing from that very last time we had talked together: *When you take a man to God and tell God you want him, you have to stay with him.*

And every time, after he attacked me, after it was over, you have never seen a more apologetic, more contrite person than Vermont. You have never heard more self-recrimination of how stupid and wrong and crazy he was, nor heard more promises of just forgive him and he will never, ever again, that it was only the depth and the power of his love unable to accept another man even looking in my direction. In a sense, if no one has ever spoken in that way, there is something flattering and almost seductive about a declaration of love like that. So you make excuses.

There were other reasons and other forces that kept me from walking out the door. This was forty-five years ago. All the awareness about domestic abuse that we have today was then almost nonexistent. With all the close friends I had, there was no one I felt I could confide in about it. They never had a clue about how beaten up I was because I was too embarrassed. When I went out, there may well have been bruises on my body but I covered them up with long sleeves and thick stockings, wearing a turtleneck or scarf to hide the marks on my neck where he had tried to choke me. I would have been mortified for anyone to know what he was doing to me.

I thought back to my old neighbor, Mr. Jones, who'd beat his wife every time she got on him for something. Everyone in the whole building could hear it, and nobody did a thing to stop him. That's just the way it was.

There was something of a prevailing attitude at this time that if a woman was beaten by her man, she somehow deserved it. There were a lot of people who plain out said, "Ain't nothin' wrong with some wife beating." It was a natural thing, a normal mean. So when Vermont started beating me, maybe there was something in me that believed somehow, on some level, it was my fault. That every time Vermont beat me up for no logical reason whatsoever, it must have been something I did to set him off. And maybe that's partly why I put up with it as long as I did.

My life had prepared me to be a survivor. If there was a problem, you tried your best to fix it. So I tried to fix me, I tried to do better and not do whatever it was that made him abuse me. To survive, I thought by fixing me, I could fix Vermont's problem, change him back to the way he was before we were married. I had fix-it-itis.

But Vermont was not to be fixed nor changed back to his old self, no matter how submissive I became. And his cruelty was not only physical, he quickly became mentally cruel. We stopped making love, and only had sex. While having sex, he would say things like, "Can he fuck you like this? Can he make you come like this? Are you thinking of him now?", all the while pounding my body with his body.

Cut to: Easter Sunday, after almost two years. In the auditorium of Cass Technical High School a major contest was taking place between The Meditation Singers and The Clara Ward Singers. For the ladies in our group, I had designed elegant toile dresses with big puffed sleeves that had cute small bows on the puff. We were lovely and the Meditation gentlemen equally sharp and smart for the occasion. After just performing a Sunday morning service, we were tuned and raring to go.

The Clara Ward Singers, known for their high-energy performances and Clara's inimitable intense style, had an advantage in this matchup because they had records out. That meant we would have to pull out our best timber and hope to shake the rafters more than they could. When they opened the program and they tore it up and walked off in triumph—as if to say, *Follow that*—Earnestine took a glance at me in concern. She said to everyone, "We need to pray right here, right now." So we prayed in our seats before we got up. Afterwards, we stood together and Earnestine began a hymn. I joined with her, then the rest of the group, and then the whole audience joined in. The spirit of God filled the auditorium and we could do no wrong.

The prize, a huge trophy, was awarded to The Meditation Singers and I was chosen to take it home until the following Sunday when I would present it to our church. I was *ha-a-a-a-appy.*

As always, when we were in public, Vermont was proud, attentive, and supportive. Seeing how exhausted I was, he helped me along with the trophy, hailing a cab and carefully putting the trophy in the backseat on one side with me in the middle of it and him. "Lay back in my arms and rest," Vermont said, sitting as he was by the door of the cab and placing his arm along the back of the seat to make it comfortable for me.

As I lay back and began to relax, I saw the cab driver look in his rearview mirror at me.

"Aren't you Deloreese Taliaferro?" he asked.

"Yes," I answered.

"I just adore you. I follow you around all the time. You are sensational."

I said, "Thank you," and felt very pleased.

Not another word was spoken as we continued on the way to our house. Once there, Vermont paid the driver and helped me and the trophy out of the cab. We walked together up to the porch where Vermont opened the door for me and what happened next, I will never know, because I woke up some minutes later in the living room with Vermont standing over me, saying, "You just refuse to respect me. You have these men right in my face. What was that motherfucker doing, telling you he adored you and that he followed you around? Like I wasn't even there."

"The man was talking about my singing and he followed the group around . . ." I tried to explain, speaking with great effort.

"Don't you lie to me, he didn't mention that damn group."

With that, the talking was over and Vermont proceeded to beat me so viciously I had to be hospitalized for the next five days.

In admitting me, the hospital asked for the name of my next-of-kin and I gave my father's name. Daddy was notified, arriving at my bedside shortly afterwards. When he saw my condition, he was so angry I thought he would burst open.

"Who does that bastard think he is, beating my daughter?" Daddy said, pacing the floor. "I won't have it. I won't. I was with your mother thirty-three years and I never hit her, and I have never hit you." He left my side only after making me promise to call him if Vermont ever touched me again.

During my hospital stay, I made the decision that Vermont would never get that chance to touch me again. I knew I had to get away from him, whatever the cost. On the morning of my release from the hospital, I went back to the house to get my things, hurrying to get out before Vermont came home. But as I was packing, I heard him coming up the front walk. Fast but cool, I stashed everything in the closet, ran into the kitchen, and started fixing dinner—as if everything was back to normal. No rocking the boat right now, I told myself, I'll spend the night and leave tomorrow.

Vermont, appearing not to suspect anything, went to the bathroom to wash up.

At that very moment, there was a knock at the door and when I opened it, there stood my daddy with a gun, an old hunting rifle. He pushed past me, shouting, "Is that bastard here?" and before I could answer, Vermont walked into the room. My father lit into him, "If you ever touch my baby again, I will blow your fucking brains out of your head, do you understand me?"

Vermont whimpered and cowered, saying nothing.

Daddy aimed at his forehead, telling him, "I ought to do it now!"

Down on his knees went Vermont as he began to beg and promise and cry. He couldn't even form full sentences, Daddy had scared him so.

That damn shotgun had to have been older than my father was. If he had fired it, I am sure he would have blown himself up.

Nevertheless, it did the job. After Daddy left, Vermont ignored me for the rest of the night and the next morning I left. Period, the end. I left the car, the mink coat, the rings, the watch, the lingerie and all the clothes he bought me. *Ever-ry-thing.* The only thing I took that I had not bought with my own money—don't ask me why, to this day I do not know—was a steam iron.

With it and the belongings that I owned before my marriage, I went back to Marie's house to live and get my ducks in a row.

Vermont called Marie, Reverend Rundless, Earnestine, George, Emory, and everyone else, pleading his case and enlisting their help in convincing me to go back to him.

And they all tried. I had done such a good job at hiding the damage they really couldn't believe that Vermont was capable of such behavior.

Marie was so crazy about Vermont, she thought I had lost my mind. "Del, whatever he has done, you've got to give him another chance. How can you let him get away? Vermont is every woman's dream." She reminded me that I had nothing when I met him, that he had bought me a car, a house, had draped me in fur, put diamonds on my fingers and in my ears. She was flabbergasted.

I understood. I knew that when Marie and everyone else saw me in public, Vermont treated me like the Queen of Sheba. They weren't in there with me when I was getting hit up the side of the head. They only saw the appearances so they thought I was making a very big mistake. Where was I going to find another man like that?

I didn't want to find another man like that, ever in my life.

No one listened to me. To my dismay, Marie and George invited Vermont to dinner, hoping to facilitate our working things out.

Before he was due to arrive, Marie asked me to go to the store to pick up some items she needed. Knowing it could spell trouble if Vermont arrived and I wasn't there, I went anyway, against my better judgment.

Sure enough, when I returned, Marie was standing on the couch screaming while Vermont walked back and forth in front of the coffee table, cursing and accusing her of being in some plot with me and covering up for me. Marie was so scared, she was trembling. Throwing down the items from the store, I started toward them and, as I did, in came George from the back door. At six foot three and two hundred twenty pounds, George readily grabbed Vermont and threw him down. In no time, Vermont became docile; he never stood up to a man.

As Marie calmed down, I pulled her aside and said, "See, I told you, he is crazy."

At last, she believed me. But now it was George's turn to think he could fix things. Directing the three of us to sit down on the couch together, he spoke with logic and authority in his deep bass voice, telling Vermont he could no longer treat me the way he had been. "If you want her back," George warned, "you'll have to change."

Vermont, sincere as ever, promised he would.

Rolling my eyes, I wasn't buying any.

"Now, Del," George said, seeing how I was reacting, "you've got to forgive and forget. You have to do your part too."

"I've done all I am going to do and if leaving him damns me to hell, hell can't be any worse than living with him." George tried to interrupt, Vermont tried to interrupt but I topped them both with my voice, stating uncategorically, "I don't care what you say or what he says, I am never going back to him."

Vermont put his head in his hands and began to moan. "I want to die," he cried. "If she's not coming back, I don't want to live . . ." The window in back of the couch was only about one quarter open, not wide enough for him to get out it. But he broke for it anyway, looking as if he was going to jump. Everyone except me tried to hold him back—Marie, at six feet, big strong George, and my strapping nephew Porgy. The three of them together couldn't hold Vermont from the window.

In the meantime, I walked around them, went and threw the window open all the way, and watched as Vermont made another break for the window so he could throw himself from the second story to his death. The minute he saw it was open wide enough to actually jump, he made an immediate U-turn and collapsed on the couch sobbing.

Seeing what a phony move it was, this suicide attempt, George finally realized everything I had been saying about Vermont was true. "C'mon outside with me, Vermont," George said, "let's take a walk."

George walked Vermont to the bus stop, waited with him until it came, and sent him home.

⌁ Back on the road for me. Literally. The last time I had needed a job, I'd gotten one driving a produce truck. This time, staying with Marie and George until I could find a place of my own, I got a job driving a cab.

Unfortunately, Vermont soon found out what I was doing and started dogging me everywhere I went. My great fear was that he would find me alone somewhere, an easy feat when I was driving the cab. I began to scout around for other employment.

On one of my trips, my fare needed to make a quick stop at the Carlton Plaza Hotel on John R Street. While I was waiting, I had to go to the restroom so I left the meter running, locked the cab and went inside to use the hotel ladies' room. On my way out, I noticed a sign on the reception desk that listed an opening for a switchboard operator. After asking the desk clerk about it, even though I knew absolutely nothing about a switchboard, I filled out the job application form, never expecting to hear from them again.

A week later, Mr. Swan, the manager of the hotel, called me to come in for an interview.

Mr. Swan, a friendly enough man, looked like a professor of some sort, as if he belonged on a college campus. He was, in fact, an opportunist and whoremonger from the word go. But to me he proved to be an angel. He gave me an opportunity, opening a door for me. I had no experience on a switchboard at all, I told him. But if the job could be learned, I said, I could learn it.

Mr. Swan liked that. "You'd start at a trainee salary," he informed me. "Thirty-five dollars a week. When you learn it, the job pays fifty."

"Good," I said, "I'll take it."

By the time he had trained me, I had a trade. I could have walked into any hotel in Detroit and run it.

After a few days of training, I talked Mr. Swan into letting me live in the hotel in a small room in the back, up on the third floor, for which he charged me twenty-five dollars a week.

In Detroit, the two top black hotels were the Carlton and the Gotham Hotel, an older establishment for the mature rich. The Carlton Plaza Hotel was a new, modern hotel with lovely self-contained suites decorated in tropical decor, a fine dining room, and a popular bar. It catered to a younger, more *nouveau riche,* exciting (to me) clientele— younger businessmen, doctors, lawyers, pimps (big money ones with Cadillacs), and their girls. In the beginning, I wouldn't speak to anyone for fear they would either get me in trouble or try to turn me out, two things I definitely didn't want to happen to me.

But I was not shy on the switchboard and soon I found that taking a little extra initiative on the job could pay off. Once I got to know the regulars, I began to cover for them. Ooooh, did I cover for them. Say, for example, one of the pimps was up in a room with someone when one of his other women called. I'd put her on hold, call the man's room and ask what I should tell her. Or, since I could see the entrance from my switchboard at the reception desk, the woman might show up and if I happened to know her man was downstairs in the bar with someone he didn't want her to know about, I'd tell her he wasn't there but had left a message for her to meet him at the Chesterfield, a bar down the street; then, I'd call him in the bar and tell him what had transpired.

If your business depended on discretion, as the pimps' often did, you would be most appreciative for the kind of assistance I offered. They began to tip me, discreetly too, passing by and slipping a bill into my hand, sometimes a twenty, or a fifty, or a one-hundred-dollar bill—depending on the importance of my services.

Working days on the switchboard, living at the hotel, and singing gospel gigs on the weekends, I was making it good. Then Vermont found out where I was and started calling day and night. Nothing I said would deter him. I was his wife, he proclaimed, and he was coming to get me to take me home and that was that.

Sounds like the perfect time for one of my angels to show up, doesn't it? But this time there was no angel. Instead, I got the next best thing: the biggest armed guard you have ever seen in your life. The man looked like a truck. Big long gun on his hip. Voice to stop you dead in your tracks. I hired him from a local security firm, explaining that Vermont was bound and determined to hurt me.

"No, miss," the guard assured me, "he will not hurt you."

The first night, the guard stationed outside the door to my hotel room, Vermont didn't come. The next night, however, he did. He arrived bearing a florist delivery box full of gardenias, my favorite flower. When he saw the guard, gentle as a lamb, he asked to see me. The guard stopped Vermont right there and knocked on my door, asking if I wanted to see this man.

"No way," I called through the closed door. After I heard the guard telling Vermont he would escort him to the elevator, I opened the door and stepped out in the hall to make sure he was gone for good.

At that instant, Vermont broke loose and ran back towards me and threw all those gardenias in my face, saying, "You just won't let me love you, will you?"

"No," I replied, "I just won't let you kill me. If what you do to me is love, I don't want it and I sure don't need it."

Next thing I knew, that Mack truck of an armed guard picked Vermont up, carried him and threw him in the elevator, got in with him, rode the three stories down, dragged him through the lobby, and tossed him on the sidewalk.

Within the month, I went downtown to the court and filed divorce papers. Vermont did not contest it. That was it. It was over. Period, the end.

I would never go so far as to call Vermont an angel. The truth is that every day, all around the world, in every walk of life, women die from the kind of behavior Vermont had inflicted on me. Thanks to God, my foremost angel, I lived through it. Daddy, Earnestine, Reverend Rundless, Marie, and George, those were my other angels who, once they realized what was happening to me, rallied in my support and were there for me with love and caring.

But I will say that the process of leaving Vermont taught me some powerful lessons. For one thing, I learned that I was never going to let any man lay a hand on me. I learned that fix-it-itis doesn't fix anything. This meant that from then on, if my man had a problem—whether it was abusing me, or alcohol, or gambling, or low self-esteem, or whatever—it was *his* problem. Not only could I not fix the problem and not fix him, I learned that fixing me wasn't going to fix it.

Most important, getting Vermont out of my life cleared the way for my own growth both as a person and in my career. My attitude was that if I wanted all those nice kinds of material things he had given me, I would have to go out and get them for myself. Now that I was starting to recognize my own strength and resourcefulness, I didn't really see a reason why I couldn't. And that belief was about to set in motion the rapid wheels of change in my life. Wonderful, exciting changes.

As for whatever happened to Vermont after that, I never knew and

I never cared. The last time I saw the man who had once swept me off my feet was that day when the armed guard swept him off his and carried him bodily from my doorway into the third-floor elevator at the Carlton Plaza Hotel. That was when, for a fleeting moment, I caught my last glimpse of Vermont. And then the elevator door closed.

6

Enter two angels. One, a Miss Dorothy Smith, Waitress Extraordinaire. And, two, a Mr. Donny Lee, Master Comedian.

Not long after I started working and living at the Carlton Plaza Hotel, I met Dorothy at one of the many clubs where she commanded a huge following for her work as a waitress. That's right—you heard me—she was a star waitress. In those days, a good waiter or waitress, like a good bartender, often had the kind of following that a singer had; and, similarly, could be in great demand to work the various establishments on different nights. A Waitress Extraordinaire like Dorothy knew what you liked, how you liked it served, and brought it to you that way. If you were one of their regulars, she or he made you feel welcome when you arrived, listened with empathy to your news, and kept you abreast on the latest happenings—who was on the scene that night, who was expected, and any dirt that had gone down before you got there.

At five foot two, Dorothy was cute as a button. She was a half-breed like me, with slanted, dreamy, sexy eyes fitting for the slow-moving sex machine she was. She worked all the top clubs—the Chesterfield, the Three 6's, the Flame Showbar—and lots of other neighborhood bars. She had such a loyal following that if she worked in your club, you were assured that most of the nightlife would probably show up and hang out. To her credit, she was clever enough to hang too, but not get hung.

The hip talk at the time was to give good friends the suffix of -ski. So Dorothy was known as Dot-ski. She called me Reese-ski.

Although she could be argumentative and moody, Dot-ski had a heart filled with love. As my friend for the next forty years until her death, she made me a permanent beneficiary of that love. She was my angel in many ways. For starters, she took me instantly under her wing, guiding me and sometimes prodding me through the nightlife scene which was so foreign to me. She proved also to be a conduit, introducing me to a variety of interesting, helpful people, one of whom was her very own mama. Whenever we had no money, we would walk over to her mother's house, where we would be fed and sent home with care packages to last the rest of the week.

Above all, Dot-ski was my first real fan. She believed in me and knew I was going to be a star long before I'd even thought about trying to sing secular music as a professional. She was convinced of that from the time she heard me singing to records on her record player. From then on, any chance she got, Dot-ski was out promoting me, telling everybody and anybody how fantastic I was and that they needed to hear me sing.

I didn't want her to push people into listening to me sing. I wanted them to want to hear me. To her that was stupid. How could they want to hear me unless they knew how well I sang?

We had very different ideas about the way I should live my life and what my path to success should be.

"Reese-ski," she loved to tell me whenever she'd stop by and find me relaxing in my bed, my favorite place to be even then (and not just for sleeping then too), "get up! Get up! You ain't gonna get no money just laying here."

"Dot-ski, I'm gonna stay in and read tonight, if you don't mind."

"Stay in and read?" she would say with disgust, her dreamy eyes no longer dreamy. "Forget it. Ain't nobody gonna come in here and give you no money. Unless you gonna turn a trick or something. Now, get up, get dressed, get out where people can see you!"

"What if I don't want to be seen?" I'd argue, knowing that if I did get up and get dressed and go to work with her, I'd wind up sitting at the bar which always bored me to tears; or, at best, if there was a show, I could hang out in the dressing room with the acts, which was always a lot of fun.

In either case, Dot-ski would inevitably be buzzing around the room, talking to regulars, nodding in my direction, asking, "Have you heard her sing? You have to hear her sing." So, after a while, audiences began to ask me to get up and do a song. The response was so good they'd call out for another song and then another. From the beginning, I sang the songs I loved—whether they were popular standards of the time, or new songs hot on the charts. That was my criterion. I listened to everything. *Ever-ry-thing.* If a song moved me, I figured other people listening would be moved too. And I was never wishy-washy about whether I liked or disliked a song. Some of my early favorites became my first repertoire of three songs: "April in Paris," "With These Hands," and "All of Me."

Whenever Dot-ski heard a club was looking for a singer, she'd tell them to hire me. Or she'd tell me to call them. Or, when I didn't want to call them, she'd call for me. Eventually, I started getting little paying gigs here and there. But nothing consequential. For my money, I was sticking to the switchboard and my gospel singing.

For almost a year after my split with Vermont, I used the professional name Pat Ferro (from my middle name, Patricia, and cutting off the first part of Taliaferro). Once I was certain that Vermont wasn't coming after me, I dropped Pat Ferro, a name that had nothing to do with me. At one of those little bars where I was booked for a week, somewhere in late 1952 or early 1953, the owner went to put my name up on the marquee and found there was no way he could make it fit. Granted, it was a very small marquee. But no matter how he put up the letters, neither Deloreese Taliaferro nor Deloreese Early was working. So, he listed me by my first name only, changing the spelling slightly and breaking it up into first and last names: Della Reese. It stuck.

"You sure can sing, Miss Della Reese," said a tall, dark, friendly fellow who approached me one night as I came off stage after one of those command performances by Dot-ski's regulars. This turned out to be Donny Lee, a popular, gifted comedian who played the top nightclubs in town. We hit it off immediately. He was pug-nosed cute, sweet, funny on and offstage, and a gentle gentleman.

The following week, Donny came to see me at one of the small bars I was playing and stayed for all three sets. He was hooked. A devoted fan. Even more important was what he said to me that night, as he was leaving. "You know, you are a funny lady," Donny said emphatically. "You are really funny."

Here was a case of a message being brought by an angel which I didn't even know I needed.

Bells could have been ringing for the significance of him telling me that. To hear it, coming from a comic of his stature, meant a lot to me. "Try doing a line or two in between songs," he suggested. "A funny story or a joke." Before that, I would simply go from one song to the next. I soon found that adding a bit of funny patter in between songs not only helped loosen the audience up, but it gave me a chance to catch my breath.

I had always thought I was funny. And I knew that I had learned a few things from Daddy about telling a humorous story. But it was Donny who really gave me the courage to incorporate that humor into my act as a singer. He believed in me enough that he began to get me work at all the places where he was booked, bringing me out at the end of his show to sing a song. At one of those clubs, a performer who worked with him on one of his comedy gags got into a fight with the owner, punched him out, and was fired. Donny decided to use me as the replacement in the gag. In the process, he taught me some of the fundamentals of comedy timing. Included in these lessons was how to hold for laughs so that you didn't talk or sing over the laughter; also how to use repetition to build the laughter by repeating whatever got you the laugh in the first place. Donny showed me how to improvise, playing off the audience, or using the particulars of a situation to create humor. The ability to turn a potentially disruptive situation into a comedy routine turned out to be a most valuable skill not only for show business but for life in general. I have both Dad and Donny to thank for that gift.

Good timing, good singing, Donny Lee, and a comedy of errors each had a hand in helping me get my next memorable gig. And it would never have happened if it weren't for the fact that Detroit itself was seen as a tryout place for almost anything new. If Detroit liked it, Cleveland and Columbus would like it and they would put it—whatever it was—out all over the country. One of those tryout things in those days was to put a small bar with a music trio into a bowling alley complex. Donny worked one of those new establishments, a place called the Oriole Bowling Alley Lounge. Telling me I would be perfect for the room, he recommended I go over there.

When I arrived, I had a very amiable interview with the owner. Unbeknownst to me at the time, he was looking for someone to work as a hostess to greet and seat customers, what they sometimes called a maitre d'ette. Unbeknownst to him, I was looking to be hired as the singer with the music trio. Throughout our interview, neither the word "singer" nor "hostess" was ever mentioned. Our conversation went something like this:

Me: Good afternoon, my name is Della Reese. Donny Lee recommended that I stop by and talk to you about working here at the Oriole. He thinks it's a wonderful place.

He: That's always nice to hear. Donny's a swell guy and as a matter of fact, I am hiring. How soon can you start?

Me: Soon as the band gets here.

He: Ha! You're funny. See you tomorrow, seven P.M., an hour before we open.

When I left we were both pleased. He thought he had hired a hostess and I thought I had a job as a singer.

The next night, I came as scheduled and rehearsed my songs with the trio. When the club opened, I was standing at the service bar waiting for my turn to sing while customers began to crowd in around the front door.

Right then, the owner walked over to me, asking, "Don't you see all those people at the door?"

Me: "Yes, it looks like we're gonna have a good night tonight."

He: "Not if you don't seat them, we won't. They're gonna walk out."

Me: "Me seat them? I'm not here to seat people. I'm here to sing."

He: "Sing? Sing what?"

The confused look on his face and the way he said "Sing?" told me that he obviously didn't have a clue about me being a singer. The owner confirmed that by saying, "I hired you as a hostess. Go seat those people."

"Want to sing."

"Well, sing as you seat them. I'll give you five bucks extra to sing, but just get those people seated now."

So that became my act: hostess/singer. I sang as I seated people, singing requests, learning their favorite songs, getting to know them as my regulars. Sometimes I sang them songs I created on the spot as I met them at the door, playing and improvising with them, serenading them to their table, all the while greeting and seating. I earned quite an impressive following. The Oriole Bowling Alley Lounge was packed from Thursday through Sunday nights.

⟋⟍ Bit by bit, slowly and subtly, my road was turning to a new direction. My family was expanding, my friends diversifying, my angels multiplying. At first, this seemed hard for others to accept. Friends like Marie and Earnestine lived in a different world than that of friends like Dot-ski and Donny. Getting everyone together was sticky for a while. But eventually, it worked out.

Blessedly, my friends knew me. They really knew me. They knew that if I had other friends, it didn't mean I loved them any less. It didn't mean I wanted to be with them any less. My friends didn't have to like all my other friends.

My friends knew my essence—that I have enough love for everybody. With me, love has never been a limited commodity. Some people only have so much love. I have an abundance. That's a funny thing about love that I've found. The more you do it, the better you get at it. Love doesn't get tired out or spent up.

For me, there are as many kinds of love as there are different kinds of angels. There is sister love, brother love, mother and father love, friend love, teacher love, lover love, individual love, all kinds—none more powerful nor dedicated than the next. This isn't something I necessarily learned along the way; it is simply the way I've always been and something my true angels have always known about me.

Others haven't been able to understand it. As I got further into this new world of secular singing, I was vigorously criticized by certain people I had known from the various churches and choirs around town. This new stuff I was singing was the devil's music, they said. They complained about me at their board meetings and, now and then, I was called in front of them to be reprimanded. What was a young Christian woman doing up on a stage in establishments that encouraged drinking, smoking, and fornication? Didn't I know I was going to go to hell for that? Many times the worst criticism would come from the person whom I had just seen looking at me the other night when I was singing, the same person I saw sitting in the audience, drinking, smoking, and kissing up on someone else's husband or wife.

Even though I knew those people were hypocrites, I began to feel confused. I knew that, ultimately, gospel singing could not provide me with a viable earning potential. But, then, I wondered, maybe I wasn't suited to the nightclub lifestyle. Besides, with the twenty-three dollars a week I was making at the Oriole Bowling Alley Lounge, secular singing didn't seem to offer a viable earning potential either.

I talked over my concerns with Reverend Rundless and Earnestine. She was in my corner one hundred percent. So was he. They both maintained that if I felt I could do a good job as a popular singer, why not try? Reverend Rundless said, "It's not so much what you do as how you feel inside." And then he added something that I would never forget: "Because you are in that world, does not mean you have to be of that world."

That was exactly the right message and the right encouragement I needed to hear at that time.

That wonderful message coincided with a wonderful surprise I got during the time I was still working at the Oriole Bowling Alley Lounge when I saw my name in the newspaper as one of the nominees for Detroit's favorite local singer. It was for a contest being co-sponsored by Stroh's Beer, the big beer company in Detroit, and *The Michigan Chronicle,* the top Detroit black newspaper.

To this day, I don't know which angel it was who sent my name in and got it on that list but I've always suspected it was Dorothy, my first, number-one fan. Knowing I didn't want her pushing me onto others, she swore up and down until her dying day that it wasn't her. As much as I loved her, I didn't believe her swearing a bit.

The way the contest worked was that readers of the newspaper were to cut ballot-type coupons out of the *Chronicle,* write down the name of their favorite singer and send it in. The singer with the most coupons would be the winner. Everyone I knew—and everyone they knew—started giving me their coupons. I went to the churches, sang for them, and asked the members to save their coupons for me. In no time,

I had coupons up the yin-yang. It took six big wooden crates that I got from some friends over at the Eastern Market to hold all those coupons, which I carted down to the offices of the *Chronicle* and presented in person. And the winner was . . . me! I won, hands down.

The prize included a makeover and a makeup kit, a gown, and a week's engagement at the Flame Showbar. That club had the right name, it was hot-hot-hot. All the top artists in the country played the Flame. The clientele was upscale and glamorous, everyone dressed in only their best, out making the scene to see and be seen. And the regular staff, if they liked you, was gracious and helpful. The gifted Maurice King, who later became musical director for Motown, was the leader of a seven-piece band in residence at the Flame. For my week's engagement, Maurice wrote my first real arrangements of the three songs I was most known for locally: "April in Paris," "With These Hands," and "All of Me."

My week at the Flame flew by. At the end of it, I went to pick up my check from Mr. and Mrs. Wasserman, the couple who owned the club. They were respectful, good businesspeople and always fair by me. When Mr. Wasserman handed me my check, I looked at the amount on it and was shocked. It was eighty-five dollars. It was almost three times as much as I had ever made singing.

"Are you sure there hasn't been some kind of a mistake?" I asked.

Mr. Wasserman shrugged, indicating he thought I wanted more but that there wasn't any more.

Mrs. Wasserman, who liked me a lot, said, "Della, maybe when you've been here awhile, we can do better by you."

She meant every word. After I went there for that one week, the Wassermans kept me at the Flame for over eighteen weeks.

The feeling I had that night I picked up my first check was one of amazement. I went home in a daze. After all these years of singing professionally, I had never made that much for myself doing the very thing I loved most. This singing business was for me, I decided.

My attitude shifted. Singing was no longer what I loved while I did other things to pay the rent; it was no longer one of a handful of things

I did to support myself. It was going to be what I did. Period, the end. No more driving trucks or cabs or switchboard. I continued to live at the Carlton and I was making all this money. Life was grand.

Dot-ski and I celebrated by going out shopping. And the first thing I bought was a present for her mother for all those care packages she had been making us. Dorothy's mama was tickled and proud.

My first stint of eighteen weeks at the Flame gave me a fast, bountiful education in the art of entertainment. As *the* club to work in Detroit, more top artists came through those doors than any other place in town. Working as an opening act for all of them, I got a chance to learn, watch, listen, and become friendly with some very special individuals.

It was at this point that everything I had learned about the art of communication from Mahalia Jackson began to have more and more meaning to me.

Sit back and get comfortable while I elaborate. It's dissertation time. Three of my greatest inspirations were Nat King Cole, Judy Garland, and Frank Sinatra. Not one of these three had any kind of voice whatsoever, at least as far as a vocal instrument per se. But when it came to the art of communication, they were unsurpassed. If Nat wanted you to be sad when he sang, you were sad. If Judy wanted you to cry, you cried. You felt those things because Judy was crying when she gave it to you and Nat had gone to that place of deep, deep sadness when he gave it to you.

Along with how much I loved Nat King Cole and Judy Garland, I am the world's greatest Sinatra fan. When Frank Sinatra sang, I could feel him. I knew that he had felt that pain or that joy or whatever it was he was singing about.

Just as Mahalia had demonstrated, these three were singing from the inside, not the outside, not showing off their vocal gymnastics, but straightforward and simple; reaching deep within so that they reached deep within you. And they were respectful of the words they sang and of the stories they told.

You've probably experienced going out to a show to hear a singer you've admired on a record or on television. They could have the most marvelous vocal range, the most wonderful voice you've heard and yet, somehow, they couldn't hold your attention. They might have hit all the right keys, sung everything as correctly as you could have asked for, but when you left, you didn't go away thinking, *Ooooh, I understand those feelings, I've been there and I know exactly what she was talking about.* To me, as a singer, that's the art of communication—taking others away, allowing them discoveries or recognitions about themselves and their own feelings.

I feel blessed to have come into my own in a time when so many great songwriters understood the art of communication in the excellent lyrics they wrote. Those lyrics could dictate how you sang, the rhythm you used, the places into yourself that you reached. The songs I loved most told stories, stories with musical messages that guided your personal interpretation. For example, "Willow weep for me," one of my favorite songs said. Now that is one sad tree. That's how I would sing it.

At the Flame, I learned from those like Roy Hamilton, the hot pop singer who made big hits of "Unchained Melody" and "You'll Never Walk Alone," from Arthur Prysock, one of the greatest balladeers of all time, and Alberta Hunter, a top-notch blues singer. Then there was LaVern Baker, another fine blues singer, with whom I literally fought my way to friendship. I became friendly with the very talented members of the Will Masterson Trio who were Sammy Davis, Jr., his father, and his uncle, before Sammy went out on his own. T-Bone Walker who sang the blues and played guitar—oh could he sing and play the blues—became a permanent big brother to me. And Billy Eckstine turned into a wonderful friend. Billy, another master in the art of communication, was one of the sexiest men to grace the Flame and he cussed worse than a sailor.

Now, to some people, this may sound like I'm only paying homage, but starting at the Flame it was the following women—Ella Fitzgerald, Sarah Vaughan, Dinah Washington, and Carmen McRae—who were most responsible for helping me perfect my style. And, rather than inspiring me to sing like them, they did it by teaching me how not to sing like them. That's how I developed my own style.

Each of these four women was so different from the others. And each was so rich and complex in her own right. The elegant, sophisticated Sarah Vaughan, for example, had a veneer of strength and independence—as we all had to have because we were working in a man's world. But offstage, in person, Sarah was a cute little purry sex kitten, completely romantic, happiest when she was in love. In each of her relationships, she really gave her all; she usually didn't get all in return.

Ella Fitzgerald surprised me too. Ella was a majestic talent. Very level-headed and even-keeled. But at the same time, she was insecure about her talent. Before going onstage, she was so nervous she would stand in the wings and tremble. She would go on and just *kill*. And Ella would come back offstage and ask, "Did I do all right?"

Carmen McRae eventually became one of my very best friends. She had the tendency to be moody, difficult, and argumentative. A fantastic musician, Carmen could not tolerate anybody making bad sounds, especially if she was paying them. Many times I saw her turn around to one of her musicians and cut him off, saying, "Now what the fuck you playin'? Just don't play. Just lay out. 'Cause you ain't playin' it right."

Sometimes Carmen didn't need to say anything. She had these looks that could kill you. These looks were so lethal they could penetrate your skin and make you want to disappear through a hole in the floor.

Carmen McRae was the best musical technician we have had in this last century. I feel blessed to have known the real her. Her angel side. As different as our personalities were, we were friends from the time we met until her dying day—during which Carmen loved and supported me as a fellow artist and friend in any way she could.

When it came to the art of communication, Dinah Washington might well have been my absolute favorite. She could hum two notes without words and have you on the floor.

Again, what I learned most from all of these artists wasn't how to do what they did, but how to do what *I* did. In that era, it was mandatory to be an individual stylist. Nowadays if you tell an up-and-comer that they sound like Whitney Houston or Madonna, they feel good about it. But back when I was coming up, if anyone had said that I sounded like someone else, I would've cried.

It was all right to be influenced by those you admired but if you borrowed too much the audience wouldn't let you get away with it. People would shout out, "That's Billie's song," or, "Leave Ella's stuff alone. Get your own stuff." Dinah would tell you herself: "Don't you be copyin' me." That was the way it was. I am glad, too, because, although my voice and register have deepened and lowered over the years, to this day when you hear me sing, you still know it's me.

In time, I was to gain a reputation as a versatile singer who could swing from pop to jazz to blues to gospel. And to this day, I don't see myself in any one category; nor do I care to be pigeonholed. Eventually I went on to do all the jazz festivals but I'm not what you'd call a jazz singer, per se. At the same time, I sing jazz and the people have always enjoyed it when I sang jazz. I sing the blues, although I'm not a blues singer either, yet the audiences have always responded and accepted that I knew the blues when I sang them. The same was true with Broadway show tunes and so-called pop music. That term still makes me laugh. To me, any song that is loved by the people and bought by the people and hummed by the people is a popular song.

In his jazz encyclopedia, music writer and expert Leonard Feather called me "a dramatic pop singer." The Guinness jazz book called me a "Gospel-influenced ballad" and "cabaret" singer. Music expert and critic Tony Sherman described me as a "razzle-dazzle showstopper," saying that I have an irresistible voice: ". . . it swoops and soars with an unabashed, big-souled hunger." And I am all those things too.

But what I really am is me, doing the music which is coming through me. Its uniqueness is my own individual style: my thoughts, my feeling, my understanding of the musical message I am receiving, and my understanding of the conversion of that into reality in me. It touches people in the real of themselves, I believe, because it is real in the real of me.

Besides all of this learning, experience and exposure I was getting at the Flame, it was there that I connected with three new angels, each of whom came bearing unique gifts. Al Green (not the singer) was the club manager and in his quiet, watchful way wielded a good deal of power. An average-looking white man, Al could usually be found in his regular booth, surveying the action on and offstage, directing traffic by signaling to staff whenever he needed something done or wanted to talk to someone. He seemed to make immediate evaluations about people based on their attitude. If he asked you a question and you replied with an iffy, negative, or untruthful response, he had little use for you. If, on the other hand, you answered honestly with a positive or direct attitude, he generally liked you and would go out of his way to help you. Fortunately, Al Green liked my attitude and liked me. Later on, he would introduce me to a very important New York angel. Early on, Al called me over to his table one night and said, "Smile."

I smiled.

"You got a great smile," Al told me. "Why don't you do that on stage more often?" It was not the first time he'd mentioned it.

I answered to the point, "Because I don't like my teeth." My teeth were crooked and not spaced well. The dentist had wanted to work on them before but I couldn't afford what he needed to do.

Well, Al suggested, I ought to have them fixed. Then he offered to help me. And he did. He found me the dentist and paid for the work.

Meanwhile, one of my other new angels, Ziggy Johnson, the permanent Master of Ceremonies at the Flame, also took an instant liking to and caring for me, teaching me how to make my entrances and exits, how to bow, how to set up my three songs, how to dress and adapt my costumes so that they would look different for each song or for different appearances. He was a true godsend. No one has ever epitomized the role of emcee as well as Ziggy. This effervescent man, a superb dancer and dance instructor, was like a little bantam rooster, full of grace and movement, never still. Ziggy kept the flow moving onstage while constantly keeping the audience involved. He knew everybody's name who came to the Flame and never forgot a birthday or an anniversary or other important occasion.

One evening, as I was getting ready to go on for my first number, I heard Ziggy say a special hello to a man who was seated in an entourage at a ringside table, women all around him. A very prestigious group it looked to be: seven-hundred-and-fifty-dollar suits on the men, the women with mink draggin' and diamonds sparklin'. When I got a peek at the man seated in the center of all this, I saw that although he wasn't really handsome or sexy, he was very distinguished looking and there was an aura of magnetism about him. His attire outshone everyone at that table. It wasn't flashy but so immaculate and expensive, I had to ask one of the dancers if she knew who he was.

"That's Daddy Braggs," she said with a sigh, as if he were some famous movie star.

Big deal, I thought, and went about my business. I had heard the women talking about Daddy Braggs before. He was a very successful numbers man from Saginaw, Michigan, who was known for the lavish parties he threw at the Gotham Hotel where he stayed whenever he blew into town. Daddy Braggs also owned the Paradise, a club in Idlewild, Michigan, one of the first black summer resorts—about a two-hour drive from Detroit. Since I'd never been to a resort before, that didn't impress me much. And I wasn't impressed by the other stories I heard about him, how rich he was and how nice he was to the ladies with gifts of mink coats and diamonds and trips all over the country if he liked you. Also how you had to be, if you were with him. Under his complete rule. After what I had been through, no thank you.

After the show that night, as usual I went downstairs to the dressing room to get changed. That basement area was a small, crowded place. There were three rooms down there along with the beer and ice storage. One of the rooms housed the photographic concession which was owned and run by the Gordy sisters, Anna and Gwen. They took pictures of customers, developed them down in the studio and, if you wanted, would turn them into matchbook covers too. All the members of the Gordy family were industrious and inventive, including Anna's and Gwen's younger brother, Berry Gordy, the future founder of Motown.

Also down in the basement was Mr. Wasserman's office and next to that, the dressing room. That was where I was when I saw Daddy Braggs making his way over to me. When all the other girls saw him in our midst, they went crazy. "Oh, Daddy Braggs, how wonderful you look!" "Hello, Daddy Braggs, come gimme a hug!" They were Daddy Braggsin' all over the place as he passed out a hundred-dollar bill here and a hundred there.

When he got to me, he said, "You're good. You oughta be a star."

"I am," I said and smiled.

Which *took him out*. He had a thunderous laugh that I liked. Composing himself, Daddy Braggs said, "You sang good but that dress you wore was pretty sad. Here, take this and get you a nice new one." His outstretched hand held a hundred dollars in it, meant for me.

"Thanks, but no thanks," I said and ended the conversation.

I don't think a woman had ever refused him before. But that was not my purpose. This was self-preservation time. After Vermont it had become my rule not to take anything from anybody. My experience had taught me that when you let them give you things, they owned you and felt they could do whatever they wanted to you.

On his way out, Daddy Braggs stopped Ziggy, telling him that I was something else and that he wanted to hire me for Idlewild.

When Ziggy pulled me aside to tell me about it, I was dubious. "This is an opportunity you don't want to miss," he said. "The money's good, it's steady work from July 4th through Labor Day, and you'll go over big there."

Adding to that, Donny Lee thought it was a good gig and said that everybody we knew worked Braggs's club so I would be on familiar turf. Dot-ski was ecstatic.

So I went to Idlewild and, true to the counsel of my angels, had a ball. I still meet people today who remember me from the Paradise shows that I did there.

Daddy Braggs was a splendid entrepreneur, a fantastic impresario with an innate vision for putting shows together. Real shows. He had a costume designer, choreographer, full orchestra, dramatic lighting and sound systems, beautiful tall showgirls, fast-dancing chorines, and great concepts around which he built the shows. Braggs was one of those rare geniuses born too soon, at the wrong place at the wrong time. Absolutely. If the place had been different, he would have had a shot at Broadway; and if the times had been otherwise, he would now be recognized as one of the great producers of the day.

The Paradise was always open and always full. We rehearsed every day and performed every night and in my free time, with nothing much to do out there in the county, I'd go over to the club and help the bartenders.

Since Dorothy had taught me about tending bar and waiting tables, I knew what I was doing and developed quite a flair doing it, mixing drinks and serving them with strong doses of humor for staff and customers.

Because I was unattainable, it seemed Daddy Braggs had to have me. He watched me at the bar all the time and soon started calling me Casey, after Casey Stengel, the crown prince of baseball, also known for his sense of humor.

"Thanks for pitchin' in, Casey," Braggs would say, passing me by at the bar.

"No problem," I'd say, keeping a friendly distance.

The bartenders were so happy to have my help that I began tending bar after the show was over until the club closed at three in the morning. Not having a car, I would need a ride home to the rented apartment where I was staying and so I agreed to accept rides from Braggs. Because I was helping him out, I didn't feel that his giving me a lift would make me indebted. We were just friends. There was really nothing more to it.

At the end of the summer, the troupe from the Paradise returned to the Flame where we put on a special show to delighted audiences. Then, with a good-bye to all, I was off to Chicago where I was hired to work Robert's Showbar. A welcoming place with a big stage and wonderful roomy dressing rooms, Robert's Showbar was a black-owned and black-loved club—me being one of the lovers of it—and a part of the biggest black-owned motel in Chicago.

It was at Robert's that I first met Dick Gregory, a smart, talented man. Although at first he drove me crazy talking all kinds of black power talk—he really loved to pontificate on the subject—I eventually came around to a few of those ideas myself. In the meantime, we became friends.

At my salary in those days, it was too expensive to stay in the Chicago hotels so I opted to stay with my sister Nodie a half-hour away in Gary. In spite of our past estrangement, we worked out an arrangement where I paid her something very nominal in return for lodging and was able to save a little money for myself.

The only problem was transportation to and from work. Fortunately, a cousin of mine, Jack McDuff, a musician who worked gigs in Chicago as well, was usually able to give me rides, at least one way. Jack, an accomplished organist, came to Robert's to hear me sing and urged me to stick with it. That felt good to hear, coming as it was from a music veteran and a family member.

To ride home with Jack after I finished my show at Robert's meant that I had to wait until he was finished partying after his work. So, I was often left with the challenge of looking for other means of transportation.

Such was the night that Daddy Braggs and entourage appeared at my show in Chicago. Same scene, different entourage.

During the intermission between shows, he came backstage to ask me out.

I told him, thanks anyway, but I had to figure out a way to get back to Gary.

"No you don't," Braggs smiled, "I'll take you."

When he returned after the second show to pick me up, he was *sans* entourage. He had taken them and dropped them off somewhere they needed to go, he explained.

After Daddy Braggs helped me into the back of his big burgundy Lincoln Continental and after he gave his driver Nodie's address in Gary, he moved closer to me on the seat.

Not someone to beat around the bush, I asked him what he had in mind.

Braggs then made his play, telling me how much fun we'd have together and all the things he could do for me and how nice he would be to me.

After listening and saying nothing, when he was finished stating his case, I told him in no uncertain terms, "I am not a prostitute. You can't buy me. I would only be with you if I loved you and you loved me. Believe it or not, I can make my own living. So, I thank you for bringing me home but I don't owe you. If I do, tell me how much and I'll pay for the ride now. I've got the money."

Braggs laughed so loud he shook the car. "Oh, Del," he said, "I think about you all the time. I miss you when I don't see you. I wish you'd take down that barrier of yours and let something nice happen to you."

I looked out the window and saw Nodie's house. The Lincoln slowed to a stop.

"Well?" he said.

"What do I owe you?" I asked again.

This time, as Daddy Braggs laughed just as hard as before, his driver started laughing with him.

Scared of him and his reputation, the only response that came to me was to jump out of his car and run into the house as fast as I could.

I avoided him the next few times our paths crossed, at Robert's and then back at the Flame, my good old stomping ground where I always had a job if I needed it.

"What do you have against Daddy Braggs?" asked Ziggy one night before it was time for the club to open.

"It's a long story," I said.

"Tell me."

We sat down on a couple of vacant seats and I told him about my marriage. The way people talked about Braggs, I said, sounded like Vermont all over again. "Real sweet at first," was how I described it to Ziggy, "then controlling and violent."

Ziggy, whom I trusted, told me, "That's not Braggs, I promise you. Daddy Braggs is a gentleman. He has never mistreated a woman and I've known him for years, Della. He must be sweet because nobody's ever had a bad word to say about him. You have no reason to be afraid of him, I promise you."

"Did Braggs put you up to this?"

Ziggy looked hurt. Not at all, he said. He had come to me of his own volition and really believed every word he had spoken.

That night Daddy Braggs was in the audience, for the first time without an entourage, just his driver. On my way out, saying hello to other guests I knew, I stopped by to say good evening to him. He bought me a drink and took me home. We dated a few times and, as Ziggy had claimed, Braggs was every bit the sweet, considerate gentlemen.

My defenses lowered, I liked him lots.

Next summer, off again to Idlewild, this time I was the star act, the headliner, with the entire show designed around me. In one of my show-stoppers, staged by Braggs, I sat on a stool in a spotlight, cocktail glass in hand, and sang "One for My Baby," creating a mood the audience went crazy for. Another crowd-pleaser was "There Will Never Be Another You" and the closing number brought down the house. It was "Headin'

Home," a song I later recorded and was well-known for. The arrangement emphasized the shuffle in it and as I sang, I walked the stage and the audience to that rhythm while the chorines and showgirls surrounded me in procession. A biggie production number.

In the audience that summer was Tony Vance, the owner of a record company out of Detroit which he had started using money from his G.I. severance pay. After being impressed with what he had seen and heard, Tony approached me about recording me. I was interested. When he told me we would have to go to Chicago because he wanted to record me with eight members of Duke Ellington's band who were working there at the time, I was even more interested.

We were going to be recording four sides, including "There Will Never Be Another You." And to really give me a push, Tony hired writer Sax Kari to write one of those songs especially for me.

This was all thrilling until I got to Chicago and heard the song. Braggs had driven me there and he thought it was as putrid as I did. The song was called "Blue and Orange Birds and Silver Bells," a takeoff of the lyric from a tune which Nat King Cole had just recorded: "When out of an orange colored sky, Crash Bam Alacazam, wonderful you walked by . . ."

The song they wrote for me was corny and dumb but I wanted to be recorded and I loved the other three songs, so I sang it. That first experience in a recording studio turned out to be a wonderful one, thanks to an angel who showed up—Clark Terry, one of the musicians from Duke Ellington's orchestra. Seeing that I was intimidated at first, Clark came over to assure me that I didn't have to be afraid. "You're as good as any of us," he told me, "we're working for you." He also gave me my first recording techniques, showing me how to stand a certain distance from the mike in the studio, unlike the way the mike can be moved around for live singing.

Tony Vance pushed those records and got a good amount of airplay in Detroit and in Chicago. Now my reputation really began to spread. By the end of the summer, I was getting calls from all over.

This was occasion for Braggs and me to have a serious discussion about our future. We really had been having a marvelous time together but I wanted more of a commitment. That was hard for him to give because, as it had turned out, he was married, even though he held out promises of divorce.

"Braggs," I told him, "I'm not gonna spend my life waiting for that day," and having told him so, subtly began to pull back from the relationship.

Daddy Braggs didn't like that. So, to prove he didn't need me anyway, he retaliated by choosing one of the chorus girls to be his lady. One of the chorus girls from the show I was starring in! I was *livvv-idd.*

She dropped so many hints that the two of them were sleeping together, I got in my car, a gift from him—a white and black Thunderbird, the first four-seater they made—and sped over to Braggs's mammoth-sized trailer. The large live-in recreation vehicles had just come out and Daddy's was probably the biggest in existence in the early fifties. When I told him how unhappy I was with his choice of new companion, he spoke down to me in a way I felt was disrespectful, and that made it worse for me. So, on my way out of his trailer, I got the biggest brick I could find and I broke every window in his beautiful burgundy Lincoln Continental.

The next morning I woke up at the rented house where I was staying that summer and went outside to find my beloved Thunderbird with every window broken out of it.

Braggs fired the chorus girl, had both our cars' windows fixed, and we resumed our relationship. Sad to say, he was never able to make the kind of commitment I needed. But, nonetheless, after we broke up as a romantic couple, we remained the best of friends for the rest of his life. He was always my angel, always there for me for whatever I needed.

A few years before he died, I went back to Detroit and spent every day for a week going to the racetrack with him. Daddy Braggs was older now but just as distinguished, with the same magnetism, and vision. As the owner of several racehorses, he was still a successful, wealthy man.

Braggs had few regrets but there was one he told me about. On one of those days as we watched the horses line up at the gate, he reached over to take my hand, held it for a minute in his and then said quietly, not really looking at me, "You were the woman of my life. I was a fool to let you go."

Believe me, in these early years of my career getting started it wasn't all fun and applause.

I was learning the ropes of being on the road, a very taxing existence by any standards. It can take its toll on even the most resilient and adaptive personalities—picking up and moving on short notice, living out of suitcases, bouncing from situation to situation, always meeting and leaving new and old faces.

In some ways I was prepared for this new phase of living. Maybe that was because I felt in a sense I had really been on the road from the time I had left home at age seventeen. But there were some places along the way that nothing could have prepared me for, lonely and difficult hours spent in out-of-the-way places all on my own. And, every now and then, there were real pitfalls and real crises, when if not for the kindness of angels, I would have ended up in a mudhole instead of back on the road again.

One such crisis occurred the first time I played the Moonglow, a club in Buffalo, New York. My opening night went very smoothly. In particular, I was impressed with the emcee there, Pinky Roberts, known as the master of the art of fast change, a talented comic who changed entire outfits between acts, holding the show together while the dancers and strippers changed. But on my second night things took a dramatic dive. After the show, when I emerged from my dressing room, there was a representative from AGVA—American Guild of Variety Artists, the performers' union.

"Can I see your union card, Miss Reese?" he demanded.

I didn't have one, I answered. In all the years that I had been working in music, not one person had ever mentioned a union to me. Unions? I knew nothin' about unions.

"Can't work without your union card," the AGVA rep told me. To get one in order to go on the next night, it would cost me $109.00.

My pay was only a hundred dollars a week and my expenses for hotel and transportation had eaten up everything I had. Panic time. When I told the owner of the Moonglow about the situation, he advanced me a week's money so I could pay for the union card. That was an angel. Man didn't know me from Adam except for the two nights I had played his club. My bind was not unbound, however, because that still left me without anything for food or other incidentals. That night, on my way into my hotel, as I was walking through the lobby, I was drawn into the lounge by the sound of an organ trio and a girl singer. After their set was over, I complimented their music, introducing myself.

"Nice to meet you," said the singer, "I'm Sadye Rowser."

"Glad to meet you too, Sadye," I said. "Best thing to happen to me all day." As a matter of fact, it was one of the best things to happen to me ever because this was my sister Sadye, an angel sister if ever there was one. Before I knew it, I was talking and talking to her, telling her about my woes; she was listening and listening, empathizing, and sympathizing. By the time we finished talking, the sun was coming up. Sadye not only helped me through that tight spot in Buffalo, but has been in my corner ever since, loving and caring for me with the best sister love around.

Later on, as my career escalated, I was able to convince Sadye to come on the road with me. For ten years, she took care of everything— *ever-ry-thing*—magnificently, allowing me to focus on my singing which I loved. Not only a girl Friday, Sadye was my girl Monday through Sunday. She spoiled me rotten. No one, try as they might, has ever been able to replace her.

After the incident with the union man, it began to be clear to me that I could probably use a manager of some kind to oversee my career. Independent though I was, there were many aspects of the business I knew nothing about. In particular, I wanted someone who could help get me some serious recording work, perhaps get me booked into some of the more famous, big-time nightclubs.

Al Green, the manager of the Flame, must have been thinking the same thing. Around the time I was in Buffalo, on his own he did an angel's deed and decided to send one of the records I had done with Tony Vance to a friend of his in New York, a manager named Lee Magid.

Lee, who managed such artists as Al Hibbler, a vocalist who sang with Duke Ellington, and O. C. Smith, a rising R&B singer, was intrigued enough to come to Detroit to check me out the next time I was back appearing at the Flame. After the show, this big, young, Jewish-looking guy approached me and told me he loved my voice and loved what I was doing. If I could get myself to New York, he offered, he'd see what he could do to help me get a real record contract. Sure he would.

Sounded like a come-on to me. Even so, making real records sounded good too. But, with work awaiting in Cleveland, there was no time to mull over doth he love me or doth he love me not enough to make a difference in my career. Putting it out of my head, I hopped on my trusty steed, the black and white Thunderbird that Daddy Braggs had given me, which was already starting to wear out from so many miles on it, and headed south to Ohio.

En route, I stopped and picked up my niece, Gloria Bolden, who was Susan's daughter. Only nine months apart in age, Gloria and I, both in our early twenties, were compatible and she helped out from time to time as my assistant on the road. Ultimately, though, the road proved much too taxing for her. She was not prepared for the demands and she missed the familiarity of home, friends, and family.

On the trip to Cleveland, Gloria was most helpful, giving me navigation tips as I drove into town, looking for the Longfellow, a new hotel that had been recommended. In those days when many top hotels would not allow blacks to stay there, even the biggest stars had to concern themselves with finding decent, black-owned or black-friendly accommodations.

The Longfellow was such an establishment. When we arrived, the main entrance led us through the doors and up a flight of stairs, at the top of which was the registration desk that was behind a sliding glass window. As Gloria and I started up the stairs, carrying the bags together, we dropped one of them and it tumbled with such a racket that the gentleman seated at the desk, stood up, opened up the sliding glass window, and looked out in concern.

This was William Bayliss, owner of the Longfellow, known to his friends as Pepper, soon to be known to me as Peppi. (This name-changing habit of mine had become chronic already; to me, he was much more of a Peppi.) At any rate, this man—none of whose names I knew yet— opened the glass, looked out to see what the noise was and saw me. And, according to what he swore from then on and what I believed, he fell instantly in love.

No doubt about it.

Peppi gave me the best suite in the building, filled it with flowers and champagne, and for the next three months took on the dictionary definition of *at-tent-tive*. I mean *attentive*. I sent Gloria home and allowed myself to be taken care of like a queen.

William "Pepper" Bayliss was my definitive angel, a God-given gift in my life, who loved me with an unconditional love. No ifs, ands, or buts. No strings attached, no expectations. Whether he was my soul mate, or the love of my life, I didn't know. It didn't matter. He would have been there for me regardless.

Peppi was medium build and height, attractive, light-skinned, successful, smart, had a warm smile, and was truly a prince among men. And second only to Dorothy Smith, he was my fan of fans. If he fell in love with me the moment he saw me coming up those steps, then that night when he came to my show and heard me sing, it was in cement. According to Pepper, there wasn't anybody who could sing any better and there was no reason to prevent me from being a star and he was determined to do everything in his power to see that happen.

To that end, we were talking about my prospects and I offhandedly mentioned what this manager Lee Magid had said to me.

"See what he could do to help you?" Peppi asked, "That's a long leap for you to go to New York on. Why don't we get in touch with him, invite him to Cleveland and see if he's for real?"

As God would have it, Lee Magid, at that very moment in time, was right there in Cleveland. Because Al Hibbler was blind, when he wasn't working with the Duke but was touring with his regular group, Lee, as his manager, went on the road with him.

We invited Lee to dinner in Pepper's suite—a superb meal which I fixed, I don't mind saying—and Pepper talked to him at length about what would be entailed in my coming to New York. I mostly listened as Peppi ran down all kinds of practical matters—what Lee thought he could do for me in the short and long run, how he was going to go about doing those things, what I needed to have to stay in New York, where I was going to stay.

Based on Lee's genuine enthusiasm for me and my talent, it was decided I would go to New York for a while. To send me off in royal style, Pepper bought me a Cadillac Coupe de Ville, hunter green with a tan top, in addition to a few new gowns he gave me for working in, and enough money to tide me over until the work was lined up.

He walked me down to the car and helped me into the driver's seat. Before closing the door and waving me off, Peppi said, "I'm here, Del, standing behind you. You need anything, just call me."

With a quick kiss, we said good-bye, closed the door and I revved the engine of the Cadillac, pulling off down the street, on my way to New York City. In my rearview mirror, I could see Peppi standing out on the street, his warm smile beaming at me as he watched me drive away.

I drove straight through to New York, and straight to Lee Magid's office in midtown Manhattan. After Lee's secretary showed me into his private office, I strode in with a lot of confidence until I saw the way he was looking at me. Up and down and all around.

"Now, look," I said, "do you want to sign me or fuck me?"

Lee's teeth almost flew out. He laughed about that for years, telling the story to so many people, it ended up in annals of show business somewhere.

Me and my mouth.

Lee, a most important angel to me, had meant no disrespect by that look. He just really thought he had a great piece of talent to represent and genuinely loved and believed in me, which was how he continued to feel for the next twenty-two years.

For starters, he put me up in the Alvin Hotel, a theatrical, residential hotel right across the street from Birdland. The Alvin was some kind of a hotel. Count Basie's band was there, Miles Davis was in there, and so was Rose Hardaway, a legend in some circles. Not too much earlier in her life, Rose was so exquisitely beautiful she would have given Ava Gardner a hard road—her face and features breathtaking, her figure sculpted in the most perfect proportions, her skin like cream. That beauty of hers was a masterpiece, a work of art. And, in fact, Rose's claim to fame was that she had been to Paris and had gone to the Louvre, where she had her picture taken standing naked next to the Venus de Milo. And Rose Hardaway put Venus to shame. The story made newspaper headlines all over the world.

Rose's running buddy, Geru Gray, was a witty woman I enjoyed meeting. The life of the party, a comic, with a communication line to whatever you needed—music, love, places to go, *ever-ry-thing.* Geru looked after Rose, who was a hard-core heroin addict. What a tragedy. It was my first up-close exposure on a day-to-day basis to see how drugs destroy inside and out. Here was truly one of the most beautiful women who had ever lived, her once creamy complexion bumpy and blotchy, dark circles under her eyes, her once work-of-art body covered with track marks, her personality always possessed, her soul being robbed from her.

For me, Rose served as an angel of warning, an example of the kinds of mistakes I or anybody else could make at any time. Especially in show business and on the road, drugs were plentiful and galore. I was never a teetotaler and, daring fool that I sometimes was, liked to try or experiment with new things, 'cause it was hip to do. But after meeting Rose, there were certain substances that I chose to avoid as much as possible.

One of my first bookings was at Birdland, right across the street. Big time, here I come! In preparation, I took the money Peppi had given me and had a new Birdland-debut gown made for myself. Ironically, I'd never set foot into the club, but why should I have? In my mind, Birdland was identical to the Coconut Grove, which I had seen in numerous movies. Large with a big stage and palm trees and tropical decor. Maybe some tropical birds too. This was not at all true. In actuality, Birdland was a small, dark basement bar with little or no decor. In fact, when I arrived for my first show, I saw that my fabulous, tropic-inspired dress was bigger than the entire stage. And when the musicians saw me coming up in this gown, form-fitting to my ankles, with fabric stretched over a wide round hoop at the bottom and covered by flowers, they looked at me real funny. Where were they gonna sit? It was time to either turn around and leave, egg on my face, or think fast. The best I could do was to stand and sing while holding up that hoop while the audience got a good look at my legs. *Emmm-barrr-ass-ing.*

Maybe I was a little more naive about this big, bad New York City than I knew.

Fortunately, though Birdland failed to meet my expectations, the next club I played, the Savoy Ballroom in Harlem, certainly didn't. Lee had gotten me a job with the Erskine Hawkins Band which played the Savoy Ballroom very regularly. And it was a ball every night. From the bandstand, watching the ballroom dancers gliding across the floor—doing fast jitterbugs or slow beautiful waltzes—was such a pleasure.

The downside was that I was given three songs to sing and three songs only: "Let Me Go Lover," "Sincerely," and "Teach Me Tonight," three songs which were on the charts at the time and made Erskine's orchestra sound modern. I went on to sing those three tunes for nine months solid. And if you don't think I learned to seriously hate those songs, then you *outta yo' mind*.

The upside of all this was that I was forced to invent a multitude of different ways to sing the three songs—articulating the words differently, changing my phrasing, adapting my interpretations, whatever it took so that I could keep them fresh for myself and sing with meaning and feeling. As a result, my work as an individual stylist advanced many levels.

Let me stop here and tell you about a crush I had.

This occurred during what for me was the best part of singing with Erskine—when we were hired as the road orchestra for the one and only Nat King Cole. Our tour lasted for thirty-four days, thirty-four of the most precious days I could imagine because I was going to be working on the same show as my idol, my angel of inspiration, my biggest and most important influence.

Not enough praise in the world can be heaped on what Nat King Cole did for black men and women in show business—and even in a lot of other walks of life. Nat almost singlehandedly broke down color barriers to the top clubs in the world; he, first and foremost, proved that not only could a black singer make records that appealed to all races, but that these records could sell millions and millions of copies. He was an angel of the highest order and he left us, at age forty-five, much too soon.

I loved him for all his accomplishments. But I loved him most for what he did for me personally.

From the first day of the tour, I was so smitten by Nat King Cole that after I opened the show, I would run to my dressing room, change my clothes, rush back, and stand in the wings and just watch him and swoon.

Nat was a gentleman, professional, wonderful and suave. He turned me all the way on. With lights flashing and bells ringing. Every night and every matinee I watched him for thirty-four days.

I really became a joke with the men in his quartet and the other members of Erskine's band. They started pointing me out behind the curtain, laughing at me mercilessly.

One night after the show, after the curtain fell, Nat stayed on stage and kept the musicians on as well. Saying nothing at first, he reached into the wings, behind the curtain to where I was standing, and he pulled me onto the stage with him. Then he spoke, telling everyone, "Leave this lady alone and stop laughing at her. She's here every show to learn. She's new to this business and I told her I would give her some pointers. So leave her alone."

Nothing could have been more thrilling. He was such a gentleman and I was so flattered, I floated off the stage. Not only had he taken up for me, he went so far as to lie for me. Of course, he had never told me anything about giving me pointers or anything. The fact was that I froze anytime he was near me, such that making any kind of conversation would have been impossible.

My stock really went up. After that, I stood backstage and watched with abandon, no one ever making a remark or laughing at me again. When Nat sang, I was paralyzed. His voice, his kindness, and those shows are some of my fondest memories.

After the tour, I decided to quit the Erskine Hawkins Band, knowing I could not sing "Let Me Go Lover," "Sincerely," or "Teach Me

Tonight" one more time. It was back on the road for me, moving on now to small clubs around New York, Long Island, and the Catskills—clubs such as Grossingers, Browns, Swan Lake, the Raleigh, and the Concorde. The money was getting better. And, in the meantime, Lee landed me the recording contract he had promised. It was with Jubilee Records, which was owned by Jerry Blaine and his brother.

My first single release with Jubilee was "In the Still of the Night," which went on to sell 500,000 copies—a substantial hit in those days. Impressive also was that it was not considered R&B, the name the record business tried to give anything sung by black artists. My record became a crossover hit, selling to the pop market and giving me radio exposure to both white and black audiences.

It was 1954. I was twenty-three years old. And I will never forget the feeling of hearing that song on the radio the first time. A short while after it was released, I was back in Detroit, visiting and working at my original launching pad—yes, you know it—the Flame. On one of those afternoons, I had gone to see my brother, R.D., and the two of us went for a ride to do some errands. We were talking like old times, talking about how things were going for me and how he was doing. R.D. had married a most loving young woman named Delores with whom he had a growing brood of kids. Delores's grandmother had been a nanny for many years to the very wealthy Vernor family, of Vernor's Ginger Ale, and they had bought her a nice house on the West Side. Delores's mother, Evelyn, owned it now, and was happy for Delores, R.D., and their children to stay there. Evelyn was another one of my biggest fans and another angel who doted on me in every way, never failing to come see me at the Flame or miss any of my latest news. I used to call her my "other mother" and that really took her *out*.

As R.D. and I were driving along in the car, talking away, the radio was playing and just as he started to say something, R.D. stopped midsentence. "Listen, Del," he said, turning up the volume, "listen, it's you."

It was me. My song, "In the Still of the Night," was coming out of that car radio at me, sounding good. Wow. What a thrill!

The excited look in his eyes and the smile on his face told me how proud my brother was.

I was proud too. For me, it was starting to be a long way from the slums.

My next big record sold twice as many copies, taking me even farther. Released in 1957, it was called "And That Reminds Me," which was a song written as an adaptation of the Autumn Concerto.

At that time, it was the norm that if a black record started to hit, a white artist would cover it. With the big record company behind the white record, somehow the black release stopped being played while the white version became the hit. Pat Boone did it, Elvis Presley did it, everyone did. Kay Starr covered "And That Reminds Me." Nevertheless, my record held on, continued to hit, and sold close to one million copies. This was a smash, a gold record!

Staying in New York in that period, I went to get the mail one afternoon and found a letter in the mailbox from Jubilee Records. Inside was a royalty check for $5,656.23. My first royalty check. I jumped up and down and danced all over the apartment. Long into the night, I looked at that royalty check and early the next morning, I was waiting at the door of the bank when it opened. After cashing it, I took the money home, laid it all out on the coffee table, and then stacked and restacked it for hours. That afternoon, I went to Saks Fifth Avenue where I purchased not one, not two, not three, but twelve new pairs of shoes. When I got home, I tried each pair on all over again, prancing and strutting in them around the coffee table and the rest of the money.

When it was mail time, I skipped down to the mailbox, wondering what new surprises awaited me. I got a surprise all right. This time, there was a letter from Jubilee saying that I owed $12,975.00.

"Excuse me," I said, as I spoke pleasantly enough on the phone to the woman in the bookkeeping department at the record company, "there seems to have been a mistake in this statement that I owe you all this money. Just yesterday, I got a royalty check."

On the contrary, she replied. The royalty check was the mistake and I would have to return it, along with the $12,975.00 I owed.

No way, José, I said, or some other version thereof.

"Then we'll simply stop the check."

"Won't do you any good. It's already cashed and spent."

Before she could finish telling me that my debt was now going to be in excess of $18,000, I had gotten dressed and was on my to the Jubilee offices, where I asked to review the books. She brought me a set of blue books, leaving me alone to look at them. There was $3,500 worth of expenses being charged against me that were for odd amounts like nineteen cents without specification of what those items were that were so necessary for making my records. When I next took my findings to Lee, he was irate and together we returned to the accounting office. When he asked to see the books, he was given a set of red books.

Now my slums were starting to show. "The books you gave me were blue," I shouted at the top of my voice.

"No," said the woman, "you're mistaken. These are the books you just looked at."

"No, I'm not mistaken," I spat back. "You're lying."

"Cool down, Della," Lee said, "let me look at these books and see what's going on." After reviewing the red books, he also found a large amount of the same kind of suspicious-looking entries.

It was now time to go see Jerry Blaine, owner and president. Unfortunately, we were told, Mr. Blaine was out. Now, I had just seen Jerry go into his office and that did it. Taking Lee by the arm, I pushed into Jerry's office and let loose all of the slums in me, as I began to walk and talk and scream and cuss and threaten and have a fit. I was a hurricane and a tornado combined in that office, scaring Lee and probably every employee at Jubilee because of those who were huddled, listening at the door and those whose offices my voice was loud enough to reach.

The words were flying from my mouth completely unedited and I remember saying, "If you don't give me all of my money, God will strike you dead right here and now," not knowing at all that Jerry Blaine had a heart condition. Well, I found out that he did when my fit caused him to have an attack. Right there, right then. Jerry collapsed, falling forward onto his desk.

Thinking God had to have heard me, I began to pray, "Lord, I didn't mean it! Oh, God, don't let me kill him and have his death be on my hands. Please God!!"

An ambulance was called and Jerry was taken to the hospital. For three hours it was touch and go, but, yes, thank God, he lived.

That was the end of my happy relationship with Jubilee and Jerry Blaine. We ran into each other several times after that but never spoke since Jerry would leave the moment he saw me coming. The money dispute ended without clear resolution. They no longer claimed I owed them money, based on their creative accounting and their two sets of books. At the same time, I never got what should have been substantially more royalties for the proceeds of a gold record.

Lee got to work looking for another recording home for me, and I, feeling cheated and abused, went to my home back in Detroit where I stayed with my angel, Earnestine, who helped me, as always, to heal and renew.

In other respects, I have plenty of positive associations with "And That Reminds Me," including the fact that this was record that helped Lee book me on my first appearance on *The Ed Sullivan Show.* And wouldn't you know? Ed himself became one of my angels.

Blessed me. As it so happened, "And That Reminds Me" turned out to be Mrs. Sullivan's favorite song, as well as their love song. Because of that song, Ed had me on the show eighteen times in one year. Every show I did, I would fly in and rehearse all Sunday for the live broadcast Sunday night, each time carefully rehearsing whatever two songs I had for the show. And then, each time, just before the broadcast, Ed would ask if I had the arrangements for "And That Reminds Me." "Do our song, Della," Ed said every time. Eventually I knew to have those arrangements with me because no matter what else we had rehearsed I would end up singing it, and be happy about it too, whether I sang anything else or not. Ed was an angel to me on his TV show, as well as later on, when I'd meet up with him further down the road and he would perform a Good Samaritan's deed on my behalf.

At the time when Lee first called me about making my debut on Ed's show, I was in Detroit, working at, of course, the Flame. And I had to leave so quickly, flying into New York and then back home the same night, no one knew where I'd gone. They found out, though, when I rushed from the airport and made it in time for the last show and Ziggy announced me, "And here she is, our very own, your very own, Miss Della Reese, directly to you this evening from *The Ed Sullivan Show!*" I was some hot stuff that night. They were so proud of me, they insisted I sing—you guessed it—"And That Reminds Me," followed by some tore-down blues and my always showstopping "April in Paris."

With the exposure I was getting, I was voted Most Promising Girl Singer of 1957 by all three major record trade papers: *Billboard, Cashbox,* and *Variety.*

For a long time I felt I could do no wrong. Feeling like I'd really arrived, I took a job on the upscale West Side of Chicago and booked myself into the Evans Hotel, one of the better local establishments. Usually I could expect to get paid by check on Saturday nights; usually I would have to wait until Monday to cash it so that I could pay the hotel bill; and usually this wasn't a problem. But at the Evans Hotel when I arrived back from my job at three in the morning with my check, the clerk had a problem. Not wanting to hear or know or give me an inch of understanding, he refused even the check as collateral and promptly put a plug in the door of my room.

I headed outside, into the cold, and across the street to the park where I would have to wait until daybreak, find a way to call Nodie in Gary, and have her come for me.

When I got to the park, it began to snow. I was wearing a thin blue suede coat with a silk lining over the skimpy gown I had worked in, some nylons, and a pair of sandals. At first I felt a rush of despair, and then I began to softly say the words of Psalm 23, the most empowering psalm I knew: "The Lord is my shepherd, I shall not want. He restoreth my soul: he leadeth me in the paths of righteousness for his name's sake. Yea, though I walk through the valley of the shadow of death, I will fear no evil for Thou art with me . . ."

Soon I was singing hymns and gospel songs of gratitude to God and I was praising Him loud and hearty for sustaining me in my time of need, for being my sufficiency in all things, as cold and wet and uncomfortable as I was. That was how I spent the night, waiting for the eight o'clock shift to change at the desk, hoping that the day clerk would be more under-standing. When I went back into the lobby, I was cold but neither frozen nor frostbitten as one would expect.

I was so in the spirit that I almost didn't see my sister Susan, who had turned a trick that Saturday night in that very hotel. After I told her of my situation, showed her the check, and promised to pay her back as soon as the bank opened Monday morning, Susan agreed to loan me the money. They let me in my room and I spent the rest of Sunday thanking God. In that instance, Susan was an unwitting angel, no question, sent to be there for me and do what she could. The very next day, Monday, I re-paid her, packed up my stuff, and drove on to Cleveland where Peppi pampered me for a few days until it was time to get moving again.

Some years later I was back in Chicago working at the Sherman House, a very fine club. Susan got in touch with me and said she'd like to come to my show and see me. This touched me very much. It was the first and only time any of my sisters had expressed an interest in seeing me perform. Susan came back to my dressing room before the show and we talked about this and that, and about how her daughter Gloria, my niece, was doing. Then Susan said, "I was wondering if you had any cash with you."

"Yes," I answered, "how much do you need?"

A couple hundred, she said. Give or take.

Fine, I said, and gave it to her and walked her to the maitre d' to make sure he sat her in a good booth where she would be well taken care of. Before I went back to my dressing room, I watched him seat her, happy that he had put her in the best booth in the room.

When the show began, I had a moment onstage to glance over in her direction to see if she was enjoying herself. The booth was empty. Susan was gone.

That was a disappointment. But nothing like the disappointment that happened with R.D. On one of my trips home, I arranged to stay at his house, thinking it would be good to spend time with him, my sister-in-law, Delores, my other mother, Evelyn, and the kids, my nieces and nephews. When I arrived, the house was cold and the children were sitting around in their coats. Inside the house. Both the gas and the water had been turned off.

R.D. had more talent in one finger than many people have in their whole body. And he tried most of the time to hustle up whatever work he could. But he was slowly giving in to the pressures of struggle and poverty, unable to cope.

This was not an especially flush time for me but I took the money I did have and paid the bills and got everything turned back on, knowing after a week or two at the Flame I would be back in the black. After my first week, I dropped off two blouses and a skirt at the cleaners. Two days later, on a Friday night, R.D. was going out to the store and I gave him a twenty, asking him to pick up my cleaning. When he returned with my three items, he didn't volunteer any change. I asked for it and Rufus said there wasn't any.

Now, right here let me mention a wise old saying they used to have in my neighborhood; maybe they had this one in yours too. They used to say there were three things you should never mess with: Don't mess with a man's hair, don't mess with his shoes, and never, ever mess with his money. Well, in regard to the latter, that's exactly how I felt too. It was my pleasure to be generous to my loved ones. But take advantage and mess with my money, all the slums in me will resurrect on the spot.

"Twenty dollars for two blouses and a skirt?" I said to Rufus, starting to get mad. "Well, I won't be using that cleaners again. In fact, I am going to call them and tell them what I think of their prices . . ."

"Don't do that," Rufus said. As I persisted in saying I felt I should call, he blurted, "I told you there was no change. Are you accusing me of stealing nine dollars and twenty cents?"

"Maybe I should be, since you know the exact amount of change I should have . . ."

I was unable to finish my thought because R.D. swung and hit me so hard, he knocked me down.

That night, I moved out to Earnestine and Reverend Rundless's house. It wasn't about the money so much as it was about much deeper problems from which R.D. suffered and my feeling that this was a betrayal of trust. Sadly, it put a wedge between Rufus and me that lasted for years. We both tried to bridge the gap but the gap kept getting wider.

In talking my concerns out with Earnestine, one of the points that she coaxed gently out of me was that the road, and the way I was living it, had begun to exhaust me. Instead of constantly having to pull up and put down stakes, she suggested, it was probably time to make a home for myself.

I agreed. And I knew New York was where I had to do it. This was going to be a change and a risk too. For Lee to pass up the out-of-the-way clubs out of town and move me up to a higher level right in New York City might mean taking a cut in the money I could get. But, as I told Earnestine, "It's time, I feel it."

She didn't care much for the idea but she hugged me and prayed for me, placing me in God's hands. And the next day, after helping me pack, she drove me to the airport.

Before I got out of the car, Earnestine said, "Del, please remember, this is your home. Don't stay there if you find you don't like it. Don't let your pride keep you from coming home."

Even as she said it, I knew that while I might come back often for visits, this was it, I was leaving home base. A lump caught in my throat. "I'll miss you," I told Earnestine.

"I'll miss you more," she said, beginning to cry. "But we're together no matter where you are in the world. Don't forget that. We will make it somehow."

We cried, hugged, and I ran to catch the plane.

New York welcomed me as a bona fide resident with open arms. I set up my home in an apartment at a great address on the West Side on 85th Street between Central Park West and Columbus Avenue.

Old and new friends appeared right away, including my much-loved sister Sadye, who lived in the Bronx and was extremely glad I had moved to the city. A new friend was Lorraine Knight, whom I met, by chance, at the mailbox. (Of course, I don't really believe in chance.) An excellent dancer who had formed her own group after dancing with Katherine Dunham's troupe, Lorraine was a definite chorine—little, lithe, lovely—and was going with Joe Louis. She loved him deeply and, I do believe, he felt the same way about her.

One of my New York goals was to work the Baby Grand, a hot, happening club in Harlem. Fatefully, Lorraine was working at the other Baby Grand, this one in Brooklyn, and helped me get work there. When the owner heard me sing, he approached and asked me the question I wanted to hear, "Wanna come up and work the club in Harlem?"

Harlem was the place to be. The emcee at the Baby Grand up there was Nipsy Russell, funny, warm, and the kind of friend in show business you love to have. And next door was the Apollo Theater, where I wanted to work most of all. The owner of the Apollo, Mr. Shiffman, stopped by the Baby Grand one night. He'd liked me ever since my days with the Erskine Hawkins Band and knew my records were starting to cook.

Well, you know what he did? Yep, he hired me to work the Apollo where the notoriously rough, critical audiences embraced me. When you did well in Harlem, you were also booked for the Howard in Washington and the Royal in Baltimore. In Washington, I worked with the delightful Cab Calloway and the gifted George Kirby who became one of my best friends and remained so until his death. In Baltimore, I continued working with George and also with the Cootie Williams Band—a great bunch.

All of this took place in one marvelous month. And it was really that next step that I had hoped for by moving to New York. I began to feel like show business for real, like I had really made it.

When I returned from Baltimore, my sister Sadye had food fixed for me and sent it to my apartment via a friend of hers named Leroy Basil Gray. What a nice welcome-home gesture.

When Mr. Gray appeared at my door—tall, black, and handsome—I took one look at him and then another at all the food and asked him, "Have you eaten?"

"No, I haven't," Leroy answered with a sparkle in his eyes.

"Looks like there's enough for two," I said, offering for him to stay for dinner with me.

It was a magical evening. Leroy was passionate, well read, and very intelligent. Trained as an accountant, he was, at that time, deliberating about whether to get his certification or to branch into a different business. We had a strong connection. After a short, intense courtship, we were married in Chicago, where I was working the Black Orchid with Johnny Mathis, a wonderful talent and friend. Johnny sang for our wedding—a small affair—along with Gene Ammons, who played for the ceremony as well.

There were many stresses on our marriage. In terms of career and money, we were in very different places. I was growing, becoming more and more successful, while his job was underpaid. He really had neither the time, money, nor inclination to get his certification as a public accountant; neither was he clear yet on what his career path should be. The more I succeeded, the harder it was on him. He felt in my way,

Leroy said, and that not having more money made him somehow less of a man.

That was irrelevant to me. "Look," I said, "I'm a woman whether I have money or not. And you are a man, money or not. My man, that I love." My words didn't help his problem.

More than anything, Leroy helped me get more in touch with my own values which were often in conflict with his. For example, he had a big problem with Lee Magid and the fact that he was white. Where Leroy came from, in one way or another, all white people were out to get you. "You have to be a fool," he said, "to let a white man handle your business. To him you're just another nigger."

I told Leroy what I had learned when I was six years old and someone called me a nigger. I had never heard that word but the way everybody laughed I knew it was very bad. Home I went to Mama. "Am I a nigger?" I asked.

"Do you have a black heart?"

"No, I been baptized."

"Then you cannot be a nigger unless your heart is black." And she got out her old raggedy dictionary and showed the word to me where it said, "Black of heart." Mama said that anyone who called me that was stupid and I should feel sorry for them and forgive them because they didn't know what they were talking about.

Young enough for her words to sink in, I accepted that notion into my mind, my body, and my being. To this day I believe strongly that to allow a vulgar name to be anything other than stupid is to give undeserved power to the undeserving.

This doesn't mean that I was unaware of the severity or the pain of racism. Nor did I disagree that something drastic had to be done about bigotry, especially then in 1958; nor was I unwilling to try to do something about it. The difference was that my launch pad was not violent hate; Leroy's was. He rocketed on that hate; I couldn't. And so the bickering began.

We both read a lot and often shared passages from our respective books with each other. When I disagreed with his point of view or that of the author he was reading, Leroy accused me of being brainwashed by the church.

He had a problem with the fact that I was a Christian and he was an atheist.

"Those are your words," I countered. "From what I can see, you are as good a Christian as any I know. You love your fellow man, you are moral and righteous. You do good anytime you can."

But he felt our ideas were too much at odds. Leroy had been raised by an aunt who beat him and told him she was doing it because she loved him. While she beat him, she claimed she was doing it in the name of God. The damage made him hate God and hate love.

The bickering got progressively worse. I continued moving forward, he came to a standstill. None of this was to say we loved each other any less than before. But I knew that my hope to see him and us happy could not be attained through me trying to fix him or trying to fix me. I had learned my lesson before with fix-it-itis. There were other mistakes I made with Leroy but that wasn't going to be one of them. All I could do, I thought, was to be patient, loving, and supportive and pray that God would help him find what he needed to feel good about himself. With only these internal stresses, we might have made it through. Unfortunately, there was an external stress: his former wife.

When "And That Reminds Me" was still soaring on the charts, she contacted us, claiming that their divorce had not been valid. And she could prove it. Much to Leroy's dismay, she announced that she was two days under the legal age of consent when she signed the divorce papers. If I paid her, she said, she would keep it under wraps. I told her to take a hike, or words to that effect. She hiked herself to court, managing to have our marriage annulled.

Despite our efforts to overcome it, Leroy and I came to the end. We tried living together for another six months and in the process, we fell apart, bit by bit, day by day.

Remembering Earnestine's words, back to Detroit I flew for her steadfast T.L.C. As in the past, she helped me through.

As I recall, it was during this time that Daddy made his first and only foray to see me perform live at the Flame. He was in his sixties but to have seen him that night you would have guessed you were looking at a much younger man. Richard Early—tall, handsome, regal—strutted into the Flame in fine King Tut form. After the show, we took a picture together and the look on his face, captured by the camera's lens, was a look of such fulfillment. He was beaming. His daughter had made him proud.

A few years back when I had started making a little money, I had gone home with the idea of buying Daddy a house. I found a very nice one on the West Side and took him over to see it.

Daddy toured the house, nodding with approval. He was very impressed. We came outside and stood together on the sidewalk, admiring the trees in the yard and the spacious front porch. "Do you really like the house, Daddy?" I asked.

Yes, he said, he did.

"Then, I'll buy it for you," I told him.

But after we talked further, my father admitted that as much as he really did like that house on the West Side, he didn't want to move away from the old neighborhood on the East Side and his friends who knew who he was and loved him. So, instead of buying him the house, for the next many years I'd send him money every time I worked a new job. It was my wish that he'd use it for whatever he felt he needed or wanted. But knowing Daddy, I was pretty sure he must have saved most of it, depositing it in the bank and keeping it there for that rainy day that you never knew when exactly it was coming.

Around the time that he came to see me at the Flame, although I didn't know it, he had begun to have terrible dental problems. For years he had worn a plate of false teeth, much longer than he should have. The plate had worn down on the nerve in his jaw, so bad it practically wore the nerve out. In 1958, the complications from it forced the doctors to hospitalize him. At that point, they found that this man of steel who had never missed a day's work in his life had become very ill. If he wanted to live, the doctors insisted, he would have to give up drinking completely. For about a year, Daddy did as they said. He didn't touch a drop.

And then one day, as I later came to understand it, he went and bought a bottle of whiskey. He also paid his numbers bill, got his clothes out of the cleaners, took care of some personal debts that were still hanging, went home, ran himself a long bath, got dressed up nice, and opened that bottle of whiskey and drank it down.

Daddy's sister, Aunt Cappy, happened to drop by that day. When she did, my father was in spasms. Cappy called an ambulance and got him to the hospital. And there he died that evening. It was 1959, almost ten years exactly since Mama had died.

News of Daddy's death did not come as the kind of shock that Mama's dying had. Even so, like all unexpected loss, it was too sudden, too soon. My grief was profound. I was his only daughter, his only child, his pride and joy. We had talked fairly often in the past year and I'd thought he was doing much better. There was a part of me that knew he was with God and that was all that mattered. There was another part of me that couldn't stop wishing Daddy and I had been given a chance to speak one last time, a chance to say good-bye and I love you. In a surprise way, I was about to be given that chance.

When I flew in to Detroit, a few days before the funeral, with family and friends helping out in the preparations, Aunt Cappy pulled me aside, saying, "I've gotta talk to you. There's something I have to tell you."

"All right, Cappy, let's talk."

"No," said Capitolia, "not with everyone around. This is private. Something your daddy wanted me to let you know."

She kept telling me she had something to tell me, each of the days before the funeral, but each time she'd say there were too many people around for us to talk. At last, right after the funeral, after everybody had come back to Daddy's place, had something to eat and something to drink, and had then all gone home, Aunt Cappy and I were finally alone.

She sat me down on the couch in the living room and handed me a letter, saying, "Your daddy told me to give you this."

It was from my father to me. In it he wrote that he didn't want to live his life the way it was. I paused reading for a moment, laying my head in my hands as the tears flowed. I understood everything. My daddy had worked hard all his life, played hard all his life, been tended and loved by an angel named Nellie, adored by his only daughter, been admired and respected by everyone who knew him. He was King Tut. How could he have lived any other way?

In the letter, Daddy wrote that Cappy would show me where everything was.

"What does this mean?" I asked my aunt. "What 'everything' is he talking about?"

Cappy got up and pulled back the carpet on the floor and there, in a square area where the matting from the carpet had been cut out, was all the money I'd sent Daddy that he'd saved all those years. In that last week of his life, he'd gone to the bank and withdrawn it all and put it up under the carpet so compactly that it had taken on the shape and the imprint of the matting.

In his letter, Daddy ended by saying that he wanted me to have the money, to do something special for myself, and that he loved me.

Richard Thad Early, one of my first earthly angels, had left me an angel's gift. I was at peace, grateful for having been given him as my father, grateful that he had been able to choose his way to go. He had made his transition, gone home to see his Nellie, where the two could be together and continue watching over me, their love living now inside me, in my heart and in my soul. Forever.

On this trip to Detroit, I learned that my sister-in-law, Delores, was very ill. She was pregnant with her sixth child and because she felt she couldn't handle another child under her roof, it seemed to me she was in total neglect of her health—in order not to have this baby. She was so sick, we were all afraid for her life.

When I went and sat down by her bedside, I took her hand in mind and spoke my heart. "Delores, I want you to consider something. If you will just have this baby, I will take the child and raise it and care for it as my own."

R.D. was all for it. Given how late it was in her pregnancy and how sick she was, she had to carry it to full term and she wouldn't be strong enough to take care of the baby when she had it. We all agreed that Delores would notify me as her due date approached and that I would come to pick the baby up.

In the interim, I was out on the road, working some newer and exciting clubs. On November 20, 1959, Delores gave birth to a healthy baby, a girl. Of course, she changed her mind about letting me take her. Though R.D. tried to talk her out of keeping the child, she wouldn't hear of it.

The matter was settled, as far as I could tell, and I moved on with my life. This was a banner time for me in my career. Lee Magid scored a record contract for me with RCA and my first release out of the gate, "Don't You Know," sold over a million copies, my second gold record, and went to the top of the pop chart.

"Don't You Know," based on an aria from *La Bohème,* was a song written by Bobby Worth, a friend of Lee Magid's, and produced for me by the fabulous writing/producing team of Hugo and Luigi. I worked with them on several subsequent records. They were godsends to me in and out of the studio.

Having been blessed with so many angels, every now and then I received an opportunity to be an angel to someone else, something that was becoming more and more important to me as I went along. In this era, now that I was starting to play the cream-of-the-crop clubs—the Copacabana, the Coconut Grove, the Fairmont, Basin Street, and a host of others—I badly needed an excellent arranger and conductor. The man I chose for the job was Mercer Ellington, the son of Duke Ellington. For years, Mercer had been kept in his father's shadow, as a member of Duke's band but nothing more. That was the way Duke wanted it. He was the star, after all. Mercer didn't necessarily want to be a star but, for years, he had been wanting to strike out on his own and lead his own band. That's why when I hired him, he thought of me as his angel. More than a few people hinted that hiring Mercer was going to displease the Duke and that there could be some unpleasant repercussions for me. I chose not to be intimidated but to stick to my guns. Mercer thanked me, I thanked him, and it worked out splendidly.

By the summer of 1961, as I celebrated my thirtieth birthday, I realized that everything in that script I had been writing in my head since childhood had come to fruition. My success had brought me travel, glamour, fame, men who courted me in great style, and more riches than I had even ever put in my script. I was not only out of the slums, I was living on the exclusive East Side of New York at 46th and 2nd Avenue, in a security building with the best amenities available, around the corner from the U.N. building. I had needed a home, and I had made myself a family of friends and angels who cared deeply for me at my root. My life was everything I had dreamt of and more. And yet, bit by bit, over the next several months, I started to have this vague feeling that something was missing. Like an itch you can't scratch. I had no idea what it was. With everything I had manifested, I wasn't at ease. Despite evidence to the contrary, I began to feel that I lacked a sense of purpose or contribution. Inside, there was just this inexplicable emptiness. In the past, though I lived a lot of time on the road, I had always found a way of feeling anchored. Somehow, even with all the best parts of my script I was living, I felt unanchored.

To fill whatever that hole was inside, I found myself partying more than was my normal mean, hanging out with a fast crowd, getting higher more often than was my habit. Sometimes the music was good but none of this necessarily made me happier or helped take the edge off. This wasn't my scene, I knew, but every time I came home from work there was nothing really to hold me there. So I'd go out and party.

If I had only known what it was I needed, I would have prayed for it. That turned out not to be necessary. God knew exactly what it was and He sent an angel to me, delivered by two other angels.

On a winter's Saturday afternoon at the Regal Theater in Chicago— where I was rehearsing for my show that night—I looked up to see R.D. and Delores with a beautiful two-year-old girl. They had named her Deloreese. I adored her instantly. And she felt the same way about me.

My angel Delores said softly, "We don't have enough to take care of the children we have at home already. I need to go out and find some work and we just don't know what to do with her."

This time I hesitated. "Delores, you'll change your mind," I said. "Just like you did before. If you let me think she is mine and then when things get better for you, you feel differently and come take her away from me, it would break my heart."

I reminded Rufus David how he felt when it happened to him. "Why would you want to subject Deloreese to that kind of pain, R.D.?"

"I know," he nodded, stating emphatically that he would not do that to her.

We talked about the ramifications of this momentous decision all afternoon. All the while, Deloreese kept cuddling me and loving me and I kept loving her. That night, after closing the Regal, I left with Deloreese—who had nothing to cover up with—wrapped in my chinchilla coat.

The next morning we flew to New York. I remember looking over at the seat next to me and seeing her—my daughter, my angel. All at once, my emptiness was filled to overflowing with a love more powerful than anything I had experienced before.

Let me say this now, to clear up any mistaken assumptions. From the moment I held her in my arms, she was my daughter, the child God gave to me. Not my ward, not my niece, not a child I was caring for. I am not her foster mother, her guardian, nor her aunt, nor any other way you would like to phrase it.

Deloreese is my daughter in every sense of the word, in every thought in my mind, in every feeling in my soul.

I am her mother.

We even look alike, like mother and daughter. And there has never been any doubt in anybody's mind that we are mother and daughter. On that airplane back to New York, she started calling me Mama and has never stopped.

Deloreese was the joy of my life. She became my anchor, my purpose, that being to whom I knew I was making a contribution. She saved me from the party scene. After I became a mother, it lost its luster. Not only that, but there weren't enough hours to work, take care of her, and still party to excess.

In fact, having her saved my life. It brought the responsibility of someone else's life into my life. Before her, I was that survivor and sometimes loner who looked out for me—my needs, my desires, my well-being. Now I had someone to love and care for, someone who needed and depended on me, looked up to me to protect, teach, and be there for her, no matter what.

That's what I have done. Unconditional love. Pure and amazing. Never had I felt her kind of love. Nor had I ever loved like that. She was so beautiful, loving, fun, and what I learned to live for.

This is the first time I have told the story of how I came to be blessed by her as my number-one angel. And I pray that it doesn't upset her or her life. I think our love and our life is a miraculous, God-filled experience that I am proud and most grateful for.

For the next four years, I took my daughter with me on the road, everywhere, twice around the globe and back. We had a marvelous time, just she and I. It was magical—Dumpsey on one hip, a suitcase in the other hand, and the world in front of us.

Thank you, God.

part
three

Acting

1961 – 1980

8

I had grown up. I had made a name for myself. The goals and dreams of these two important volumes of my life had been fulfilled. Now, a new unwritten volume was beginning, this one commencing with all the hopes and prayers I held for my precious child.

I got deep into the mother thing and I loved it more than I can say. I still do. There was so much I wanted to give my daughter, so much I wanted to protect her from. This is not to create the impression that I had a terrible childhood because I didn't. Mama and Daddy were my first two angels, and through them, I was ultimately able to rise above hard circumstances, against the odds. They would have given me anything; they would have given me more if they'd had more. With what they did have, they gave everything they could have.

But I wanted my baby's childhood to be the basis for her life—love-filled, joy-filled, with enough of everything all the time. I didn't want the mark of the slums on her with an outside world saying she could never amount to something. I wanted her to know all of her needs would always be met and that she was an extraordinary human being; to know she was loved unconditionally; to know that, no matter what, she could talk to me and that God, she, and I could handle anything that happened.

Only the best was what I wanted for her: the best environment, surrounded by the best people, people with depth and creative understanding; the best schools, the best opportunities. Just the best of the best. For the four years that she traveled with me, I hired an excellent tutor who came along with us on the road. It was important also that with all our coming and going, she had a sense of stability and normalcy. I wanted her to be free, to be independent without an attitude of the star's spoiled child.

It wasn't going to be easy, I knew. She was a child taken out of poverty and placed in a new environment with new ideas and expectations, one who had left a large family of sisters and brothers to come to a family of just me. The absence of a father. The changing of mothers. The moving around where she had lived in one spot. The unanswered questions and the wrong assumptions made by others.

It was difficult in many ways for both of us. But our love for each other was and is so strong, we made it through. Our struggles only made our love stronger and brought us that much closer.

There was trouble at first dealing with R.D. Once Deloreese and I were settled, he called to express his fear that since he and I weren't getting along, I might take those feelings out on the baby. Which was crazy. He made similar calls a couple more times, causing me to say, "Look, R.D., if you're gonna bug me, I will bring the baby back."

He sure didn't want to hear that. From then on, he left me alone.

Another problem which arose almost immediately was the congested area in which we were living. Every time the nanny took my daughter to the park and I happened to hear a truck squealing to a stop or some other loud sudden noise, I would go ballistic thinking something had happened to my baby.

For my own peace of mind, I decided to buy a house in Westchester County, which was not far from the city. In New Rochelle, I found a lovely Tudor house, with rolling hills for a lawn, and a big back yard for Deloreese to play in. I knew it was perfect the moment I saw it. After I bought it, I discovered to my shock that there were no other black people in the neighborhood except Willie Mays and me. Even more shocking was the stink which buying that house caused. After all, this wasn't the South or anything. It was New York, an upper income and supposedly progressive place.

Well, they may have been progressive enough not to throw bricks through the windows but every time I went out to the market, or the drugstore, or the dry cleaners, the looks people gave me were just as bad. If I started down a shopping aisle filled with other shoppers, suddenly they'd all clear the deck. When I parked my car to go into any of the local stores, I'd notice people huddling and pointing, as if they'd never seen a black person before. Pretty soon, I started ordering my groceries by phone and having them delivered. The same with drugstore supplies and the dry cleaning.

Although a few hateful individuals tried to mount an effort to somehow legally question my right to own property there, I refused to even deal with them and turned everything over to my wonderful New York lawyer, Benjamin Sneed, who was my first lawyer from the time I started to make a little money. An angel he was, through and through, and a very dear friend. A fatherly black man of great integrity, from the islands, Benjamin was a brilliant lawyer, looking after me and my legal affairs as if I was his own daughter. He took care of me for the first fifteen years of my career when I was living on the East Coast, never once in that time telling me that there was something he couldn't handle. And with him, everything was always handled absolutely correctly, including whatever the complaints had been about my moving to New Rochelle.

And so, in spite of the lack of a community welcome, we held our heads high and dug our heels in, making a home for ourselves that we loved very much.

We had been there for just over a year when Deloreese, at about three and a half years old, made a most important request of me.

It happened on account of our staircase. Inside the house, leading from the first floor to the second story where our bedrooms were, there was this long, high staircase. To get down it without falling, Deloreese taught herself to turn around and sort of crawl/climb backwards down the steps. Careful as she was, it was hard work for her.

Now, in my household whoever works there is considered part of the household. And so, rather than referring to me as Mrs. Reese or Miss Reese, our housekeeper Zena would call me my given name. But whenever Zena would call to me from the kitchen up to my bedroom— "Deloreese!"—my daughter would hear her and proceed to back down the steps and then go all the way into the kitchen and say, "You call me, Miss Zena?"

And Zena would say, "No, I was calling your mama."

After this had been going on for quite a while, these trips down and up the stairs began to really infuriate my little girl. Of course, I didn't know what the matter was but I'd see that pretty face of hers with frowns all over it and know something was really making her mad. I think if she coulda cussed, she woulda cussed.

One night, after we'd eaten dinner and everybody else had gone home, she came into my bedroom wearing that perturbed frown on her mouth. I said, "Baby, what's the matter?" And we had this very adult conversation that, if you'll pardon the grammar, I'm going to write the way I've told it for years:

After I ask her why is she upset, she sez, "I don't have a name." And I sez, "You do have a name, your name is Deloreese." She sez, "No, that's your name."

And I said, "But it's your name, too." She sez, "No, that's your name and Miss Zena knows it's your name but she keeps callin' it all the time and I keep goin' down the stairs and it makes me tired and I want my own name."

So I said, "Well, okay then, don't get upset. What would you like for your name to be?"

And she said, "Dumpsey."

I looked at her and said, "You sure?"

She said, "Yeah."

I said, "Well, go downstairs and get the broom."

So she backed down the steps and went to the kitchen and got the broom and crawled back up the steps with the broom and came into my bedroom and handed it to me. And I said, "Get down on your knees," and she got on her knees and I held up the broom, touching it lightly on each of her shoulders, and I said, "I dub you Princess Dumpsey."

And it made her so very happy. She smiled dreamily, curled up on the floor, closed her little eyes, and went to sleep. And ever since that night, she has been called Dumpsey.

Treated and greeted like the royalty she was, Princess Dumpsey saw amazing sights traveling the world with me in those early years—Italy, England, Australia, Brazil, *ever-ry-where.*

Now, Rio de Janeiro, that was an adventure. On my opening night, the concert house where I was playing was packed to the rafters and the audience appeared to be most attentive. Despite the language barrier, I could tell they felt everything I was singing about. But then, just after my last song, as I went to take my bow, things started flying out at me from the dark. Because I was standing in a spotlight and all those things being thrown at me were landing on the darkened stage, I couldn't tell what they were.

Not that it mattered. It was enough to know that people en masse were throwing things at me. I was crushed. Never in my life had this happened. I turned, ran offstage and hurried into my dressing room where I promptly locked the door and began to cry. Moments later there was a knock at the door.

"Della, it's me, Mercer," said my conductor, Mercer Ellington.

Oh, Lord, I thought, now they're throwing things at Mercer.

Opening the door only wide enough for him to get in the dressing room, I pulled him inside and locked the door behind him. "There," I said, "we'll just stay locked up in here 'til they all leave."

Mercer shook his head, as if to say that wouldn't be necessary, explaining, "They're throwing bouquets at you. They love you. They're giving you a standing ovation."

I went back out on the stage and saw, sure enough, that it was covered with bouquets of all different kinds of flowers. Once I understood what was happening, it was completely thrilling. Later, the owner told me he had never seen them so pleased with any other star who had come there.

That night, we partied in grand fashion. After riding the elevator up to the penthouse somewhere around four A.M., I checked in on Dumpsey who was fast asleep, sent the babysitter home for the night, and then tumbled into bed myself.

In this frame of time, there was some sort of government upheaval going on in Brazil. We had been warned by the American consulate to beware and we were given instructions as to how to behave in case of a disturbance.

At nine A.M. that morning I was jolted out of sleep by a serious disturbance. It was the explosive sound of a cannon being fired. I leapt out of bed, grabbed my baby, grabbed my coat and jewelry bag, and headed for the elevator. It descended and stopped on the next floor where Mercer got on, all of his stuff crammed into his bag. On the next floor, the drummer got on the elevator, equipment in hand. Two floors down, the bass player got on the elevator, lugging his bass. The pianist, packed to leave, was the last to get on. No one said a word to the others. The minute the elevator doors opened on the main level, we flew out and through the lobby, pushing and knocking our way in between the various hotel guests who, until we showed up, seemed to be relaxing and milling about happily. Now they looked as alarmed and concerned as we did. Not stopping to chat, we hurried to the desk, where I asked as calmly as I could for the American consulate—which happened to be just next door. Hearing that they were open, we rushed out of the hotel, pushing through another group of arriving hotel guests and alarming them, and into the consul's office. Everyone was talking at once, frantically asking for information about how soon we could leave Rio.

The consulate officer helping us asked, "But why do you want to leave?" He knew from our papers that we were scheduled to be performing there for two weeks yet had only been there a day.

In unison and almost in harmony, we replied, "They're shooting cannons and we want to get out of here!"

The man smiled slightly and said, "Miss Reese, and company, that cannon is shot every morning at nine A.M."

Exchanging glances, we stood there looking and feeling completely foolish. And then we had to go out and go back in the hotel, across the lobby, past all those people whom we had alarmed and confused and bumped into. Talk about first-class embarrassment. We were mortified. Everyone, that is, except Dumpsey, who thought it was just another adventure with her mama.

The highlight of that trip came later in the week when I went to see the Christo Redempto, the statue that stands high on a mountaintop overlooking Rio. At the time, the steps had not yet been completed all the way to the top. So I climbed what steps there were and then hiked up this long dusty road with stones jutting out from the ground. It was exhausting and though I really wanted to turn back to head downhill, having come that far, I had to continue. And just when I was too tired to make it any farther, I turned the corner and there was this enormous statue of Christ. It was a spiritually monumental experience. As the years went on, I often used the power and the lesson of my climb to help me through very difficult times when things became hard and rocky and dusty, reminding myself that just ahead Christ would be there and, knowing that, I could always make it a little farther.

The goals of this new life chapter included higher, broader horizons for myself as an entertainer, with aspirations to break into acting and to continue growing as a creative person. One of the ideas I began to have was to incorporate gospel music into my nightclub act, something that nobody had tried to do. Nowadays popular stars like Whitney Houston, Natalie Cole, and Michael Bolton often include gospel songs in their concerts. But back in the sixties, gospel was considered to be just for church and not something that would have a broad-based appeal to general audiences. I didn't buy that. To me, general audiences had just never heard gospel music. And if I gave them a chance, I was sure they would love it.

In 1962, while working at the Copa, I had an opportunity to test my idea by including in my show a group of some of my favorite angels, the Meditation Singers. It was so gratifying to be singing and working again with Earnestine and Marie and the rest of the group. And true to my expectation, our gospel music went over big, delighting the audiences and reviewers. Based on that success, my idea began to grow. Why not take gospel music to Las Vegas?

That got me flak from both sides. Many in the gospel community were horrified. Gospel belonged in the Church, they claimed. Their attitude was that to take it out of the Church and to Sin City, USA, of all places, was a one-way ticket to hell on an express plane. I disagreed. I also disagreed with the top tour promoters who said that while gospel might have a novelty appeal, it could never draw the large crowds necessary to fill the big showrooms in Vegas. Why couldn't it? I said.

Before long, I was given a shot to prove it could with a two-act show called "Portrait of Della Reese." In the first act, together with the Meditations, I introduced gospel music, followed by a set that showed the evolution of the blues; in the second act, I sang selections of gospel, blues, pop, and jazz standards, along with songs for which I was known from my albums. RCA recorded the show as an album release and it was filmed as a TV special by National Telefilm Associates.

In Las Vegas the show was a phenomenon. The first room we played was a hotel lounge from which we could be heard throughout the casino. Pretty soon, there were so many people in the lounge listening to us, all the gambling had come to a stop. In no time, we were booked into one of the big showrooms the skeptics thought we could never fill. Well, we not only filled it, but we played to sold-out houses every night.

As the first person to bring gospel into the mainstream, successful though I was at it, I wasn't given the credit for it. On one hand, it bothered me. On the other hand, it couldn't take away from the pride I had in myself for paying tribute to my musical roots and to those angels like Mahalia Jackson, Willie Mae Ford, Beatrice Brown, Roberta Martin, Eugene Smith, and others who had inspired me along the way.

The other angel who deserves thanks here is Mr. Ed Sullivan, without whom I might never have played Las Vegas. Some years before, in the late fifties, it was Ed who'd first brought me out to Vegas with his TV show.

In those days, black entertainers could work the strip but we couldn't go into the casino, nor could we eat or sleep in those hotels. The only place to stay was all the way across town at a hotel aptly named the Dust Bowl. Then, a doctor by the name of Dr. West, along with his wife, Dottie, a former chorus girl, saw the need for a black physician in Vegas and moved there. They also went on to build a motel and several houses so that black stars would have decent housing. Happily, I was able to rent one of those houses.

One night for Ed's show, I was late getting to the club. I ran into the dressing room which I was sharing with Blossom Seely, a gifted ballroom dancer who performed with her husband. I changed as fast as I could and rushed out on stage just in time for my entrance. Since I hadn't eaten beforehand, when we finished the eight o'clock show, I was *huuunnggrrry*.

So I pick up the phone and call room service to send me back a cheeseburger.

Cut to: 10:30 P.M. No cheeseburger. Blossom now decides she'll call room service for me but they refuse her. She is *livvv-idd*.

Cut to: 11:45 P.M., still no cheeseburger, and the second show goes on at midnight sharp. Blossom now is having a fit. So much so that when Ed Sullivan walks by, he hears and comes in to find out the problem.

Blossom says, "This child is hungry and they won't serve her a cheeseburger back here in the dressing room."

"We'll see about that," says Ed.

A cheeseburger arrives in minutes but now it's time for me to go on so I'm stuffing down this burger. Mr. Sullivan sees me and says, "Please, Della, take your time and eat," and proceeds to hold the show up until I had eaten. To arrange for a cheeseburger to be delivered to a black person performing in a casino was like parting the Red Sea. But Ed did more.

After that, every night Ed and his wife took me out to every restaurant in Las Vegas, walking in with me, sitting me down at the best table in the middle of the restaurant where the three of us had dinner. All-white restaurants. The looks were to kill but he was Ed Sullivan and there was nothing they could do about it. That was an angel's deed, an act of goodness he didn't have to do, but one he could do and one he did.

The owners of the New Frontier saw me on the Sullivan show and hired me on my own to play there. That was where Morris Landsburg saw me and booked me to work the Flamingo. My tenure there lasted nine consecutive years, twenty-six weeks a year.

For the first few of those years, Dumpsey was still traveling with me, along with my sister Sadye, my number-one road assistant. This was an especially blessed time in my life. Since my show at the Flamingo lounge was the latest in town, everybody working the strip would come over to jam or sit in or just hang out with me after their shows were over. That's how I came to meet and sing with another one of my idols, Mr. Frank Sinatra (wow!). Some of the other regulars included Dean Martin,

Sammy Davis, Jr., Sarah Vaughan, members of Duke's band, Basie's band, Louie Prima, Keely Smith, Billy Daniels, Billy Eckstine, the Treniers, Shecky Greene, Don Rickles. This was some *go-o-o-d* music and some *go-o-o-d* fun.

My daily routine was a challenging one. I'd arrive at the Flamingo at 11 P.M. and work until 5 A.M., which allowed me to get home just in time for the baby to get up. We'd have breakfast together, play for a while, and then Sadye took over so I could sleep, wake up, get ready for the night's work, and have some time to see the baby and play with her before she went to bed. Challenging though it was, we bonded even closer as a result. My attitude was and is that if God had sent me this angel child and He had given me all this work, He would provide me with whatever ability, energy, and stamina I needed to be the best mother I could be and the best singer I could be.

That was my attitude and that was what happened. For four years straight, God gave me the opportunity to take Della Jr., as I sometimes called her, on the road. Then, when she was almost six years old, the state of New York intervened, insisting she be registered in a school. It broke my heart to leave her. My phone bill equalled the national debt for the next twenty years.

On one of my first Las Vegas stints without Dumpsey, Lee Magid brought his new client, Lou Rawls, over to my show at the Flamingo. I knew Lou from my gospel days and when he came up to jam with me, it was a musical and soulful click. Together we sang some blues duets and, oh baby, did we rock the place. He started sitting in with me regularly and pretty soon, the booking people from the Thunderbird heard him sing with me and hired him. Lou continued on as my buddy and we hung out between our respective shows.

It was a completely platonic friendship. But not according to a fellow I was dating at the time who had just flown in from New York to see me and, unbeknownst to me, not only spotted Lou and me leaving the Thunderbird together in Lou's car, but followed and watched us. Nor did I know that Sweets Edison, a trumpet player and friend of this man, told him that he, Sweets, had personally seen me in Lou's motel room, sitting on his bed. Which was true. The room wasn't big enough to hold anything more than a bed, one chair, and a dresser. So, sure, I was sitting on the bed but apparently, Sweets made it sound like I was in the bed.

That night, when I arrived at the Flamingo for my last show, this man I was dating—whom I thought I knew—rushed into my dressing room with a gun in his belt which he flashed first and then pulled on me. Sadye, who was there with me on that trip, was shaking like crazy. But I just kept on dressing. Don't ask me how because I was shaking just as crazy on the inside, somehow maintaining my calm on the outside.

Pointing the gun, he said to me, "You don't believe it, but I will kill you."

I said, "Well, you'll have to do it after the show 'cause I've got to go on now," and I walked out of the dressing room and onto the stage.

Time for angels? You bet. And there they were, all of them, every single member of the audience that night. Seeing all those people, there was nothing the man could do. My show was one of my best ever, my angels responding with standing ovations and applause for several encores. It broke the man's spirit, moving him to decide not to use his gun on me. At least not to shoot me. He did use the threat of it to force me into my car so we could drive to the Thunderbird to confront Lou.

When we got there, Lou was finishing up his show. No sooner did he walk off stage, this man accosted him too, flashing and pulling out the gun again, scaring Lou beyond words.

"We have nothing to fear here," I repeated in a steady voice. Lou, however, was past reassurance. Then it was decided to go back to the motel room so I could pick up a tape player I had loaned Lou and I could show the man with the gun why I was sitting on the bed.

"See?" I asked him.

He nodded solemnly, realizing that there really was no other place for me to sit.

From there, I drove him straight to the airport for a plane back to New York.

In the car, he apologized for the misunderstanding, asking, "Will you ever be able to forgive me?"

"I forgive you now," I said.

That was the end not only for that fellow but also, sorry to say, for me and Lou Rawls, who has not been my friend since that night.

On a happier note, this was at the same time that Reno and Tahoe opened up for me. So for most of those nine years that I played the Flamingo in Las Vegas, I would move right on to Harrah's, which I played in the other two resort cities. The work from just those three gigs kept me busy most of the year, except for the time I spent making records here and there. RCA did well by me for quite a while, giving my releases strong support. Along with my biggest-selling single, "Don't You Know," I had several other hits including "Bill Bailey" and "It Was a Very Good Year," which both went gold, as well as biggies such as "Not One Minute More," "Sunny," and "Games People Play."

My plate was full. Work was plentiful, financially and creatively rewarding, and I was hearing my music on the streets. The only hitch was that, except for Christmas and summer vacations, it was a real task getting home to New Rochelle to see Dumpsey. After a year and a half, it bugged me so much, I started contemplating a move to Vegas. Then again, I didn't really love being there. It was dry and dusty and so confining. As an alternative, I began to consider Los Angeles, which was one of those hot tropical-type settings I had loved since childhood. Plus, it was only a forty-five-minute flight to any of the resorts I was working, which meant I could come home on my day off during the week and Dumpsey could fly to see me on Fridays after school, giving us at least three days a week together.

When I was out working in L.A., also checking out the living situations and debating when exactly we should come out there to live, I met an angel who helped accelerate the move. He materialized at the Palomino, the club I was playing in the San Fernando Valley. His name was Bobby Bryant, and he was a trumpet player who was playing backup for me. Bobby played with such a love for the music. He was so good, he *took me out*. Tall, well-built, with medium-brown skin and a pencil-thin mustache, he was a joy to look at and to be with. The Jolly Brown Giant, his friends called him. The attraction was mutual, deep, and potent. After playing for me back in Vegas, he left with me to play on an overseas tour of military camps in Germany, Holland, and England. Our romance intensified and while overseas we became engaged.

At first, I really thought Bobby was THE ONE. And, as it so happened, he lived in Los Angeles. Now that I was on my way to being his wife, there was no question about where I was moving. After the tour ended, our plan was for me to come out and stay with him until we found a place of our own, and then I'd send for Dumpsey and ship our belongings out.

To my joy, I found out I was pregnant while I was in Amsterdam. Bobby was as thrilled as I was. Six weeks later I suffered a miscarriage. It was hard on me physically and emotionally. But the next month, in Germany, we celebrated the wonderful news that I was pregnant again. Two months later, in Frankfurt, I had another miscarriage. The pain and the sense of loss were overwhelming. In both instances, the medical services I received were excellent but the doctors were at a loss as to why these miscarriages were occurring. When I turned to Bobby for comfort, perhaps sympathy, his only solution was for me to stop singing.

"Like I told you, you're just workin' too hard," he said.

Granted, Bobby was from rural Mississippi and knew nothing about the science of reproduction or the medical causes of miscarriage. But deep down, I could see that what he wanted was a reason for me to stop working and stay at home to have a baby so he, too, could stop working the road.

After growing up in Mississippi, his experience with racism made him uncomfortable working in all the white clubs in which I performed.

"Bobby, I have my own discomforts," I told him. "But I'm too ambitious to allow it to get in my way. And I'm not gonna let it take away either my conviction or my courage to work through it toward my dream."

"That may be, Del," Bobby agreed, talking in his slow country boy way of talking. "And I applaud you for that." But, he reminded me, he made more money working as a studio musician where he didn't have to deal with the white clubs. That was his security, even though it was not offering him a chance to grow. Because Bobby had an honorable sense of responsibility to help out his parents and to provide for a son he had from a former marriage, he was not willing to risk going without that steady work in order to move to a higher ground.

We literally made and wrote beautiful music together. And yet, he never really listened to it for the true potential it had. He couldn't visualize the kind of future for himself that I saw I could have for myself, nor did he want to take a chance to go after it; just the opposite for me, I had to follow the certainty I knew in my heart and soul that my journey was just unfolding. I was operating from faith; Bobby was operating from fear.

Against my better instincts, when the European tour was over I did go home with him to L.A., which was actually his mother's home. As a guest in her house, I never felt at home. After some weeks passed, I awoke one Saturday, packed up my things, and went to Fred Sands's office, one of the better realtors in town. One of the first houses I saw was on Warbler Way, in the fashionable hills above Sunset Strip, and I leased it on the spot with an option to buy. As soon as I could, I flew to New York, packed up the house there, and returned to Los Angeles with Dumpsey.

Even as I settled into my own place, Bobby Bryant and I did not break off our relationship right away. In the hopes of making him more comfortable and more secure, we opened a bar together called Marty's On the Hill, along with some partners. For a while, building the bar and running it did bring us closer. But it was not too long before we knew that the relationship had played itself out. Once again, I chose not to lapse into fix-it-itis. If Bobby didn't see the same future I did, our futures weren't meant to be intertwined, and so I moved forward on my own.

Many years later, Bobby told me he finally knew what we could have done and been together. He was ready. But I had paid my dues and

made my mark by then and was already heading into yet another frontier.

As I was coming to understand more and more, timing is everything.
That was one message that Bobby, as my angel, had brought me. Though
patience was never my strong suit, it was becoming clearer and clearer
that there is such a thing as God's Time, which may not always coincide
with our time. And while there may be the best laid plans of mice and
men, God is always in charge of a better plan. This helped me see my way
through a variety of disappointments—whether they were related to
love, work, the weather, whatever. Of course, when things didn't pan out
as I had hoped, I'd have my regular fifteen minutes of blues. After that,
I'd hit the trail again, knowing that God was absolute good and that He
wanted only absolute good for me, trusting that in His Time, all would
be better and more than I had hoped for.

God sent me Bobby as an angel to give me another message that He
had been trying to get through my thick skull for years. After Bobby, for
the first time in my life, I realized that I could make it without a man. A
major breakthrough. As you will recall, where I came from, the message
I learned was that a woman without a man was not complete. The way I
was raised, if you didn't have a man, it was due to something lacking in
you; if you did have a man, your value was based on his. Bobby served,
without knowing it, as the angel to bring me to a place of recognition that
I was complete in and of myself.

I didn't transform overnight and take a vow of celibacy. But from
then on, slowly and surely, I accepted that the man in my life wasn't
there to define me or give me my worth or to make me whole. For all
the truth of these revelations, they were not reached painlessly. There
was a part of me that Bobby had really crushed. And so there was a period I went through in which I felt very low.

One of the two people who really helped me to heal and get me back
on my feet was a woman named Molly Toliver. I met her not long after
Dumpsey and I moved into the house on Warbler Way. As it happened,
that house was a cantilever which hung over a steep hillside, offering a

high, wide view of the city below. The first woman I hired as a house-keeper, besides not being able to clean to my satisfaction, had some sort of fear that the cantilever was going to fall down the hill, taking her with it. It was two days before she'd even look out the window which caused her to say, "Oh, no, I can't live with this." She removed her apron, collected her things, and headed for the door. But before she left, she was nice enough to recommend a friend for the job. That turned out to be Miss Molly, who I knew from the beginning was to be so much an angel in my life that I wouldn't have been at all surprised if she had flown in on wings.

Molly Toliver was not only a first-class housekeeper; she brought to my home a spiritual influence and presence that gave me the peace of mind to go out on the road, knowing that Dumpsey would be safe and nurtured in my absence, kept close to the spiritual aspects I was not there to give her all the time. Though there was a nanny who lived in while I was gone, Miss Molly actually doubled as housekeeper and nanny, becoming a second mother to Dumpsey. Whenever I was gone, she handled any crisis that arose. And whenever my imagination got me going about my daughter's well-being, I comforted myself that if anyone ever meant my daughter harm I'd sooner come home to find Miss Molly dead at the door, having sacrificed herself for Dumpsey. She was that protective of my child.

She worked for me for twenty-five years and in that time, I never saw anyone who came into my house who didn't love Miss Molly. If she had not recently made her transition, Molly would still be with me today. I really—add a thousand more *really*s to that—don't know what I would have done without her. She was much like my mother—a little doll, a short, chubby, loving, Christian woman who sang and moaned, praying in her way, all the day long. Like my mama, she knew that God was absolute good and she praised His name, singing happily about life every day. It was a joy to have her in the house.

And so, no matter how low my spirits were after Bobby Bryant, Miss Molly lifted them day by day, bit by bit.

The other angel who helped, first as a friend, later as more than that, was a gentleman named Anthony Jordano. He, too, was very important in giving Dumpsey a sense of groundedness in her young life. From the very start and for the next eight years, Anthony was a father to my daughter. He loved her, treating her as if she was his very own, while she adored him and I appreciated his love for her. We soon had a nice family thing going. And now, with my different mindset, my relationship with him was different from others in my past. He was my friend first as well as my partner. He was who he was, there to share with me but not to determine who I was.

Anthony Jordano had a mixed background ethnically. A Heinz 57, I liked to call him, with maybe some Italian, some black, some white ancestry all mixed . . . He was light-skinned, fair-haired, slender, very handsome, kind, caring, interesting, and entertaining. When I met him he was a bartender but he decided shortly thereafter that it would look bad for me, a star, to be with a bartender.

"However it looks, I don't care, because I'm with you," I assured him. "And you might as well do what you know how to do."

Anthony couldn't see it that way. But, working only at various intervals, neither could he seem to find anything he really wanted to do to support himself. Instead, he spent most of his time traveling with me— giving me a much-appreciated reprieve from the loneliness of the road. When we stayed at home, while I slept to rest up for my night's work, he took care of Dumpsey, taking her on fun outings and afternoons at the park—all of which I was most grateful for.

As the expression goes, be careful what you wish for because you just might get it. Let me amend that to say, you always get exactly what you ask for. I had asked God for a man on whom I would not be dependent to make me feel complete. And that was the very angel He sent. Not only was I not dependent on Anthony, for eight years I supported him. In the end, I just got tired of doing that. I wanted someone to support me. Or at least contribute to our mutual welfare. I wanted someone who was as secure in himself as I was in myself, someone who had interests and passions of his own, someone who was pursuing his dreams.

Feeling that in the eight years I had clearly shown him my gratitude for everything he had done for me, I decided we should separate. Regretfully, we were never able to be friends again. That was disappointing. But in my life, with a few exceptions, once an angel always an angel, and I could never discount what good we had together.

Flashback: 1957, on the movie set of *Let's Rock,* a youth-oriented film starring Julius La Rosa. Four weeks earlier, Julius and his girlfriend had come into the nightclub where I was performing at the time. Julius was a rising star in those days, mainly from his appearances on *The Arthur Godfrey Show.* After my set was over, Julius came backstage, introduced himself and his girlfriend, and asked, "How would you feel about doing a movie?"

A movie? My eyes lit up. This was just the break into acting I felt I was ready for. I told him, "I'd be very interested in doing a movie."

Julius went back and talked to the producer and director of his next movie and before I knew it I got the word that I was making my official film debut.

Some debut it turned out to be. What my part amounted to was singing a song. That's it. For four weeks, they had me work on a scene in which all I did was stand still and sing while Julius drank a drink and suffered the words of the song.

"How's it going?" Lee Magid's upbeat voice asked over the telephone as he checked in with me on the set.

"Awful," I grumbled. "This was supposed to be an acting gig. Well, it's got nothin' to do with no acting. I thought this was supposed be, you know, a part." With all the comedy and acting I did in my live show, I certainly felt I had the credentials for it. Plus, I reminded Lee, I had two big hits already out and other singers were being given shots at acting all the time.

Lee could hear that I was pissed off and disappointed. "Okay, Della, okay," he said, "don't worry, you'll get your acting shot."

Even though Lee didn't deal that much with the acting aspect of the business, he was right. And that was a lesson I was about to learn. I would get my shot. In time. In God's Time.

At first, like other black singers, my many television spots were limited to singing only.

But in one bold stroke, thanks to Merv Griffin, this was to change. Earlier, I had done his radio show where we formed a warm, professional bond. One of Merv's regular bits was to do the weather report to music. So the night I was on the show he did the weather to "And That Reminds Me." He started playing and spoofing it. Fearing not, I jumped in with both feet. We had a ball making each other laugh. Merv was so smooth, starting up a song like "Tea for Two," for instance, singing: "On Friday, in Washington, it's true . . . it's going to be forty-two." And I would sing a quick ad lib along the lines of: "Yes, and in Milwaukee . . . they say it will be forty-three." The listeners loved it.

The next time I saw him was on his television show, which was broadcast from New York. That night, when my number was finished, Merv invited me to sit on the couch and talk to him. Completely unheard of at that time. In those days black artists with hit records were hired to sing on TV shows but were never invited to sit on the couch and be interviewed by the host. So that night when Merv beckoned me over to the couch and not only congratulated me on my song but also began to talk with me, I was almost incredulous. That gesture was most certainly an angel's. He invited me back whenever I was in New York and later, when his show moved to Los Angeles, I practically became a regular.

In turn, I quickly hopped on a busy circuit of variety-show guest-star television, in time doing more than three hundred appearances on the shows of those such as Mike Douglas, Jackie Gleason, Perry Como, Andy Williams, Steve Allen, Joey Bishop, Pat Boone, on Hugh Hefner's *Playboy After Dark* variety specials, and on the *Hollywood Palace*. Getting on that circuit paved the way to the big kahuna, Johnny Carson and his *Tonight Show*. Johnny is truly one of the funniest men alive, as well as an angel who helped launch many careers. What he did to help me was not only make me a regular guest but to invite me to guest-host for him on numerous occasions. Hosting his show was always a blast.

In 1968, eleven years after my disappointment over my non-acting debut, I finally got the chance to show what I could do in a real acting part. It was on *The Mod Squad.* On my first day of work, the director, Gene Nelson, turned to one of the producers and said, very loud, "My God, this woman can act." Coming from Gene, a top director who had worked his way up after starting out as a dancer, that was all I needed to hear to vindicate me for what I had been trying to tell people for years. Gene continued to use me in acting roles whenever he could and recommended me to others. By the seventies, I was getting hired in guest acting roles in other TV shows and later on, as a recurring character or series regular.

Game shows were also a plentiful source of work and *Hollywood Squares* became a regular gig whenever I was in Los Angeles. When I did the pilot for that show, the other guests included Hollywood columnist Hedda Hopper and comedian Allan Sherman—well known at the time for his hit song "Hello Muddah, Hello Faddah." At one point in the taping, Allan was sounding off about women's inadequacies, sarcastically saying how we should stay in our place and how we made a lot of mistakes because we were too emotional.

"Well, we make a lot of mistakes," I retorted. "I'll grant you that— one of us made you."

He: "My father had something to do with that."

Me: "He just dropped you and let her do the rest."

Hedda laughed so hard, we had to stop the tape. She wrote about it in her syndicated column which was carried all over the country. The publicity soon got me recognized as a wit, opening many new doors for me.

In the meantime, back when Mike Douglas started his show, which was broadcast from Cleveland, Ohio, I had been one of his first guests and went on to work his show for years. This was where I met a very important angel, Woody Fraser, the show's producer. Woody was a major fan and was influential in my being invited back often; eventually he had me as a co-host with Mike whenever I was on, which was very successful.

Although I never knew what happened, the next time I saw Woody, in early 1969, he had left Mike. It was on a night in Chicago where I was singing at the Sherman House.

Woody Fraser, a kinetic, high-energy individual, arrived with a group of his friends to see my show. Afterwards he came back to my dressing room, raving about my act. We had a couple of drinks, during which he said to me, just this simply: "Would you like to do a TV show of your own?"

Just that simply, I said, "Of course!"

He said, "Then we'll do it."

To myself, I said, *I hope someone else is driving 'cause he must be drunk.*

We said our good-byes and I never gave it another thought.

Less than a month later, Woody showed up at my house on Warbler Way with sketches for scenery and master designer Rocco Urbisci—the best in the business who went on to be a major director and producer—and several other production people, everyone with plans and scripts and all the other details involved for the preparation of this show to be called, simply, *Della*.

I was speechless. I hadn't seen him since that night in Chicago and here he was, ready to go. Once I was able to speak again, I said, "It looks wonderful, Woody. I like it. When do we go on the air?"

"Oh," he answered offhandedly, "in about two weeks."

Two weeks? That was nuts.

Well. We went on in two weeks. But not without more than a few moments that made me seriously doubt we'd make it. Woody, angel and champion that he was to me, was also three different people in one body. He was, first, a pure creative force with original, brilliant ideas; second, he was a great producer with skills at leadership and the ability to be in control; and, third, he was very childish; about four and half years old, it seemed. In the middle of an intense meeting, out of the blue, Woody would pick up a book and throw it high into the air, impulsively, and then rejoin the meeting. Or he would give precise directions about the way he wanted a segment handled and when we did it that way, he'd say, "What are you doing? That's not what I told you to do," and proceed to change everything around. Afterwards, he would begrudgingly admit that the changes didn't work. Then again, he'd add, it was different and it was always good to be different. Plus, Woody liked to mix it up amongst cast and crew, subtly pitting people against each other or him. There were times when everybody was mad at somebody and there Woody was—off in a corner laughing about it.

Once I got used to his habits, it wasn't a problem for me. What was a problem was producer Rick Rosner—who later scored big by being involved in the creation of *CHiPs*—and on my show was to be second in power only to Woody. Where Woody, impulsive and mischievous, always believed in me no matter what, Rick didn't seem to have the same confidence. I suspect where that came from. After all, I was not only going to be the second woman ever to host her own variety talk show, I would be the first black woman to do that. Somehow, it seemed, even before Mr. Rosner had met me, he assumed on that basis that I might not have the proper polish to be able to handle it.

Woody was confident that once he met and got to know me there would be no problem so we arranged for me to take Rick to dinner at a local restaurant where I brought along my sister Sadye.

Rick, though on the young side, was the stiffest man you'd ever want to meet. He was so uncomfortable, I decided to try to loosen him up and make him feel more at ease by telling him some jokes. Cute ones. Funny ones. Nothing moved him. All the people sitting at the adjacent tables were laughing hysterically. He didn't even chuckle.

Pronto, he reported back to Woody that he was very concerned about my language and repeated some of the colloquialisms I had used in my jokes.

Woody told Rick, "Sure, offstage she tells jokes like that all the time.

Not on the air. Everybody knows her and loves her. She has a spotless reputation. She's a class act."

Rick said, "But what if she slips and talks like that on the show?"

Woody tried to convince Rick that I was a pro and knew very well how to present myself to the television audience, reminding him about all the shows I had done before and never slipped. But Rick continued to fret so Woody got Rick and me together, telling me, "Rick is concerned about your language and I want to let him know that he has nothing to worry about. Why don't you let him get a chance to hear that you know how to handle yourself in front of the camera? Maybe you could give him a couple minutes of the kind of language you'll be using on the air."

What I did to respond was not right. But by this point, I was *o-ffend-ed.* I mean, *offended.* This was a producer who was making judgments about me based on nothing. He didn't know me. He didn't know my work. He hadn't taken the time to do his homework and see any copies of the shows I had guest-hosted for Johnny, any of my hundreds of radio and TV guest appearances. So when Woody asked me to give Rick a sample of how I was going to talk on the air, I couldn't help myself but to just stick it to Rick.

"Well," I said, poker-faced, "I was thinking of opening by saying 'Good afternoon, motherfuckers . . .' "

Rick Rosner went into shock. He really thought I was going to say that.

As the days passed, Woody needled Rick to make him worry more. And every time I ran into Rick I'd go off on him. Rick was so frantic, he began to break out in sores. The day of the first taping arrived and when I stepped out of my dressing room, there was Rick, his back against the wall, waiting for me.

I smiled at him and said, "Well, here we go, Rick," and then, taking a beat as if to step away, I turned back to him with an even more charming smile, composed myself the way I would before starting my opening monologue, and said, "Good afternoon, motherfucker."

Me and my mouth.

At that instant, this big bump on Rick's face went POP! He was that terrified. Of course, I went on that day and every day for the duration of the show which ran for the 1969 and 1970 seasons, and each time presented myself perfectly fine.

Rick Rosner calmed down eventually although he was never really comfortable around me. In time, Rocco Urbisci—who was a fantastic idea man—stepped up to a director's position, which gave him more creative input, while Rick stepped up to have more responsibilities in the office, dealing with matters less stressful than me.

In spite of those hectic two weeks of preparation, those two years of doing *Della* provided me with a most wonderful and endearing experience, a period I count as one of the most precious of my life. It was heaven.

We aired five nights a week, taping three hour-long shows a day on taping days, ultimately doing 292 shows in total. A syndicated show, *Della* was seen in almost every major northern city, as well as nine southern cities. In all the markets, the show received top ratings.

We had the best orchestra available. And since all the best musicians wanted to be on our show, all the best singers and dancers wanted to sing and dance with those fabulous musicians.

We had the best crew available; Woody went top flight all the way. He set a wild, frolicking pace to the show. It was an anything-goes, laugh-a-minute, touching, dramatic, exuberant atmosphere. Our format incorporated musical variety, guest interviews, cooking, animals, and whatever else Woody turned up that might be of interest. One of his more innovative segments was about health food, a new topical concept just coming into its own. The guest was Leigh French, a popular comedienne of the day, sort of a hippie type. In the segment, she was going to be pro–health food while my part was in opposition, speaking in defense of meat and against the substitution of soy beans for it. For the payoff, I was to reach behind the curtain and lead this cow out with butcher marks on it, as I proclaimed my loyalty to stick with all these various, delicious cuts of beef.

This was typical of Woody Fraser's inventiveness. As it so happened, the man who rented us the cow brought a bull on the day of taping. As it also happened, the bull didn't like the sound of trumpets; and that day, it happened, we had a musical bit with *five* trumpets playing. When the bull heard them, he began to stomp and kick which the owner had to quiet by hitting the bull with this hard, thick rope soaked in oil with a huge knot in it. Bull did not care for that either. Between the knot and the trumpets, he got so mad he decided to relieve himself all over backstage and everybody back there.

Cut to: me, unaware, as I reach behind the curtain for the cow and, instead, this raging bull—literally—comes charging out covered with feces! Swinging himself from left to right, the bull tore up almost all of the scenery and props onstage. It took six men helping the owner to get that bull offstage and out to his truck. What a frightening yet funny scene that was, trying to clean up and continue with the taping.

There was always something funny and strange and exciting happening every show. I interviewed some of the most interesting people in the world and had the chance to sing with everyone from Carmen McRae, to Sarah Vaughan, with Billy Daniels, Billy Eckstine, Bobby Darin, the Righteous Brothers, Tony Bennett, Joe Cocker, Kenny Rogers (it was Kenny's first TV show), and everyone with records on the charts at the time.

We had the greatest guests available. My first guest was Vincent Price. He was wonderful. This great actor whom I had watched in movies all my life was just as great in person being himself.

Everyone was terrific but nothing could really top the day that Ethel Waters came on as a guest. My idol since childhood! When she arrived at the studio, I met her at her car, assisting her into the theater and to her dressing room. After she was all set up, as I started to leave, Ethel caught me by the hand, saying, "You will have to help me through this. I'm depending on you to get me through this."

I was flying high when I left that room. And she held onto me all through our segment together. When the show was over, Ethel hugged and thanked me, telling me, "Della, I would have never made it through without you."

My idol had needed me! What more could I ask for?

Yet there was more. When she was ready to leave I gave her a gift of perfume. Having been told that her favorite was White Shoulders, I'd gone out and bought the biggest bottle I could find. Ethel Waters broke down in tears as I presented it to her, hugging me and thanking me some more. She told me, "You have no idea how glad it made me and how much it means to me that you would have me on your show."

She had no idea how much those words and those moments with her meant to me. That, to me, was definitely a time when I was touched by an angel in passing. I floated for weeks.

Towards the end of my second season, during hiatus, I decided it was time for a move. With my house being so close to Sunset Boulevard, it seemed everyone I knew had taken to dropping in on me at all hours of the night after cruising the strip to look at the hippies who were hanging out then in throngs. That was the big nighttime entertainment once the hippies began to take over Sunset. When my friends showed up, sometimes as late as three or four in the morning, they didn't even apologize. They gave me the classic line, "Oh, hey, we were in the neighborhood and thought we'd drop by . . ." as they headed in before I could remind them that Dumpsey had school in the morning and I was taping early too.

That was one concern. Also, as Dumpsey was getting older, the house seemed to be getting smaller, in addition to the fact that she had learned to swim like a fish and I was constantly trying to find a friend's house with a pool where she could go swimming. It was time to go house-hunting again, hopefully with the possibility of finding something affordable that had a pool of its own.

That's what I told June Eckstine (Billy Eckstine's former wife), who was an excellent Los Angeles realtor. And I added, "I'd like a house so off the beaten track that when people show up unannounced, I can shut the door in their faces because there will be no way they can truthfully say they were in the neighborhood and thought they would drop by."

That was exactly the house she found me, a lovely house high off the beaten track at the top of Bel Air Road, with a magnificent view of mountains and lakes and an indoor pool. Perfect. I bought it and have enjoyed living there ever since, almost thirty years now.

One night not long after moving in, I went out to the pool where Dumpsey was going to come and join me. She had been talking about wanting to go skinny dipping which I couldn't let her do at someone else's home. Now that we had our own pool, she insisted we just had to skinny dip. On my way out to the pool first, I left the sliding glass door open for her. Swimming along, I didn't notice that when she came in, she had closed the door behind her. We had a delightful, refreshing swim. When it was time to get out, I knew how chilly it was outside the heated pool so I told Dumpsey, "Baby, you stay here in the warm water while I go get us some towels."

In my mind, I suppose, the sliding door was still open. It wasn't. Moving at a fast pace on account of the cold air, I walked right into the glass door. On impact the center of the glass shattered and fell out on either side of the window while I lost my balance and fell on top of the jagged bottom piece of glass. As I scrambled to stand up, every time I changed position that glass was cutting deeper into my stomach. The harder I tried to regain my balance, the more the shattered glass that had fallen on the one side was cutting up my hands while I slipped and slid on the shattered glass under my bleeding feet. Unaware that the top piece of the glass was seconds away from falling straight down and decapitating me, something inside of me was screaming that I had to find a way to get up. There was no physical way I could do that.

A split second before that top glass plunged down, my mother who had died in 1949, Nellie, my angel, reached around from behind me, taking hold of my head and shoulders, and lifted me up onto my feet and told me to sit down in a chair.

Now, I realize some of you might be saying, *How can that really be? How could you have known it was really her?*

How did I know it was my mama? Because it was her smell, her smell only, that wonderful-smelling mixture of Ponds Cold Cream, vanilla, and spices. As she lifted me and told me to sit down, that scent overwhelmed me, as if I was wrapped in an airtight capsule of it.

Dumpsey, in the meantime, jumped immediately out of the pool and ran for a towel with which she tried to mop up the blood but soon saw there was too much to do any good. After all those years as a child when I had refused to learn anything from my mother about healing, I didn't know anything about how to wrap wounds or what to do in a crisis like this. That night, Mama spoke to me, her scent still all around, telling me what to say to Dumpsey to show her how to make a tourniquet for my leg. And then Mama was gone.

Dumpsey took over in the position of lead angel. Almost naked she raced down the hill to my next door neighbor, Dr. Harvey Cantor, a general practitioner and surgeon, who was relaxing in his shorts. She pulled him out of his house, pants in his hand, and dragged him up to our house. If he wasn't an angel put there for me by God that night, I don't know who was.

When Dr. Cantor looked at the bloody mess that I was, he gasped, called for an ambulance, and took my body in his hands, literally holding it together that way until the paramedics arrived and all the way down the hill as the ambulance sped to UCLA Medical Center. When I got there, I was in shock and they took me straight to the emergency operating room.

Several doctors were standing around me talking.

"Who signed her in?" one of them asked.

One the others said, "The only family member with her is a daughter, nine or ten years old."

"We need to have an adult relative sign her in," the first doctor said.

Of course, these doctors were really more of my angels. Together with Dr. Cantor and the marvelous Dr. Rose, the two of whom oversaw my treatment, they were instrumental in helping me through. But at that moment in the operating room, they were starting to make me mad. That is so stupid, I thought, sitting atop the large medical cabinet, listening to them discuss me as if I wasn't there. This was a definite out-of-body experience.

The second doctor said, "She's lost so much blood, we'll never get enough back into her in time."

Did that mean I was going to die? Unh, unh, not 'cause of some damn papers. Now I was very angry. So I left my perch on the cabinet, came back to my body and looked up, saying, "Give me the papers, I'll sign them myself."

Their eyes bulged as if they were seeing a ghost.

"C'mon," I repeated, "lemme sign the papers."

The doctors later told me that I shocked them into movement. They had been so sure I was a goner.

I signed quickly. After that, I blacked out, not knowing what happened next.

    I didn't regain consciousness until the following morning. But deep down in my unconscious mind as I slept, I knew I had been saved. I knew my angels were with me. And I knew something else, something which came to mind this past Easter as I happened to be writing this very chapter. It is on Easter that we celebrate the resurrection of Christ and as I prepared my lesson to give for Sunday's service, it occurred to me that all of us, in one form or another, must rise many times in our life. Some of us every day. And we can. We have within ourselves that same Christ-like ability to be reborn, renewed, transformed, to rise above what is physically or realistically possible. We can do the miraculous.

I had lost seven pints of blood; I only had nine to begin with. I should have died. But I didn't. I rose. A miracle.

That same recent Easter Sunday, a group of us went out after church for brunch. At the restaurant, after twenty-seven years, one of my angels was there, an angel who had been there for me on the night I almost died. He walked up to me as I was waiting to be seated and said, "My name is Bill. I don't know if you remember me but years ago when you walked through a plate glass door, I was one of the paramedics in the ambulance."

"Hello, Bill," I said, recognizing him, "thank you. God bless you."

"You know," Bill told me, "when we were coming down the hill, Dr. Cantor and I were holding you together. He was holding the bottom part of your body and I was holding the top. And, I can tell you this now, you looked terrible. I wasn't sure you were going to make it. But I wanted to say something to make you feel better. It was something like, 'Don't worry, Della, you're going to be fine.' And you looked up at me, right before you went into shock, and you said, 'I know it. Because God is inside of me.' "

"I remember that," I said, nodding.

Looking at me that fine Easter day, in the pink of health all these many years later, Bill the paramedic angel said, "You know what? You were right."

9

I awoke the morning after the accident bandaged all over with my leg tied to the ceiling, not knowing who or where I was. The pain was more than tremendous. There was no comfortable way to lie because I had a thousand stitches now holding me together.

I wasn't going to die after all. But the question at hand was whether I would walk or not; and, if I did, would I have to drag my left leg, the one in which I had come within an inch of severing the tendon.

When they released me from the hospital, I was confined in bed at home for three weeks. With my leg still tied to the ceiling, I was unable to do anything for myself. But, never fear, an angel was swift to the rescue. This was Marie Sayles, my very dear friend as well as a marvelous singer and pianist. When Marie got news of my condition, she promptly closed her house up and came to take care of me, bringing her family as assistant angels to help. She assigned her husband and son to the upkeep of the yards and her oldest daughter to the house cleanup. Marie herself worked nights but, after sleeping only a few hours, she was up early to cook my breakfast and start dinner, give me my medications, catch another nap, get up, finish dinner, and leave for work, returning late and then starting all over the next day. It was very tiring for Marie and her family, but they refused to leave me. Even their youngest, my goddaughter, three-and-a-half-year-old Della Maria, helped out by sitting at my bedside and coloring pictures for me.

Many vital lessons emerged from this experience. It confirmed what I believed about God sending angels at the times when you most needed them. It taught me that the willingness to accept the help is also a gift you give in return to your angels. They can't do the work they want to do without your acceptance. More than anything, I was about to have a real eye-opener about priorities.

One very sunny afternoon when those hot blustery Santa Ana winds were blowing, Marie and her family were all outside trying to cool off. Dry and thirsty as I could be for a glass of cold water, I couldn't even reach over to the pitcher beside my bed. The only thing I could reach was my bell which was what I rang whenever I needed something. RING, RING, I rang, waiting for someone to arrive. No one came. Obviously, they couldn't hear me. *RINNNGGG!!! RINNNGGG!!! RINNNGGG!!!* I rang so hard, the bell broke. Still, no one heard me.

I wasn't being neglected or ignored by any means. Given the layout of my house and my back yard, it really was unlikely that they could have heard me. And they simply didn't. Although I realized that, it didn't solve my problem.

By now, on top of my thirst, I had to go to the bathroom. This was always an ordeal. Because I hated that bedpan, I had to be assisted, first by lowering my leg down and then by walking me to the toilet. So my bell was broken, my voice couldn't be heard. Desperation time. I was looking around the room to see if anything gave me an idea for what I could do to help myself. And as I did, I saw my jewelry box filled with diamonds, pearls, and other precious stones, my gold and silver pens, bracelets and earrings; I saw my closet and the minks and chinchillas hanging there. Then it hit me.

These were things I'd sworn by as proof of my successful steps from the slums to the top of Bel Air Road. But what good were they to me in my moment of need? They couldn't ease my thirst. They couldn't lift me from my bed and help me to the bathroom. In that moment, it finally dawned on me how unimportant these material things were and how, in the past, I had placed more importance in them than I should have. Not anymore. This was a lesson that put my priorities in proper perspective. And they still are.

Within minutes of my having this revelation, little Della Maria came to bring me a new picture she had just drawn. Hearing what I needed, she went to the back yard and called everyone back in to help. My angels came to my side quickly.

At the end of the three weeks, I went to have the cast taken off. "When I remove your cast," the doctor warned me, "don't be upset if you can't move your leg. Don't worry, just relax."

That was easier said than done since the movement of my leg would determine, medically, if I would be able to walk again.

Once the cast was off, he explained, "If you can move your leg with some therapy, it's a good indication that you will walk." As he spoke, he took my leg in his hands and began to manipulate it, up, down, and from side to side. Then, he bent it at the knee and I almost jumped off that table in a supine position.

Giving me his prognosis, he said, "You are a lucky lady, Miss Reese. You will, in time, be able to walk again."

So thankful to God, I told him, "No, Doc, it's not about luck. It's because God held me in his arms."

"I don't mean any disrespect, Miss Reese," the doctor said, "but he almost dropped your ass this time."

We laughed and laughed.

I went to therapy for a month and I was walking once more. I walked and walked and walked, praising God as I did, praising the angels He had sent. Feeling so much closer and dearer to God, I sensed more deeply than ever not only my love for Him but His love for me.

My first live performance was at the Westside Room of the Century Plaza Hotel, here in Los Angeles. Towards the end of the show I sang a medley I had arranged of "Wade in the Water," "Bridge Over Troubled Water," and "I'm Proud to Praise the Lord," a song I had written with my leg tied to the ceiling and which I sang to my angel Marie Sayles to write down the music for me. As I sang the medley, I told the story of the accident to the audience, feeling all the emotions I had felt when I lived through it. They felt it every bit as well. For all the audiences at the Westside Room and for me, this was quite a spiritual, memorable experience, written up with much praise in all the reviews for the show.

⟶ "Excuse me?" I said to the man from King World, the distribution company that sold *Della,* as he delivered his monthly report to Woody Fraser, Rocco Urbisci, and me. He had, in effect, just announced that the show was being canceled. The news was disappointing enough, though not entirely unexpected. What really bothered me was one of the reasons he had given for why he was unable to sell the show.

It had nothing to do with the accident. When I had gone back to work, we did a successful job at hiding any unsightly scars or my initial difficulty in walking. At first, I wore wigs that covered the abrasions still healing around my hairline and neck. For a change, instead of being on my feet as I often was during some segments, I stayed stationary, seated behind a desk.

Far from being hurt, the ratings moved up. In fact, in states like Tennessee, a southern state that was thought to be a tough market, we went to number one.

But, according to this man from King World, that wasn't good enough to sell to the sponsors. I knew this was the climate at the time, especially because I was a woman and I was black. That was never said although with each of his monthly reports there was some complaint about my hair or my clothes. This time, however, it was pretty blatant. The reason he was simply unable to sell the show, he had finally said, was because my gums were blue.

"Because her gums are blue?" Woody echoed. "What does that mean?"

"It means I'm black," I said. Gesturing to my producer and director, I shook my head with a sigh, saying, "C'mon let's get out of here."

Woody and Rocco were as appalled by that comment as I was. At the same time, we knew the cancellation had been coming. The cost of producing the show was up to $85,000 a day, $20,000 higher than Woody had first proposed. Our main sponsor, General Tires, thought that was ridiculous. Somehow or another, they were going to pull the plug eventually. Once again, timing was everything. Ten years later, God bless, the climate would be much more receptive to a black female hosting her own show.

As was my habit, after my show was canceled, I went through a day's worth of depression. Then, not forgetting that I was a single mother, a working mother, the next morning I picked myself up, dusted off my hands, rolled my sleeves up and put out the word that I was available for work.

What was the response? Yes—you are right again—it was back on the road for me. One of my first stops was a two week booking at Mr. Kelly's, a jazz room in Chicago, which I often worked a few times a year. Opening for me during this stint were Tim and Tom, a black and white comedy duo represented by Lee Magid. Tom Dreeson was the white comic and Tim Reid the black comic.

After Mr. Kelly's, as we were both managed by Lee, we worked together on several jobs. I thought very highly of their talent and was happy to become a sort of sponsor for them, promoting their cause whenever I had the opportunity. It was all just about friends until I started getting heavier vibes from Tim.

As it was, there was little any kind of vibes could have done to penetrate a wall of self-protection I had built up. I was at a place where I didn't trust any man. Period, the end. Too much abuse and disappointment and bad timing had accumulated. Besides, it hadn't been long since my last relationship with Anthony Jordano had ended; before that, I had gone through a real letdown with Bobby Bryant. In my attempt not to fall into old habits of fix-it-itis or of allowing a man to determine who I was, I felt that wall of distrust towards men was necessary.

Tim Reid was the angel who managed to find a way through this cement block wall I'd built to protect myself. With gentle kindness, love, and lots of humor, Tim literally insisted his way through. He was such a dream to me that my resistance began to seem pretty silly. We started dating and I grew increasingly fonder of him. Good-looking, smart, ambitious, confident, positive, funny, and talented, Tim was on the way to achieving his goals. His love was direct from God, just what I needed at that time.

After extensive overseas touring together, we returned to Los Angeles and Tim started acting classes, wanting very much for me to go with him. He felt acting class would be his means of making the transition from stage comic to television actor, a decision that was to bear him much fruit.

But I had already made that transition and really had no interest in going to acting class.

For the first time, significant differences between us began to show. The fact that I was much older than he began to make a difference, which wasn't in evidence before. We were alike in our passion to pursue our dreams but we were at different stations in our journeys. Tim was still climbing while I was settling into position. I saw in him, for the first time, my struggling self: My running here and there, trying every road, hop-

ing each turn would be THE TURN; each promise would be THE
PROMISE; each person entering my career THE PERSON.

As my angel, one of the realizations Tim was put in my path to help
me see was that none of them were the THE's I had hoped for; and how
I set myself up for disappointment each time.

Seeing the old pattern so clearly and having become more consciously aware that God was in charge of my life, I was ready now to stand
still and let the Lord's salvation lead me. It seemed too simple to even explain. I called it a God thing. All I had to do was to stand strong on my
faith, in one place, and be, just be. I knew God had a plan and, in His
Time, I would mount upon wings like an eagle.

A God thing? Tim liked the sound of it but couldn't really relate. He
was not at that place at that time.

And I could no longer relate when he starting laying out his plans we
should use—acting classes, meeting names that were said to offer the key
to success, discussing the whys and wherefores of these plans. "I don't
need that anymore," I told him, "I've had my training. I've been training
ever since I started singing. When I sing the blues, I act blue, and I'm not
necessarily blue. When I sing a happy song, I act happy, and I'm not necessarily happy. As a lyricist, I live those words I'm singing. And what I've
found is that I can transfer those abilities and do it all without music. The
principles are the same."

"Della, I can see where that could be true. But don't you want to
stretch, get new insights?"

"Of course, but not from an acting class."

We went around and around. Although he saw my point of view, he
thought his way was THE WAY. And it turns out it was THE WAY for
him. He went on to get a series, *WKRP in Cincinnati,* and then later, *Simon
and Simon.* After that he produced *Frank's Place,* eventually becoming one
of the top black producers on the scene.

Our paths were diverging and I believe we both were looking for a
way out, even though, as Gladys Knight sang it so well, neither one of us

wanted to be the first to say good-bye. Then, while I was working out of town, Tim went through my desk and took exception to some old letters he found from other men, dating back to long before I had known him. Upon my return, when he questioned me about them, I refused to defend, deny, or comment, other than cussing him out for daring to go through my things.

In a way, this was probably the convenient last straw for both of us. We said our good-byes at the same time, both feeling somewhat wronged until a short period passed and we got over it. Today we are really good friends. He and his wonderful wife, Stephanie, are a lovely couple, meant for each other and very happy, God bless.

In previous times when I was moving on from a relationship, I often ended up feeling so let down that I would shun men by default, building up my wall of distrust and skepticism. But after Tim, I decided that this time, I really preferred to be alone by conscious choice and so I chose to be celibate until I felt otherwise. Otherwise turned out to be three and a half years! Though I was in my early forties, my sexual prime, it didn't bother me at all. That may seem crazy to you but trust me, it was a blessing. It, too, was a God thing. In fact, during this time, I began to really know and love myself, and to finally reach that place where I did feel complete in who I was. Happiness was truly an inside job, I learned, as I discovered much to be proud of myself for, really appreciating what I had accomplished.

This was a time not of spiritual awakening because I was already awake, but of spiritual deepening. As I got to know myself better, I came to a more conscious awareness of the Christ in me. From that I saw how, as a survivor, I had long been spurred from need; now the Christ in me could show me the way to be moved from love. Love of others, love of my angels, love of strangers, love of the earth, love of all humans and all life, love of self. And, in turn, as I realized just how gifted I was, I saw more than ever that God lived in me—not only for emergencies but all the time—and He loved me and would always take care of me and that there was nothing too big or too hard for Him to do. The knowledge of my own godliness gave me strength, courage, and the peace that surpasses all human understanding.

How grateful I was to Tim for bringing me to that place, a place I needed to be for the troubled waters ahead.

In the mid-seventies, my career was no longer moving at the pace I had always known. I was working, making a living and getting by, but there was significantly slower movement. I had parted ways with one of my long-time angels, my manager Lee Magid. After twenty-two years together, times had changed and the music business had changed. Lee saw the new breed of Young Turks coming into power as disrespectful and un-knowledgeable, which meant they weren't giving him or me the recognition Lee felt they should. In 1965 I had left RCA, going on to record for ABC and then Avco Embassy, where, in 1972, I had something of a disco hit, "If It Feels Good Do It." But for the last few years my records hadn't done so well. Coming from the more grounded place that I was, this didn't bother me as much as it might have in the past. Better and bigger things were in store for me, I knew, especially in the arena of acting where I had only begun to get my feet wet. Unfortunately, Lee wasn't really prepared to manage an acting career. He became harder and harder to deal with; whenever we talked, everything was being turned into a screaming match.

My leaving him was painful for both of us, but I knew it was the best thing in the long run.

I was still with the William Morris Agency, which had represented me since the early sixties. Although my agents there were in accord that it was time for me to move into the acting arena, while they began to scout out opportunities, I faced an inevitable lull.

That was when I discovered that the man who had been working as my lawyer and to whom I had given full power of attorney, had stolen $253,700 from me. A black lawyer, he had also represented himself as my friend for ten years.

This man is not to be confused with my much-loved New York attorney, Benjamin Sneed. Benjamin, an angel, was like a father to me, a man who had gone far beyond the call of duty for me, never taking a cent from me that wasn't his reasonable fee. He was honest, protective of me, and a fantastic lawyer.

Perhaps that's why, when I got to Los Angeles and needed a local attorney to handle my affairs, I gravitated to this other black lawyer, thinking somehow I could trust him as I had Benjamin. That was naive on my part and this so-called friend exploited my naïveté and robbed from me.

It gets worse. There had been another individual, an accountant, whom I had trusted, who also pocketed money of mine. During my many years on the road, I would regularly send him portions of my paychecks with which he was to pay my taxes. He didn't. Instead, he bought himself some apartment complexes.

This came to light around the time that I find out about the lawyer stealing the $253,700 from me. Just as the dominoes start to fall, the Internal Revenue Service informs me that I owe them $485,000 in back taxes.

So, you know me, when there's a choice of being the victim or giving it my best fight, I definitely ain't gonna lay down and die. No, I say, I can handle this. I'm big and bad. And I did what I always did—put my nose to the grindstone and found work, taking whatever I could get, almost working myself to death. But my mistake—and here is where information is power—was that when I sent money from these gigs into the IRS, I should have been noting on those checks that they were for the current tax year. Well, the IRS was applying those payments to what I owed for ten years ago which was accruing interest faster than I could ever be able to pay them, all the while that my current taxes were now going unpaid.

I didn't have this money and I sure didn't see a way to ever get this money. So I went out and found an excellent accountant, a Dane named Mods Bjerre, who did the best he could to sort things out although the books that the previous manager kept were indecipherable. Mods told me that I needed a tax attorney, referring me to the offices of Slate & Leoni.

The firm is top notch and Mr. Slate managed to clear up a few of my tax problems but couldn't dig me out of this hole. "I think I've gone as far as I can go," he said at last. "But there is a guy on Wilshire Boulevard, another tax attorney, you ought to check out. I think he might be able to help you."

"Fine," I said, "if he can help me, I can be helped."

"Good," he said, almost as an afterthought, "otherwise the IRS is probably going to take possession of your house and your car and your other valuables."

By this point, I was starting to feel a little anxious. Or should I say, a lot anxious. For moral support, Dumpsey, now in her early teens, came with me to talk to this tax attorney on Wilshire Boulevard. After reviewing my papers for a minute or two, this attorney looked up at me and said, "It is impossible for you to owe four hundred and eighty-five thousand dollars. You've never made enough money to owe four hundred and eighty-five thousand dollars."

No one, so far, had said this. I like him. I didn't know it yet, but this man was my angel.

"Give me a few days to look into this further. I'll see what I can do."

In the elevator on the way down, with my daughter at my side depending on me to get us through this one, I leaned up against the wall and closed my eyes and talked to the Father. I prayed that this man would be able to help. I admitted, at last, I couldn't handle this mess. I couldn't handle the pent-up anxieties anymore. Didn't want to. Didn't want to think about losing my house, my car, and everything I owned. And on the elevator, out loud, I said, "Father, you got it. I give it up to you. You gave me my house, Lord, and if you don't want me to have it, you'll find me another. You've always given me a car because you know I don't like to walk; if you don't want me to have this one, I know you'll give me another car. I'm not suffering through this anymore. It's your battle, not my battle. You know I'm not trying to cheat anybody out of anything. I let go, I let you. Right now, right here, Thy will be done. And Father, if I have to live in a truck, it's okay."

From that moment on, the wheels began to turn. My Wilshire Boulevard angel called three days later, as promised, saying, "Great news. I have them down to two hundred thousand dollars."

"Might as well be two million because I don't have two hundred thousand dollars."

"All right, let me go back one more time."

"Better go back two or three or four more times because I don't have that kind of money or near it."

A week later, my angel called me up to his office to tell me he had them all the way down to $100,000.

I said, "Same. Different day."

It was as low as he could get it. But a solution was immediate. It came from my accountant who said, "Actually, I think I know where I can get the hundred thousand."

"What do I have to do?"

He explained that I could borrow the money against my house and he could set up a deal where I could pay it off in a timely but not immediate fashion. Problem solved. Period, the end. Mods went to the bank, picked up the check, and handed it to the IRS.

I never saw the money. I never had to take a dime out of my pocketbook. The taxes were paid. And when I looked back at that $485,000, I saw that it was only an appearance; I didn't have to have that money. So what I had thought was this very big tumultuous monkey on my back turned out to be some meetings, some conversations, and God sending me the right angels to give me what I needed. It was over. The idea of Let Go, Let God had always appealed to me but never before had I tested it to that extent in that way.

It gets better. More angels were about to appear.

⌒— Enter: Ernest Borgnine. He was starring in a pilot for a series called *Flo's Place*. It was set on the waterfront in Long Beach, California, where his character hung out and worked as a tugboat captain. My part was Flo, owner of a seafood restaurant with food so good it drew the elite of the city to my place. The stories revolved around the interactions in my restaurant between the uptown crowd and the waterfront people who lived in the neighborhood. Flo was a hard-headed Hannah with a sweet, loving heart that she hid under her gruff. The acting involved was a real stretch, giving me the chance to reach a full range of emotions.

Ernest was a joy to work with. Considerate and a great teacher, he never patronized me or made me feel dumb.

Although the pilot didn't sell, it turned out to be an all-important stepping stone. My agents at William Morris sent the tape of it over to Jimmy Komack, the producer of *Chico and the Man,* who was looking for an actress to be a regular on the show. Got the job! The series starred Jack Albertson, Freddie Prinze, and Scatman Crothers. Our director, Jack Donohue, had directed many of the *I Love Lucy* shows.

This group of talents became my new family.

Jack Albertson was unbelievable, a virtual library of punch lines. He remembered every joke he had ever heard or told. Scatman, a delight, was a mandolin player and played and sang all the time. Freddie was a bundle of energy, always in motion, and a loving boy. We got along famously. He used to stop by my house to play backgammon with me and he could never beat me. But he hated to quit and after each game he would say the same thing, "Play me just one more game so I can beat you." It was always late at night when I'd finally get him to leave.

Jimmy Komack, an excellent producer, was also producing *Welcome Back, Kotter* along with a couple of other shows at the same time. I became good friends with him and with his wife, as well as with Jack Albertson and his wife.

It was a wonderful family of angels, and a wonderful job. *Chico and the Man* was shot in Los Angeles, so there was no traveling for a change. On top of which, it was a hit. What more could you ask for?

The question I am often asked is one I will answer here. No, I do not believe Freddie intended to kill himself. He was a kid and a clown who loved to shock people with outlandish stunts and pull odd tricks to get a reaction from others or to upset them. When he mortally shot himself during a party at the Beverly Comstock Hotel, it was Freddie trying to pull off a trick that got out of hand and backfired.

Drugs may or may not have been involved. In any event, Freddie was a victim of too much, too soon. He had gone from the barrio to the White House in about a year, a transition that gave him no time to prepare for success. He had no chance to work off the energy of his ambition. His dreams came true before he finished dreaming them.

A tragic waste. We all felt the pain and loss of it. I was snowbound in Cleveland when I saw the news on television. I had to get back for the funeral but the airport was closed. Although the city was frozen in, I was able to get a car, drive to Toledo, take a plane to Chicago, and fly home from there. I went from the airport directly to the funeral and together our work family faced the media and supported Freddie's family and each other through the circus.

On the show, we tried to carry on by saying that Freddie's character had gone back to Mexico. A younger boy was introduced and we continued for a while. But it was never the same for us or the audience without Freddie Prinze.

A short while later, Jack Albertson died. And now Scatman has gone home also. Those three were all such gentlemen, separate and distinct, but all gentlemen. I miss them and yet I know they've each joined the team watching out for me from above.

With Freddie's death, a chapter had ended. It had been three great years, a flow of so many fun-filled days.

Time again it was for a slowdown in my career. Not a standstill, just a move into lower gear. So I hit the highway. Yes—you are exactly right—it was back to the road for me.

Or, I should say, it was off on the waves for me. On this next leg of my journey I started working the luxury cruises. I went to the Caribbean, Rio, Alaska, Bermuda, St. Thomas, across many seas. I love to cruise. The service on the cruise liners is the best and I love being served and catered to. And there is a peace on the water that I find most refreshing. The movement is like a rocking chair—soothing and comforting. It's a perfect place to think and read and dream and make love.

Now, just 'cause I say that, I don't want you to jump to any conclusions. During the period we're talking about, as you recall, I hadn't yet ended my vow of celibacy. So I'm just speaking hypothetically.

Whether my journeys took me on cruise ships or to exotic foreign places or to closer, more familiar destinations, I'd learned over the years to love the road. For a long time, it kept me from being bored. Just when I'd feel myself falling into a boring old routine, it would be time to leave for another place. What kept the road the most fun for me was a group of special angels whom I would be remiss not to mention— musicians. I've sung with many of the top orchestras and symphonies in the world. I've sung with legendary bands like those of Erskine Hawkins and Woody Herman. And I've sung with solo accompanists and small trios. In each of these contexts, the often unsung musicians are the ones who make the singing possible. And so, to pay tribute to them as a group, following are a few names I must acknowledge and a memory or two taken from across the years.

Musicians are a rare breed, to say the least. When they love you, they love you. They tend to be very protective of themselves and those they love. When they don't love you, they still work for you but in a different way. They'll play all the notes correctly and yet they won't give you the music in their souls.

One of those who gave of his soul and more was Marvin Jenkins, my accompanist and fellow traveler for twenty-five years. Marvin was five foot four, if that, and the perfect size for his size. A snappy dresser and a hell of an accompanist, he seemed to know when I was going to breathe and how long my breath would last.

Much great music and much laughter came from the very gifted Allen Jackson—tall, jet black, with sinewy muscles. Allen traveled many a mile with me and never overcame his habit of comparing everything foreign to things at home. He was a bad American tourist but a joy to me.

Then there was this brilliant drummer named Floogy who played for

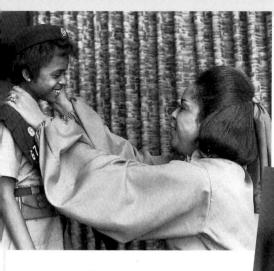

My biggest joy in life has been raising my daughter, Della Reese, Jr.

Being a single parent isn't easy, but it is a blessing still.

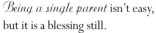

I can't get enough of showing off my baby. Who ain't so little here. My hair after the brain operations gave us mother-and-daughter naturals. *Photo by Tony Korody*

I have run the road for years with my play-sister, Sadye Rowser. She was road manager, wardrobe mistress, cook, bodyguard, baby-sitter, but above all a lifelong friend.

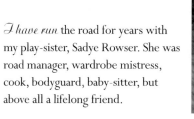

The Della Reese Show, cohosted by Sandy Baron *(left)*, had the best artists of the day. Here we had jovial George Kirby, putting a smile on Jack Palance's face and mine.

I cannot think of a greater untrained, can't-read-a-note pianist than Erroll Garner. Just being in his presence was almost as wonderful as singing with him.

Soupy Sales gave me my first appearance on television, in Detroit. Turnabout is fair play, as he appeared on my show in Los Angeles, fifteen years later.

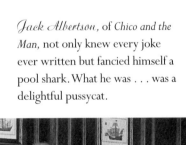

Jack Albertson, of *Chico and the Man*, not only knew every joke ever written but fancied himself a pool shark. What he was . . . was a delightful pussycat.

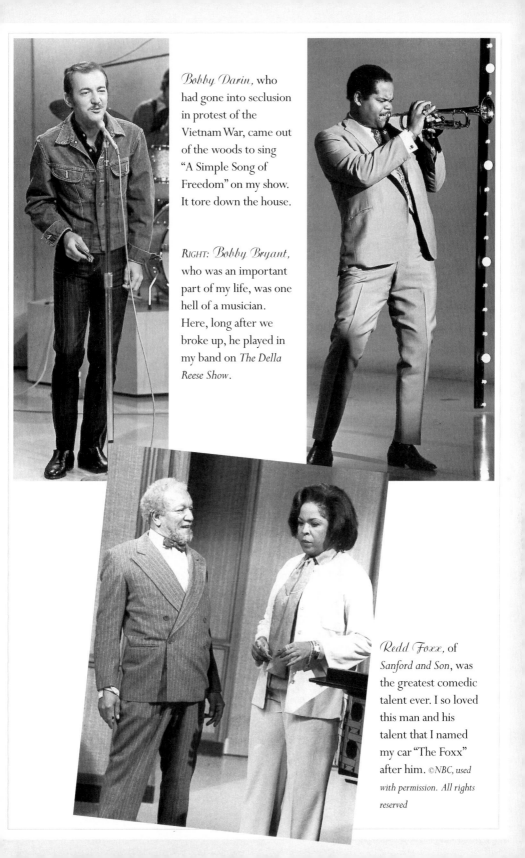

Bobby Darin, who had gone into seclusion in protest of the Vietnam War, came out of the woods to sing "A Simple Song of Freedom" on my show. It tore down the house.

RIGHT: Bobby Bryant, who was an important part of my life, was one hell of a musician. Here, long after we broke up, he played in my band on *The Della Reese Show.*

Redd Foxx, of *Sanford and Son*, was the greatest comedic talent ever. I so loved this man and his talent that I named my car "The Foxx" after him. *©NBC, used with permission. All rights reserved*

Four ladies of music on ABC's *Love Boat* special. Even though we had the *Love Boat* regulars, and guest stars Van Johnson and Cab Calloway, it was a "girl thing," with me, Carol Channing, Ethel Merman, and Ann Miller. *Photo by Gene Stein, used by permission of ABC, Inc.*

Gospel is my favorite music, and when the opportunity came to sing with Andrae Crouch and Ernie Ford on *More Gospel Sounds* for PBS, I jumped at the chance. *Used by permission of KOCE, Huntington Beach, CA*

This was Mr. Chicago, Irv Kupcinet. His entertainment column helped my career tremendously.

The nice thing about performing on cruise ships is the days off. Franklin, me, and my accompanist of twenty-five years, Marvin Jenkins.

The surgeon who performed the two brain operations on me was cherubic, twinkle-eyed Dr. Charles Drake. When he told me that God held his hand during operations . . . well, he could have cut me anywhere, and I'd have smiled.

Two weeks after my second brain operation, I was doing commercials for Campbell's Soup. Ain't God grand!

Photo by Tony Korody, used by permission of the Campbell Soup Company

I went back to do a benefit concert with the Meditation Singers for New Liberty Baptist Church in Detroit. With the proceeds, the church bought this van for the elderly (*right*).

This is Queen Mum Odessa Lett, to whom I will be eternally grateful for giving birth to my husband, Franklin. She was as independent and feisty as she was adorable. Look how happy she is to be with her son, whom we both love so much.

The wedding party: (*girls, from left to right*) Talon Jordan, Monique Chambers, Malika Jones, Precious Chambers; (*behind them*) my good buddy the Reverend Johnnie Colemon; my son, Dr. James Barger; me; my man; and my daughter, Dumpsey. *Photo by Isaac Sutton, property of Johnson Publishing Co., Inc. All rights reserved*

Mr. and Mrs. Franklin Lett, Jr., being serenaded by my best girlfriend, Carmen McRae, at our wedding reception.

My buddy and spiritual leader, the Reverend Johnnie Colemon. She, along with God, is responsible for my being a minister.

My star on the Hollywood Walk of Fame is shared with my family. *Back row:* three of my four children: Deloreese Owens, Dominique Lett, Frank Lett III; *front row:* my husband, Franklin Lett; my grandson, Sean Ewing Owens; and yours truly.

I was extremely happy when Roma Downey, my costar on *Touched by an Angel*, asked me to officiate at her wedding to David Anspaugh. And I am also the godmother to their daughter, Reilly Marie. *Photo by Gregory Cannon*

Through the grace of God, I came from the "black bottom" of Detroit to the top of Bel Air, California.

me for only a brief stint starting with a gig in Hawaii. Like all human beings Floogy was an expression of God; albeit, a very different expression of God. Floogy was slender and very black and greatly confused. Every morning in Hawaii Floogy would get up and go out to the pool and in front, directly in front of the door from the Hotel Biltmore out to the pool, he would spread out the whitest towels you can imagine. And then Floogy would set up his manual typewriter and a stack of papers and a fifth of vodka and he would begin to look like a writer—moving papers around, thinking, and drinking the vodka.

A few curious tourists would ask him what he was doing and he would explain to them the theme of his great novel, at length, until he drew a crowd. By the time he finished his oratory, he would have also finished the fifth of vodka. He never wrote a word. And by one o'clock every day, from every window in the hotel, you could see Floogy lying on those white towels out cold.

And that was only the beginning of the adventures we had with him.

Another most important musician to me was John C. Cotter. Ours was a match made in musical heaven. John traveled with me for six years, including working some of my Vegas stints. I will never forget one of our gigs there when, as usual, I had rented a house from Dr. and Mrs. West. Staying with me there was one of my dogs, Saucy Peggy, along with the other members of the band. At the time, I was raising dachshunds, the sausage dogs, which was what Saucy Peggy was.

Now, whenever we practiced in the living room there and John was playing the piano, Saucy Peggy would swoon and lie on or under the piano. This dog would really swoon and sing when he played. Saucy Peggy fell in love with John who at that time was dating my hairdresser, Alpage Terrell. If Alpage was in the room, she would chase Saucy Peggy away and and the dog would sit off to the side and growl under her breath. But as soon as Alpage left the room, Saucy Peggy would go right back and lay up under the piano and bark and howl to John's playing. One night, on our way to the gig, Alpage chased Peggy away so bitterly that I reprimanded her for speaking to the dog that way. Saucy Peggy scampered into my bedroom and got under the bed where she pouted and whined and didn't even acknowledge our leaving.

When we returned at five in the morning there was a surprise waiting. Let me note that Alpage Terrell had a very generous bust. And, somehow, Saucy Peggy had gone into her bedroom, found one of her bras, dragged it to the door of the bedroom and turned it up so the cups could be filled. And fill them Saucy Peggy did. From the back door of the kitchen where the garbage was, all the way through the kitchen and through the living room and into Alpage's bedroom, Peggy had transported garbage, piece by piece, not dropping one speck of it anywhere else but in those bra cups. There each of them was, filled to the brim with garbage.

John was out parking the car when Alpage and I came in to see Saucy Peggy sitting smugly by the bra, as if to say, *Yes I did it.* And when John came in, Saucy Peggy jumped up in his arms and started licking his face and purring. Like a kitten. None of us could keep from laughing. I laughted 'til I cried, all the while that Saucy Peggy was in dog heaven in John C. Cotter's arms.

Peter Meyers, my conductor and arranger, was a true angel. From Manchester, England, Peter came to work for me in Las Vegas and we continued for the next fifteen years. About five foot eight and pale, as many English I've met tend to be, Peter had a huge talent and marvelous sense of humor.

It was Peter Meyers who set me free musically. Until he came along, I'd become very inhibited about expressing my musical ideas and insecure about my lack of musical training. Although I had the ability to hear arrangements in my head, I wasn't able to explain them. Still, I had an excellent ear and because of my understanding of harmony and my years of arranging gospel choirs, whenever I planned the way I wanted to sing a new song, I could hear in my head the instrumentation that gave me the feeling I wanted. By mentally transposing what I knew from vocal arranging, I might use the soprano part for the trumpet, or the alto part for the strings, or the contralto for the higher saxes and the baritones and bass for the lower saxes. And so on. But whenever I told an arranger what I wanted, I'd have to sing the riff I heard, rather than writing down the notes. Invariably, I was told, "You can't do that," or, "That's not musically correct." Feeling inferior musically, I would back off, which was frustrating because I could so clearly hear it in my head. Sometimes, I'd even pay an arranger to write out arrangements for me and I'd skat sing the sections I could hear in my head and they'd write out the notes in the correct way.

Early in my association with Peter Meyers we were working out a new song and I made an arrangement suggestion, skatting it for him. Before he could say anything, I caught myself, saying, "But I guess that's not musically correct," as if to withdraw the suggestion.

"What do you mean?" Peter asked.

"Well, uh, you can't do that, huh? I mean, I know I can hear it, but it can't be played, right?"

Peter said, "If you can hear it, I can play it. Just sing me what you hear."

I did and he played it. Just the way I'd been hearing it. What a revelation! When I told him about everyone who told me my suggestions were incorrect, he said, "What they should have told you was that they weren't capable of doing it. Because if you can hear it, it is musically correct. It wasn't you, Della . . ."

That freed me. I was no longer afraid to express what I heard and thought the music should be. Hello! We did the blues, classical music, jazz, show tunes, bits of humorous material, *ever-ry-thing*. He was a wonderful teacher. My experience made me realize how destructive the power is of a person in authority telling another that they can't do something they'd really like to do. It's what happens to children when they're told they're no good at something. What magnificent angels the parents and teachers and friends are who convey the opposite message: *You CAN; if you can dream it, you can do it.*

⌒ God was so good to me. I grew up dreaming of other places and He took me to other places. He filled my pages with laughter, love, and characters. He gave me strength to weather storms. And when I couldn't, I had given Him my load and He carried it for me. I asked for help and He sent me angels. I needed work and He provided. Then, without my asking, God decided to send me another angel that I hadn't even asked for: a son.

Many years earlier, during one of my stints at the Reno Harrah's, where I was working the lounge, I kept noticing the face of this boy who looked too young to be in the place. He came, every show, every night, watching from the bar where he sat close to the waitress station. The manager, not wanting to have his license revoked for serving a minor, asked me to speak to the boy and find out how old he was. When I did he introduced himself as James Barger, a pre-med student at the university there in Reno. He insisted he was my number-one fan.

"James, thank you," I said. "But your coming in here like this underage, you're messin' with the license and therefore messin' with my job. You can't do this."

His face fell. "But I won't drink. I just want to come and see you."

I thought for a second and decided it would be all right to invite him to come see me in the afternoons at my hotel. The next day and the day after that and for the rest of my stay, James came to visit. We'd sit and talk and enjoy each other's company.

That was how we began a friendship that continued to grow over the next few years, given the frequency that I was in Reno. Even when I stopped working there as often, he kept in touch, letting me know, eventually, that he had completed medical school and would be coming to Los Angeles for his residency.

When James arrived in town, he came to see me at my house. Only the two of us were there. He told me about his plans to become a psychiatrist, which pleased me very much.

"You'll make a wonderful psychiatrist," I told him. "You've got all the right stuff. You're so interested in other people and their concerns. You take their problems so to heart, I know. James, I mean it, you are genuinely interested. If this is what you want to do, you can do it. You're intelligent, unique, loving, and I'm very proud of you."

James smiled and became very quiet. After a few minutes passed, he stood up, paused for a second, and got down on his knees in front of my chair. Looking up at me, he took me quite by surprise as he said, "I want you to be my mother."

"But you already have a mother," I said, still not sure whether he was serious or simply expressing his fondness. In fact, not long before, when I was performing in Indianapolis, James had taken me to meet his mother and father in Shelbyville, not too far from there. This was a big deal. A big deal to the whole neighborhood. A black woman, a show business black woman, arriving with this young white man and being received in the home of this white, upper-crust family? The community was up in arms and baffled too. They acted as if they'd never seen "one" before. On the other end of the pendulum, James's parents couldn't have been more welcoming to me. They were lovely people and I was not about to usurp his mother's place.

Watching James's serious face, I reiterated, "You don't need another mother."

Then James explained, "My mother is very ill and she won't be here much longer. When she goes, I want you to be my mother."

"But we're already real tight. That's all we need."

"It's not the same. I want you to be my mother."

"Okay," I said, sort of fluffing him off, "I'll be your mama."

After that, we saw each other now and then, but he didn't bring it up again and I assumed the matter was forgotten.

A short while later, James brought his parents to California for a visit and we arranged to get together for a bite at my house. Throw some burgers on the grill, I told James, a casual hello. When his parents arrived, I could see that his mother's health wasn't good. James's father, a circuit court judge on the bench for thirty years, made me laugh right off by calling me "Sir," on account of my deep voice. While James and his dad were enjoying a swim, his mother and I were left alone on the patio. She turned to me lovingly, saying, "I'm glad you'll be here for my son, because, you may or may not know this, I won't be here much longer. He loves you very much and I believe you love him." She let me know that she was in accord with his desire for me to become his mother. When she said, "It makes my going so much easier, knowing that I won't be leaving my son all by himself," well, that took me *all the way out.*

James and his father came back from swimming and no more was said about it. We ate our burgers and when they were ready to go, I walked them out to their car. As James helped his mother into the front passenger seat, his father paused before getting into the driver's seat, saying to me, "Sir?"

"Yes?"

"It's a good thing you're doing for the boy," he said, just like that, and got into his car.

That was it. That was how God sent me my angel, Dr. James Barger. From that moment on, he was my son. And I was his mother.

A beautiful daughter whom I adored, a son whom I cherished, what more could I have asked for?

There was nothing I could think of. But God could.

10

"*Nice to meet you*, Mr. Lett," I said, extending my hand to shake his, just as the maitre d' gestured for us to follow him to our table.

This was a business meeting at the Ritz Carlton in Chicago. Mr. Franklin Lett, one of the top advertising executives in the country, and one of the very first black ad execs, had been looking for a crossover spokesperson—a celebrity with name and face recognition who appeals to all races—to represent a new Borden's macaroni product.

Previously, I had been successful as a crossover spokeswoman for Kraft Barbeque Sauce, and the producer of those spots, Frank Smith, had been insisting Mr. Lett really ought to consider me for the Borden's account.

Mr. Lett, however, wasn't familiar with me and had been declining the recommendation. But after considering a slew of candidates, he had yet to find what he was looking for.

As God would have it, I was working on a three-city tour with the fabulous Ben Vereen and one of our stops was at Mill Run, just outside of Chicago. It was a theater in the round and, I must say, Ben and I put on a really good show.

Refusing to give up, Frank Smith let Mr. Lett know that I was in town performing, urging him to at least come out and see me at Mill Run and consider taking a meeting with me.

Finally Mr. Lett agreed, came to the show, saw that I could sing and that I had a presence and warm rapport with the audience. It seems that he was impressed enough to feel a meeting would be in order.

Hence, our first face-to-face was taking place at the Ritz Carlton. From the get-go, I found him to be an exceptional businessman. Sharp, warm, friendly, professional, very well-spoken, impeccably dressed, he exuded a great energy and an up attitude. There was a part of me that was wary. After my ordeal with the black attorney who had raped and pillaged my business affairs, and stolen money from me on top of that, along with a few other less than satisfactory associations with black businessmen, there was something of a bitter taste in my mind for their brand of business. Yet Mr. Lett was different and I felt I could work well with him. He was prepared for my questions, his answers were honest and direct, and his paperwork was *to-gether.*

The meeting was a success. I left Chicago expecting to hear favorably from him soon.

Not one inkling of Franklin Lett in any romantic context entered the picture. Nor, I'm sure, any of me for him. It had been a business meeting, no personal or sexual over- or undertones about it. Besides, he was not my type. Too fair. Based on my track record, you'll remember, I liked big black men. So I entertained no thoughts about him whatsoever, except what a well-organized businessman he was.

Over the next few months, he began to call fairly often to update me about the account, which was momentarily stalled because of internal changes going on at his agency. We also started chatting about other aspects of our lives. I was still trying to retrieve the money that had been stolen from me and Mr. Lett was able to give me some great advice which, when I tried it, worked beautifully. As he confided some of the problems occurring in his business, I was able to give him my unbiased opinions. Because we had no agenda other than friendship, we found it easy to accept the other's help.

We became friends over the phone. Two thousand miles apart. We began to talk at least two times a day. We'd start each day with a conversation in the morning; in the evening, we'd talk again, comparing our days. This went on for months. We really came to lean on each other, trusting one another completely. I found myself taking his words to meetings and quoting them with verve. He found my words triggered new awarenesses in him.

As we got to know each other, we also found out something rather interesting and amusing. We were both born and bred in Detroit. Although he had grown up on the West Side—in a more middle-class black family—we had both visited each other's neighborhoods on many occasions. And when I started moving westward, there were periods when we went to the same grocery store, same drugstore, same cleaners, even the same movie theaters. Yet our paths had never actually crossed. Not only that, when he moved to Chicago and lived there for years, I was in town all the time working, hanging out at the same places, eating breakfast at the same diners. We'd never seen or met the other.

Is timing everything, or what?

One late night, as I was enjoying my first private moment that week, sitting at my desk going over paperwork I'd been trying to finish for days, the phone rang. It was Franklin calling me from his office, about one A.M. Chicago time, and he talked to me for the next forty-five minutes. When we hung up, it dawned on me: he had taken forty-five minutes to tell me he didn't have anything to tell me about any decision from Borden's, but when he did, he would call me back. Hmmmm.

I called him back, catching him just as he was about to leave, and I talked to him for another forty-five minutes, telling him towards the end what I had called for: "In case you do have any news, I'm putting your name at the top of my call list. So wherever I am, my secretary will reach me immediately."

"Very good," Franklin said.

"Good night. Sleep warm," I said.

"Good night. You too."

Aha. The dance was beginning.

He continued to call every day, still without a decision from Borden's. Somewhere in this period, the language changed. More personal, more affectionate. Hello!

Meanwhile, back at the ranch: After three and a half years of celibacy, I awoke one morning and everything in me wanted to be held and kissed and loved by a man. Enough was enough. I needed a man. That early morning, I spoke to the Father about it and I said, "I need a man but you know I choose badly. Will you choose for me?" That was it.

Mr. Lett wasn't even a consideration. In fact, I made no considerations of my own. This was a God thing. It was His choice and He could do the considering for me.

So I began to prepare for the man I knew God was sending me. I gave away the round bed I adored so much, along with the specially made bed linens. My new bed to be shared only with my new man was an automatic king—which has two twin beds together on a king-sized frame, allowing individual operation for raising the head or foot of the bed. I bought new bed and bath linens. Changing the bedsheets regularly, I would not allow anyone to sit on or even touch the bed and I was so adamant about it, family and friends thought I was losing it completely. In the past, I had always entertained in my bedroom, where everyone was used to hanging out on my bed or laying across it. Nineteen-year-old Dumpsey wasn't too worried until I started to speak of this man I knew God was sending, as if he were already there. Then I began to say, "Good morning," to this man, and "Good night," too. Everyone was sure I had flipped.

⌒— "I'm heading out to L.A. next week," Franklin mentioned in passing one night. He was going to be pitching for the Charlie Tuna account. "It would be great to get together but it's just in and out. Evening meeting and then I leave the next morning."

"Why don't you come to my house for a late supper after the meeting?" I offered.

"That would be nice," he said, "but it would be eleven by the time I could get there."

"Eleven it is," I said, giving him the address and directions.

The next day I received a call from Lon Fontaine, a longtime friend who had also been one of the choreographers for Motown. Lon was producing a benefit show for the Ebony Theater, which was founded back in the days when there were no black theaters in L.A. Lon asked me to come and take part in the press conference scheduled before the show.

"I'd be happy to do you the favor," I agreed. "But I'll have to leave after the press conference because I'm expecting guests at my house that night."

Lon said, "No problem. Thanks for coming. I need you. If the press knows you're there, they'll definitely show up. We'll send a limo to pick you up around seven."

Everything went smoothly until the press conference ended and I asked for my limo to take me home, only to find out that it had been hired to take someone off on a one-way trip.

Okay, I have no car. I call a cab, even though I know good and well that in Los Angeles, unless you are at a hotel or a cabstand, calling a taxi is a joke. Now I have no cab, no limo, no way home. It's now nine-thirty, it's a forty-five-minute trip to my house, Franklin is arriving at eleven, and I can find no one willing to take me.

Finally after I had a couple of fits, a man with a brand-new Cadillac allowed his son to drive me.

As we were leaving the father told his son, "Remember now, it's a new car and it shouldn't be driven over forty miles an hour." Which was *stuu-pid,* of course. New cars hadn't needed to be driven slower for the last thirty years.

But I'm not too worried, thinking surely that the son knew better and like most kids couldn't wait to rev the engine and let her fly.

Not so. We pulled onto San Vincente, a wide-open boulevard, and he kept the speed down at thirty-five. "You know," I suggest, trying not to get furious, "you could probably drive faster."

"No," the son said, slowly, almost in a monotone, "my father said not to drive the new car over forty miles an hour. To be on the safe side, I think thirty-five is even better."

"But, really, that's actually not correct," I say, through gritted teeth. "In the nineteen-forties, yes. But nowadays brand-new cars can be driven as fast as you want."

"No," he repeated in his drone, "my father said not over forty."

"Well, that's just sort of stupid," I muttered to myself, allowing him to hear.

"No, that's not what my father said."

We're poking along and the clock is ticking and I am getting more ticked off each minute.

On Sunset Boulevard, where there are hardly any other cars on the street, I start to beg, "Please, please, could you just step on it?"

"No, I can't. My father said not to drive fast and it's his car."

Now I want to kill him. We finally start up the long winding road to the top of the hill where I live. It's very dark and this young driver is afraid of the curves and slows down even more. Behind us is a car that wants to pass, but the son of the owner of this new Cadillac won't pull over.

The car behind us is making me mad too. Everything is making me mad. *Fi-na-lly,* we pull into my driveway and the car behind us pulls in too. Probably to complain about how slow we were going. Excuse me? Some nerve this person has.

I jumped out of the Cadillac and walked to the car to tell the man or woman that this is a private driveway and to get out. As I approach the car, breathing fire, ready to unleash all my pent-up frustrations of my disastrous evening, I see the driver start to get out and begin hot and loud, "Listen, do you know that this is . . ." until I see that it's—can you guess?—yes, it's none other than Franklin Lett, my dinner guest. My whole demeanor changed instantly mid-sentence, mid-walk, as Miss Charming appeared: ". . . such a pleasure to see you."

Waving the driver of the Cadillac off, I called, "Thanks so much," and invited Franklin in.

We sat down in the living room, drank some of the wine I had put on ice before leaving earlier, and started playing backgammon. For the first time in his presence, I took in this man with all my senses, and felt my body begin to warm. As I looked at this guy whom I'd considered not my type, I noticed now how masculine he was, how his lightish eyes had an alive sparkle in them, how beautiful his tan-colored skin and light brown hair was, how his mellow voice had a rhythm of music when he spoke, how his laugh billowed up out of him every time I said something even halfway funny. More than anything, he had a particular scent that almost enveloped me, some unknown blend maybe of his cologne, aftershave, soap, shampoo, and a sweet-spicy subtle aroma that came from his skin.

This was not a feeling to easily ignore. Making the most of the moment, I had on a cashmere wrap skirt which I began to conveniently let drop open now and then, fixing it back at the appropriate times. After a bit, I suggested, "There's a backgammon set in my bedroom that has better light. Let's give it a try."

In the bedroom, we sat down at the table in front of my window seat which did, indeed, have a very warm overhead light. Sitting underneath it, as I leaned to make my backgammon moves, that fantastic skirt worked out. Soft and moving. Unintentional. But maybe not. We played for hours, talking not so much as only friends anymore. The talk was something else now. Implying but never stating, yet offering possibility, opening the way.

He had to catch a plane at six in the morning and at two A.M., he was ready to go. As I walked him to the back door, I knew the goodnight kiss would be something spectacular. I opened the door, let him step out, and leaned my face to his, closing my eyes and preparing for the kiss. And then I heard the engine of his car start and saw him wave to me as he drove out of the driveway. *Ooooh,* egg-on-my-face time.

But as they say, it ain't over 'til it's over. He called the next night, warmer and more personal than ever. Before long, our phone calls became sexy and steamy. Yet we kept the friendship, a friendship that has only grown deeper and stronger over the years.

In early 1979, I was in Philadelphia doing a musical play called *The Last Minstrel Show,* a very good piece with a fine cast, including Gregory Hines. Right around the time it closed, I was asked by David Tebbit, then the president of NBC, to perform for a private fundraising dinner he was hosting at the Pierre Hotel in New York.

As it so happened Franklin was going to be in New York that same weekend, scheduled to stay at the St. Regis. When I told him I was going to be at the Pierre, he said that as soon as he got off the phone he was changing his reservations to stay at the Pierre as well.

Having made a prior commitment to get together with my friend Barbara Sharma who was doing a Broadway production of *I Love My Wife* with one of the Smothers Brothers, I agreed to meet her in my room at the Pierre at two in the afternoon. I arrived from Philly that day at noon and Franklin wouldn't be getting in until around four.

After Barbara and I caught up with each other, I confided, "There is this man coming here to see me and when he comes, I want you to get out of here as fast as you can."

"You got it," Barbara said with a smile.

"And don't seem to be pushed," I added. "But whatever you do, don't linger. Find a good time and split."

She understood completely.

As expected, Franklin arrived, I introduced him to Barbara, we had a quick drink, and—I told you, timing is everything—Franklin said he had to stop back at his room to get his notes and make some important phone calls. He left, giving Barbara the perfect opportunity to leave as well.

By the time Franklin returned I was a changed woman. Before I had been wearing a daytime suit of some sort, from which I had changed into floor-length silky lingerie, which was really not much more than some lace at the top and some lace at the hem, with the sheerest available piece of material to hold the pieces of lace together.

When his knock at the door came, I walked into the foyer, an area from which the rest of the suite could not be seen. I opened the door wide and there I stood in all my splendor. The sight took his breath away and while he was gathering himself, I pulled him into the foyer, closed the door, and pressed him back against it with my body.

Not realizing that Barbara had left, in the midst of our entanglement, Franklin kept pointing to the living room, which I ignored altogether. I was on a mission. Don't forget, it had been three and a half years. When he understood that Barbara had gone, well, what happened next is none of your business. But it happened for three days and three nights. Except for my performance at David Tibbet's fundraiser, about an hour and a half with bows included, we never left that room. No maid service. Just clean towels and room service trays in the hall.

By the fourth morning, we agreed that we really ought to get out of the room, each trying to show the other that this was not just a sexual situation. We showered, dressed, and hired a limo. On our way out, we stopped at the bar downstairs and each ordered a Kir Royale—a light, delicious drink made of champagne and creme de cassis. Looking out the windows, we had our first sight of daylight in days. It was a lovely, un-usually sunny day for a February in New York.

When we stepped into the limo, Franklin asked that we be driven around Central Park. The entrance to the park, at 59th and Central Park East, was only a block away from the Pierre at 60th and Central Park

East. After riding around 110th Street and heading back down on the west side, when we reached 59th Street, the driver buzzed back, asking, "Where to now, sir?"

As if on cue, we both said, "The Pierre."

Back we went to the room and locked up for two more days and nights.

I now knew he was THE ONE. My husband, the man God had chosen for me, an angel He had sent even before I asked for him. I was ready, fully and deeply committed beyond anything I had ever known.

Franklin, however, was in a different frame of mind. Only separated a year and moving out of a nineteen-year relationship, with two children to consider, he was going through major divorce anxieties. And not a man to take commitments lightly, he had promised himself, God, Peter, Paul, James, John, and all the other prophets and saints that he would never be married again. He had never expected what was happening with us to happen this way, this deep, this full of unconditional love, this magnificent sex, this friendship, this all-encompassing joy.

On our last morning together, before we had to leave, we sat down to have breakfast together. My first words to him, spoken across his eggs, were, "Do you have a mistress?"

He almost choked. After he regained his composure, he answered truthfully, though with an air of try-to-be-coolness, "Yes."

"What are you going to do about her?"

He swallowed, thought for a few seconds, and then said, "I guess I'm going to go home and find a way to tell her it's over. If it really meant something to me, I couldn't have been here this way with you."

I really did enjoy that breakfast.

We rode together to the airport where we caught different flights. Franklin walked me to my gate. We kissed a long kiss good-bye and as we came out of it, I grabbed his head and bit his scalp. Don't ask me. To this day, I don't know why. It really got to him, but not in a bad way. Even now, he refers to it occasionally.

Leaving him made me miserable. Not only because I wanted to be with him but I was so sore, walking was a bummer and sitting on that plane was something else. But it was worth it. I would gladly pay the price all over again. Any time, any place.

Our romance unfolded better than in the movies. Soon we were spending every available weekend together, me flying to him or him flying to me. Wherever we met, when we checked into the hotel room, beside the bed were two Sonia roses; wherever we went out to dinner, there were two Sonia roses on the table. He'd have them shipped in no matter where we were all across the United States.

One night over dinner, we were talking about a plan for him to come to Los Angeles the next weekend. Now that he was coming to my turf, I felt he should know about my past relationships that had occurred there. Not to dangle them, but to arm him with the knowledge so that he didn't hear it on the street. You know, at a party or at a show, when some supposedly well-meaning person decided to come up and point out someone else I had been with. But as I began to talk, Franklin stopped me, saying something that I'd never forget. "It's not important what brought you to the table," he said. "I'm just thankful that you're at the table. And what matters now is what you do at the table."

In spite of his outgoing demeanor, Franklin was and is a shy guy—a romantic, sensitive, deeply caring person—which I found more charming every day. And I still do. I saw that he had a capacity to love unconditionally, neither demanding nor oppressive of me but genuinely supportive and encouraging. He wasn't intimidated in the least by me, my fame, or my fans. It was *soooo* refreshing.

When you ask Him, God sure does know how to pick husbands.

Oh, by the way, Franklin didn't know yet that he was going to be my husband. I knew and, of course, now you know. It was a God thing. No escaping it. And by now I was all the way up in love with him. I was *serio-us,* and really into the *us* part. He loved me too but he was scared of how serious we were becoming.

In the meantime, his business world was falling apart. On top of which, he was missing his children, whom he loved beyond explanation.

In both the work area and in his personal life, Franklin was caught in a struggle between finding his own happiness and doing the right thing by others. With not an evil bone in his body, he could never bring himself to knowingly hurt anyone. Whatever was happening, he'd look first for the good side of an issue and the good in others—and second and sometimes third. But once he lived up to his word and was through, he was *thr-o-o-u-ugh*. And once he'd given you your chances and did decide he was finished with you, he wouldn't so much as piss on you if you were on fire.

I discovered early on that Franklin is an honest man almost to a fault; even if he has to suffer a loss for the sake of his principles, he will. Whenever I saw him try to deviate from them—at times when it would have helped him at the moment—what impressed me was not that he wouldn't but that he couldn't! Instead, he would talk to me, mulling it over into the night, actually talking to himself until he talked himself back in line with his principles.

I witnessed and learned, thank God, from this tremendous ability Franklin has to verbalize a situation in its entire form, discussing both sides objectively to the point of debate and argument. Truth and fair judgment always won out.

"Sit down, we have to talk," he said to me as I was getting ready to take a bath one evening during a weekend romantic excursion.

I sat.

He sat. Then he spoke, "You are the most wonderful woman I have ever known and you deserve someone who can love you the way you should be loved. My work demands so much of my time. Sixty, seventy hours a week. Not to mention the travel required. What time I have off, I need to spend with my kids. That's unfair to you. You're the kind of woman who should have someone there for you, to take care of you. Maybe it would be best if you found someone else."

I put my tongue between my lips and blew a spit-filled razz-bubble. Saying nothing at all, I stood up and walked on into the bathroom and started my bath.

Franklin came to the bathroom, into the open doorway, and just stood there, looked at me, and shook his head.

He never tried that again. Oh, but he tried other things. He really thought he could get away.

Our first real impasse came on one of the weekends when I had flown to Chicago. This entailed my catching the redeye from L.A. on Friday night, arriving in Chicago at six the following morning, spending all of Saturday with him, and then, Sunday morning, he'd leave me alone to go spend the day with his children, only returning in time to take me to the airport.

Finally, early on Sunday morning, I raised the issue. "It seems to me we have so little time together that you could find another time to have breakfast and see your kids than when I'm in town."

"But when I don't take them to Sunday breakfast, it makes me feel too bad," he said, subject closed.

"Well," I said, not done, "it makes me feel too bad sitting in a hotel alone after flying all night from L.A., after working all day."

For the first time, we couldn't seem to work it out. And when I saw him getting dressed to leave, I told him emphatically, "I won't be here when you return. In fact, don't bother to return because I'll be long gone."

I began to pack. Before he strode to the door, he said, "We'll talk about this when I get back," kissed me and left.

Finished with my packing, I checked out and took a limo to the airport for an earlier flight, a drive on which I cried *pro-fu-u-u-sely*. I mean, *profusely*.

At the gate, I checked in and the ticket agent arranged for me to board the plane early where I could wait for departure. Sitting there still crying on this empty plane, I looked up to see the stewardess at my side. She said, "There is a gentleman outside the plane who said he'd like to speak with you and, Miss Reese, he looks very upset. Maybe you should see him. He says it's an emergency."

Leaving my things, I got off the plane and saw Mr. Franklin Thomas

Lett standing there looking pensive and upset. Then he saw me and burst into a very relieved smile as I rushed into his arms. We sat together in the airport until the plane was ready to depart. There were no apologies, no reprimands. His being there settled the problem and we both knew it.

The impasse was past and getting through it made us even closer.

A few weekends later, this time at a hotel in L.A., I raised the issue of wanting for us to have more than just the span of a weekend together. I had to figure out a way for longer periods of time with him. Regular days. Time to talk face-to-face about what happened at work. Waking and sleeping with each other, just being together without the pressure of a plane to catch. I wanted to know him better, to show him my depth and my abilities, to let him see how beautifully I could take care of him.

As Franklin was getting ready to head back to Chicago, I presented him with an idea, sort of a ploy. "You know," I began wistfully, "I really wish you lived here or had a place where I could cook for you."

"Are you a good cook?" he asked, as if surprised.

"I'm really good," I answered. "You should have the pleasure of my cooking some time."

"What's your specialty?"

"Whatever is your favorite meal, that's my specialty."

Not properly impressed yet, he said, "You probably have never heard of my favorite."

"Try me."

He grinned and said, "Chess pie."

He was right, never heard of it. But he would never know that. Grinning too, I said, "One chess pie, coming up."

Cut to: My house where I'm on the phone with the public library trying to get info on chess pies, only to discover that there's a chess pie recipe in a cookbook by Minnie Pearl, an autographed copy of which Minnie herself had given to me when she appeared on my show. The hitch? It's buried in my storage shed in a box somewhere. I ask Ron— the man who takes care of my house and helps my life run smoothly— to empty the shed. Which doesn't thrill him at all.

Please pause for an angel identification: Ron Hearin. About a year earlier, I had hired a secretary who came with good references. I was a little put off by her nails. They were so long they must have curled around themselves two or times. How could she type, I wondered. But she turned out to be a fine typist and seemed to do an adequate job. Then I came home from an appointment one day and walked in on her copying my Rolodex into her personal address book. Unh, unh. I don't play that. And when I caught her, I practically chased her out, but not quite. I kept her phone book, told her to call for her ride—since she didn't have a car—and get her things together.

While she was doing that, I went outside to simmer down. The boyfriend, I assumed, arrived to pick this woman up. As he was waiting, he took a look around my front and back yards, and then commented to me, "Your yards here could use a little work, you know."

"Yeah, I know," I said, "do you know anything about gardening and yardwork?"

He said he did and that he thought he could give me a couple or three days a week, if I wanted.

"That's fine," I said, "you can work here. But don't you bring this woman back here, if she is your woman. Unless that's a problem for you."

"Don't make no difference to me," he shrugged, telling me that they were only casual friends.

So that was how Ron Hearin, my angel, came to work for me and never left. He started off doing the yard work and went on to take care of my house when I was on the road, living in the guest room, and keeping a thorough eye on everything, protecting it as if it were his own. Never once in all these years have I come home to find one thing missing. I've left money, jewelry, furs, you name it. In the times when Dumpsey and I were there alone, having a man about the house gave me an added security. Also, I'd found that whenever I called for some sort of work estimate around the house, contractors were always prone to up their bid when they got there and found a woman. But when Ron called, as if it were his house, having a man greet the contractors always seemed to bring the prices down. Nice-looking, in his early middle age, he was wonderful at greeting guests and helped answer phones as well.

Like my angel Miss Molly, Ron became part of my family, as did his own family members. Ron's son, Dioñ, grew to be another angel to me and worked for many years as my personal hairdresser. Between Miss Molly, who couldn't do some of the heavy work, and Ron, who helped her out in those instances, my home could not have been tended more lovingly and happily than if they were the owners. Both of them really knew me. They knew my patterns, knew my wants and my needs, and took care of them before I'd even ask.

Back to the featured story of the chess pie: After hunting down Minnie Pearl's recipe, I added a few touches of my own and, on an early Friday morning before that day's work on a TV show, baked the most beautiful, incredible chess pie you've ever seen, took it with me on the plane to Chicago, and presented it to Franklin the moment I stepped off.

"Here you go," I said, hoping he was properly impressed.

Him: "What's that?"

Me: "What did you ask me for? A chess pie."

It floored him. Then he floored me, saying, "This is so sweet. If I'd known you were actually going to do this, I would have told you my real favorite."

Kill, kill. But I bounced back calmly. "Well, what is your real favorite?"

Him: "Deep dish apple pie. I love that."

Me: "One deep dish apple pie, coming up." It really was one of my specialties.

Cut to: The following Thursday night at home in Los Angeles as I finished creating this deep dish apple pie to end all deep dish apple pies. It was HUGE—14″ long by 9″ wide by 6″ deep—and baked with the finest ingredients that could be found: whipping cream, five kinds of grated cheese, cinnamon, brown sugar, a variety of spices, and a crust so flaky even Nellie would have been satisfied. I beheld and smelled my creation made from love and saw that it was good. Very good.

The next night when it was time to go to the airport, the pie was so big and heavy, no suitable boxes could be found, so I covered it with tinfoil and made a kind of sling for it. I had to have the always helpful Ron go to the airport and assist me onto the plane with it. Taking my seat in the second row, I slid it under the seat in front of me, realizing that there was nothing I could do to disguise its intoxicating aroma which was now smelling to high heaven. When the gentleman sitting in that seat was settled in, he began to look around, thinking perhaps as he peeked behind the curtain of the galley it was coming from there. After we took off, the smell thickened, permeating the cabin, especially where he was sitting.

Mid-flight, sandwiches were served. The man ate them but continued looking at the galley. A piece of cake was then served which he knew was not what he'd been smelling and he dismissed with a look that said, *What is this crap?* "I'll wait," he told the stewardess.

Upon our arrival in Chicago, I had the steward help me pick the pie up from underneath this man's seat, and, at last, he saw where the haunting smell had been coming from for the last three hours. He gave me a dirty look that Carmen McRae would have envied. If looks could kill, that one and the scowl he gave me later at the baggage counter would have knocked me dead.

It was worth all that and more. Franklin was more than properly impressed. Let me tell you, I was well-appreciated for the pie and the loving that night was more than par excellence. For the rest of the weekend, he showed off the pie to everyone he knew at the hotel where he was living. An entire dance troupe staying there came by the room, one by one, to taste this now legendary deep-dish apple pie.

In the spring of 1979, after looking high and low for some way to be able to spend more time with Franklin, exactly the right opportunity fell in my lap. It was a Chicago production of *Same Time, Next Year* in which I was to co-star with Adam Wade. It was a real actor's piece, no singing at all, with a chance to flex my acting muscles comically and dramatically. Also, between rehearsals and the run itself, it would keep me in Chicago for six weeks. The show's producers put me up at the Lake Point Towers, where my room had a gorgeous lake view from every window. I felt that having my own place yet being on Franklin's home turf for those six weeks would tell us—or me, rather—something about how we would do on a long-term basis.

I didn't know it yet, but there was other knowledge I had come to Chicago to find, and a new angel was being sent to guide me to it.

The name Johnnie had been cropping up in my conversations with Michael Robinson, my hair and makeup man for *Same Time, Next Year* who had also done hair and makeup on *The Last Minstrel Show*. Back in Philadelphia, Michael used to feel comfortable confiding his problems in me and whenever I told him what I thought, he'd say, "You talk just like Johnnie."

After a while, I finally asked, "What's a Johnnie?"

"Johnnie Colemon," Michael had said. "She's my minister." And he told me how wonderful and inspirational she was and what a joy it was going to her church which was on the South Side of Chicago.

Now that I was there in Chicago, Michael insisted I go to one of the services. That first Sunday that I attended, Johnnie Colemon was conducting what she calls Panorama of Truth—or P.O.T.—a five-day gathering for all the various churches across the country and the world who are part of the Universal Foundation for Better Living, which Johnnie founded, with her church, Christ Universal Temple, as the mother church. These five days include seminars, music, and guest speakers from all walks of life. For the service I attended that first Sunday, Johnnie invited me to speak which felt marvelous. Just being in her presence was marvelous. Johnnie was and is a God-filled-to-the-top-and-running-over-dynamic-piece-of-God. She got my complete attention.

After the service, on the way to the elevator, I stopped her, gave her a hug, and whispered in her ear, "I'm gonna be your buddy for the rest of our lives."

Beautiful, serene, powerful Johnnie gave me a bemused look, asking, "What does a buddy mean?"

I told her a buddy is the one who is there when everybody else runs away. The one you can always count on.

"Well, we'll see," she said, almost with an attitude of—*Oh really!*

Later in the day, when I saw Franklin, I was bursting with my news about this wonderful church and this incredible minister. Before he could get a word in edgewise, I asked, "Could we go together next Sunday? I know you'd love it."

"I do love it," he said with his melodious laugh as he explained that it had been his church for years. "I'd be glad to take you next week."

In fact, when Johnnie found out we were coming together, she sent a car for us. At the church, we were ushered into her office and welcomed warmly with coffee and pastries. She was still sort of looking me over as she talked to Franklin.

When it was time, we went into the chapel and took our seats. That day, the choir—directed by the Reverend Robert Mayes—was really cooking. And Johnnie was stupendous. She put into words everything that I'd always believed about God, the same things that I was put out of every church in Detroit for believing: that God loves you and thinks you are the greatest thing He ever created; that He made you in His likeness; that you can have, do, be anything you want to have, do, and be. Johnnie let you know the choice was always yours—between the high, positive, productive, prosperous road or the rut or the mud hole.

When she finished her sermon, she asked me to sing. Reverend Mayes, or Bob as I came to know him, had been playing a song during which the offerings were to be gathered. When he asked me what I wanted to sing, I said, quietly, "If you'll tell me the lyrics, I'll sing what you're playing now."

It shocked him that I would ask to sing a song I'd never sung before but he did as I asked. It was a song called "Only Believe," and the lyrics went perfectly with the moving music I was hearing and the words that were spoken that day. It took Johnnie and the church *all the way out.*

At another service, Bob arranged for the choir to background me. Johnnie started to look at me differently after that service. In a short amount of time, she and I became such close friends that certain members of the staff and the church experienced some jealousies, voicing them under the guise of protection, as if to suggest that because of my profession, she might be hurt. I fluffed it all off, knowing my reputation was a great one and that Johnnie was my angel, my mentor, and my friend for life. We did, as I'd predicted, become buddies, and have been in one-ness for almost twenty years.

As closing date for the play approached—July 6th, my birthday—I was trying hard not to become maudlin and moody. The show was a success, my getting to know Johnnie Colemon a godsend in every way, and my time had been excellent with Franklin.

A note: From this point on, Franklin will be known as Daddy, which I call him. In fact, I never call him Franklin and I should have said so before.

Daddy and I had spent the six weeks playing house together in that apartment on Lake Michigan that the producers of my show had rented for me. We ate together, made it homey for ourselves, hanging out and playing there just the two of us, and even entertaining various friends like my Chicago girlfriend Aurlyne Jordon who'd performed in the Idlewild review with me twenty-five or more years before.

Now, with a birthday celebration planned after the show on closing night, it was time for me to go back to L.A. Our time together had shown me just how compatible Daddy and I were; and that we could live together in a permanent nest. And yet, with nothing said or decided, those morose feelings were creeping in around my edges; Daddy seemed to be affected similarly.

At last, four days before my departure date, we sat down to have a where-do-we-go-from-here talk.

He presented his concerns. Daddy had made the difficult decision to close down his agency and was fielding job offers in Washington, D.C., and New York. And I lived in L.A., a city he had experienced, he said, as mostly a lot of palm trees, flakes, and phonies. He made it obvious that he really wanted us to be together but as a man and father he felt a deep responsibility to his children. Which I could only respect.

My position was simple and clear. I just wanted him. I knew it was right and that we could make it work. How could it not? He was the man God had sent me.

He stood, telling me, "Listen, I need to go for a run. I need to run and think and sort some things out." He changed into sweats and headed out, leaving around 12:30 P.M.

Feeling edgy, anxious, hopeful, scared, I knew there was nothing I could do to force the outcome. I did the only thing I could do, settling myself into bed, and putting myself into a state of gratitude and praise for all of God's goodness to me. Then I talked to the Father, telling Him that I was going to let Him determine the outcome, putting it in His hands. Letting go, letting God. Whatever this man I wanted so decided, I knew God would give me the strength to accept it. In a place of calm and faith, I waited with uncharacteristic patience for his return, talking to God to still myself whenever a hint of panic or negativity set in.

At 2:30 P.M., two hours later, he returned, drenched in sweat. Wiping himself with a towel, he sat down on the side of the bed and said, "I thought it over."

"Yes?"

"And what I want . . ."

"Yes?"

". . . is to go to L.A. and be with you." He paused and then quickly added, "If that's all right with you."

I jumped out of that bed, half-laughing and half-crying, and grabbed him and almost smothered him with hugs and kisses.

The celebration after the show closing night was manifold: for a successful run, for my birthday, and for the beginning of our lives together, Franklin's and Della's.

In the three days since the night he'd made the decision, he'd packed up his business and his personal furnishings and put them into storage. And the next day, July the 7th, 1979, a glorious, historic day, he came to be with me in L.A.

In early 1980, the two of us took a trip to our hometown of Detroit where I was performing and where we could have a chance to see old friends and family. Things hadn't been so easy for us over the past months. Daddy's move to L.A. had been a major one, full of sacrifice and risk, radically altering the path his life had taken until then. Behind him now was the multimillion-dollar business he had built up from nothing, an individual feat as well as one that helped open doors to the advertising world for other black executives and companies. Given the resistance, the opening may have well been a tiny crack, but he had climbed the corporate ladder in spite of the obstacles—and maybe because of them too.

With most of his connections in Chicago, here he was in California, starting all over from the beginning at the age of forty, a time he had once envisioned as the point at which he could start working less and enjoying more.

It would take four years until he mastered this hard transition and dealt with his personal challenges. Eventually, he would work out his divorce and hold onto positive relationships with his children, despite all the negativity which surrounded the divorce. He would be more than fair, which is his normal mean.

In time, he would also discover a new and much more rewarding career path. One of the many wonderful things about Daddy is that he is forever evolving, never setting limitations as to his varied interests, talents, and capabilities. In college, to please his parents, he initially pursued a pre-med major, switching towards the end to visual arts which he loved, going on to specialize in portraiture painting. But with a wife and two kids to support, he'd left that creative field and turned to graphic arts, which soon led him to the lucrative field of advertising.

Eventually, in addition to becoming my manager, and a fantastic one at that, he would be able to draw from all of his career experience, using his visual, storytelling, and marketing skills to become an ingenious business entrepreneur, and ultimately, a producer and writer for stage and screen.

The time that this process of cleaning up the past would take, as he called it, was often for me a hard, dusty, rocky road. But I held on, never forgetting he was my angel, the man God had sent me. And the holding on increased my faith which gave me patience; which as I've said before is not an innate ability for me. In the beginning, with all the agonizing over the divorce, my patience was worn thin often. I didn't feel I owed anything to the former Mrs. Lett. Their marriage was over and they had separated before I even met him. Watching the lengths to which she went in order to oppose the divorce, I couldn't see her point of view or her perspective or her condition or her anything EXCEPT her in my way.

Though he and I argued about it, with sleepless, tearful nights for me, we stuck it out through this first adjustment period.

Then came that trip to Detroit. There is something about going home, any time, that tends to bring up strong feelings both good and bad. I loved seeing my hometown angels and performing to crowds who had cheered me on in the very beginning. But other sights made me blue. So many things had changed, gotten old. Things that once looked so big and imposing now seemed small and insignificant. It wasn't just that Detroit had changed, I had changed. I had grown. I had gotten on with my life.

That was exactly what I felt Daddy and I needed to do—to get rid of the baggage and get on with our lives. And that's what I told him while we were there in Detroit, calling for a showdown.

Nothing doing. He flatly refused to go through changes with me. "I love you," he insisted, "and I'm going to spend the rest of my life with you. But we have to wait . . ."

Interrupting, I said, "Fine. We'll wait. But you're gonna be sorry for this. Life could end any moment and we're messing around and wasting it."

That was the end of the discussion. But what an uncanny choice of words I had made in speaking about the possibility of life ending at any moment. Little did I know how real and how imminent that possibility was.

By the next morning, in flight back to Los Angeles, I was over my anger and feeling all bubbly. That day I was going to be doing Johnny Carson's *Tonight Show* and a few days later Franklin and I would be leaving for a much needed vacation. Doing Carson was its own kind of homecoming for me. I knew everybody there; they liked me, I liked them. It was lots of fun.

For this taping, Richard Dawson, also a friend, was filling in for Johnny as guest host. After my first song, I went to the couch where Richard and I joked and laughed with fervor. Then it came time for my second song, "Pieces of Dreams." Some people call it "Little Boy Lost." A fun, challenging way to sing the song is with only the bass as accompaniment. The melody and rhythm are all in that one instrument. In order to pull this off as a singer, you have to be able to hold your own. Naturally, I had to do it that way because it's what all the heavies did; and, of course, I was one of the heavies.

The bassist played a four-bar intro and I began to sing. For the next six bars, I sang gloriously and then, to my horror, I hit the worst note I have ever sung in my life. My body began to twitch. Doc Severinsen saw me twitching so violently, he thought I was dancing. I could feel by now that I was about to fall down. Not knowing what was going on, I still knew something was wrong, very wrong. As I fell, I put myself in God's hands and fainted.

As I lay there unconscious, a navy nurse who was out in the audience rushed down to the stage, where she began to work with me, directing Daddy and the show's production people to take me to the nearest hospital, St. Joseph's, a block from the Burbank studio.

Because I was very heavy at the time, the emergency care doctors at the hospital immediately assumed that the collapse was caused by high blood pressure or one of the other disorders of obesity. But after checking my vital signs, which were good, they couldn't figure out what had happened to me.

Daddy called my personal physician, Dr. Jack Wohlstadter, who had me moved to Hollywood Community Hospital, where he practiced. Dr. Lavet, who worked in Dr. Wohlstadter's office, arrived with my medical records and worked over me all night. Since I was an entertainer, out of routine, they looked for drugs in my system. Finding none, they were really confused.

What they didn't know, partly because I had never included my mother's cause of death in my own medical records, and because I was unconscious and couldn't tell them, was an important clue from my family history. The very thing that had killed my Mama on her way home from the movies thirty-one years before had happened to me: an aneurysm in my brain had burst. A part of my brain had exploded.

What the doctors did know was that it was serious. Daddy was warned to expect the worst. Most likely, they said, I would be dead by dawn.

Daddy, my certain angel, refused to leave my side. He prayed over me all night long, never once doubting that God would answer his prayers.

And God heard them and went to work, calling forth an army of angels, both familiar to me and not, sending them to save one of His children, me, whose life was very much in the balance.

Teaching

1 9 8 0 – 1 9 9 7

11

The Lord sustained me and I awoke at dawn. Though I was disoriented and groggy and not aware of my circumstances, my doctors decided I was stable enough to be moved to Midway Hospital where, they believed, the diagnostic equipment would better enable them to find out what was happening to me.

The next thing I remember was arriving at Midway and being put in a dark room. After I was told to lie still, I was sedated, as everyone tip-toed around the room looking concerned. When I woke up, I focused on faces for the first time. At the side of my bed were Doctors Lavet and Wohlstadter; at the foot of the bed was Daddy, telling me, "I'm here, baby, you're gonna be just fine."

They began the tests and the X rays which finally revealed what had caused my collapse, not that anyone explained the diagnosis to me. Next, a new doctor was brought on the case, a doctor who was reputed to be the best neurological surgeon on the West Coast. What he was best at was coming to my room every morning to explain how dire my status was, telling me about the 3% to 7% chances for not surviving. He never once spoke about the 93%–97% chance for success. He seemed more worried about a malpractice suit than getting me well.

Day after day, I held on. But the more this doctor focused on the worst aspects of my prognosis, the more the confused, disoriented, and afraid I became. Parched from the need for some kind of information that never seemed to come, I felt myself falling away. I was more frightened by that than I'd ever been in my life.

On one of those dark, dark days, my longtime angel, our house-keeper, Miss Molly, came to see me in the hospital. Before saying anything, she prayed with me, which gave me some comfort. But my tears soon began to flow, as I told her through a weak voice, "I don't know what's happening, Miss Molly."

She took my hand.

"And I'm not afraid to die," I said, "I just want to die as a Christian. I don't want to be in here alone screaming and begging. I want to lean on God and die with Him there for me."

Molly spoke to me, and as she did, I heard echoes of Nellie. She said to me, "You're not going to die, you hear? I'm prayin' every day and God has told me that you gonna be all right. What I want you to do is not worry in here. I want you to stand strong on your rock. Trust God. And He'll bring you out of here."

After that, whenever the doctor of doom came to talk to me, an invisible shield went up between us and although I could see his lips moving, I couldn't hear a word of what he said. At that point, God would speak to me in a manner I could understand—in music or in Scripture.

What do I mean by that? For example, this doctor started to tell me they had decided to operate and that, *if* I survived, my family should know I might come out of surgery "visually impaired," "dragging my leg," or "mentally disturbed." He was unable to say what he really meant: dead, blind, a cripple, or crazy. Right then, everything he had said so far went over my head and as he continued, the shield went up and what came into my ears were the words of a song called "Turn to the Light," which says:

> *You've got to turn to the light*
> *The light that shines from within*
> *You've got to turn to the light*
> *The light that shines in all men*
> *I've got the light, you've got the light*
> *Shining in our soul*
> *It makes the pathway brighter*
> *And higher still our goals*
> *God is that light . . .*

It was a rhythm song and as I let it fill me up, I must have looked like I was nervous or twitchy or something. When, in fact, it was just me grooving with God.

"Miss Reese," the doctor announced one morning, on one of those days he seemed to feel was going to be my last, "you need to have an arteriogram."

A what? I'd already had a CAT scan, along with every other test. What test was this?

He explained that this test would allow them to look at my brain by running a tube in me which would release a dye to cover the actual place where the blood vessel had ruptured so that when it got time for surgery, they wouldn't have to search around with my head open. "The tube will run from your groin to your brain," he went on. "It's a necessary test. But we have to find the right man who can do the test by finding the best route."

With every inch of my physical strength, I rose in that bed to a sitting position, repeating back what I had just heard. "Are you telling me you want to run something through my body and you don't even know the route?" Before the doctor could answer, I turned to Franklin and told him, "Daddy, if you let that man cut me, you better hope he kills me because if one drop of his negativity falls on or in me, I'm gonna kill you."

Daddy calmed me down. He held me and stroked my forehead as he said, "Don't worry, baby, I'll handle everything." Knowing how tired I was of hospital food, he offered to go pick up some steamed vegetables at the Chinese restaurant across the street.

While Daddy was gone, I began to pray silently, telling God in my silence, *Father, I don't know what decisions to make. I've never heard these words before. I don't understand the language.*

At that moment, the door to my room opened. Standing there in a shaft of light from the hallway was a man in green hospital operating gear—or scrubs, as they're called—his shoes covered in paper slippers, and a surgical mask hanging down. The man said, "Miss Reese, I was just passing your room and something told me to stop. May I come in?"

"Yes, you may," I said, liking his manner.

He approached my bed, telling me he was from arteriograms, and sat down in the chair beside me. "I hear that you'll be with us tomorrow."

I nodded tentatively.

He went on. "I realize that sometimes patients don't know what decisions to make. They've never heard these words before. They don't understand the language. So, if you don't mind, I thought I'd explain the process in everyday language."

"Please," I said and listened to a much less complicated, less intimidating description of what would be done and what I could expect. I already had a good hunch this doctor was an angel but it was what he said next that confirmed my suspicion.

"You don't have to worry about me," this angel in scrubs said. "I know exactly what I'm doing. But in case I'm not there, you'll have the doctor who taught me everything I know; and he didn't even teach me everything he knows. So, either way, you're in capable hands." He stood from the chair, saying, "There's only one thing we need to ask of you, Miss Reese. You must be still. Can you do that?"

I nodded with complete certainty as my favorite help from the Bible came to mind: "Be still and know that I am God."

Seeing the confidence on my face, he turned and left.

I am now in conscious awareness that God had been in my room. God Himself as an angel in disguise. He repeated to me the silent prayer I had only just prayed. He put me in mind of *my* favorite prayer verse, the message He needed to remind me of.

Daddy returned with the food to find me crying and praising God. Filled with the spirit, I looked at him, breathless, and said, "God was just in this room, Daddy."

"He's always with you, baby."

"I don't mean like that. I mean in this room, in that chair you're sitting in."

"Just relax now, babe, everything is all right."

"No, no, no. I tell you He just left this room." After I described what had transpired, we held each other, thanking God for the timely comfort and information He had given me.

The next day I was wheeled downstairs for my arteriogram, a procedure that took an hour and a half. I never felt a thing. Not a pain, not a doubt. Not a fear. I was still, still and safe in the knowledge that God was God.

Nine days went by and the best neurological surgeon on the West Coast had yet to do anything about the surgery. Because this man had probably assumed I was going to die under his hand, he had made himself too afraid to operate on Miss Della Reese. So, stalling for time, he continued his morning reports of gloom, making it one of his functions in life to tell me why, statistically, I wouldn't survive surgery. Every day, he ran down the statistics, how three out of a hundred didn't live, how seven out of a hundred had something drastic go wrong. He wasn't lying. That was what his book of medical references stated. But I was working out of another book that said God would never leave nor forsake me and that I could touch the hem of His garment and be healed. I was reaching for that hem.

All the angels in my family were helping me reach as well. There was Daddy with me around the clock, along with frequent visits from Dumpsey and my son, Dr. James Barger, plus the calls, cards, flowers, and gifts from friends and fans everywhere. Johnnie Colemon had been with me on the phone from the beginning, promising to fly in whenever I asked. Dr. Jack Wohlstadter kept in frequent contact, never simply turning me over to the other doctor, but continuing to be involved in the case.

"Jack," I finally told him, "something's not right. I am tired of not knowing what's going on and when or what they're gonna do, whatever they're gonna do."

At that point, Jack went and got the famous neurosurgeon and rounded up every other doctor involved so far on the case and had a meeting. At last, in clear, straightforward, matter-of-fact language, they told me about the aneurysm, about the medical reasons for my needing surgery, about the risks of surgery and the risks of not having surgery. That knowledge freed me from my limbo. As was my normal mean, all I needed was to know the problem, then I could get to work and make decisions.

The first decision was to get an outside opinion, so Daddy and my son, Dr. B., took my various tests and X rays to an expert at the UCLA Medical Center. After reviewing them, the expert said, "These are the clearest X rays I've ever read. Frankly, if your surgeon can't operate by them, you need to find another one. And soon."

The one aneurysm that had burst was leaking blood into my brain. The X rays showed there were also two other aneurysms on the other side of my brain which, although they were what he called "passive," could become a grave concern if left unattended. The UCLA expert said there was a great surgeon in Switzerland, but explained that the fourteen-hour flight might be too long. If I wasn't given the right medical doses to coagulate my blood, there was a high risk that it would overflow in my brain. Instead, he thought the five-hour trip to Canada to the London University Hospital in Ontario would be better. He advised

Daddy that the doctor there, Dr. Charles Drake, was considered an expert's expert in the field.

My dearest angel Daddy had known me now for little over a year. The day before my collapse on *The Tonight Show,* he had made it clear that he wasn't going to be rushed into any specific plans between the two of us until he had taken the time to work through his own career and personal challenges. Now, he put all of that aside, devoting himself completely in body, soul, mind, and everything else, to pull me through this.

Wanting me to have the best possible medical attention, he began looking to hire the best available medical plane for the trip. On speaking to one of the pilots, the gentleman recognized the destination and volunteered, "London University Hospital? The patient must be going to see Dr. Drake. I like taking people to Dr. Drake because I always bring them back too."

That was Daddy's assurance.

On the morning after the decision had been made for Dr. Drake to perform the surgery, I awoke to the smiles of Johnnie Colemon and her assistant, Helen Carry. Johnnie had chosen this moment as the time to come. Throughout the day and into the night, she sat on the edge of my bed, holding me, and praying with me. Johnnie worked to help me release the tensions that had been building, helping me to let go of the frustration from the delay in decisions, aiding me to banish the old confusion. As she helped me clear the way, she reminded me of my principles and of my inner-knowingness that not only would everything be all right, but that everything was already all right.

From that knowledge, I also knew that whatever the outcome, I needed to get my house in order. With Daddy, I went over my instructions as to how I wanted things handled—just in case—and told him where he would find the $60,000 I had in cashier's checks and insurance papers, and other business paperwork.

It was my decision not to be transported by ambulance or a hospital plane to the plane that would be flying me to Canada. I wanted to walk out of that hospital and onto the plane under the power and the strength of God. There was no advising me otherwise. I needed to do that to know I could do that. Johnnie prayed with me on my intention, helping me through our prayers to accept that I could do it.

"Thank you, Johnnie. God bless you for being here."

"Thank you, Della, my dear," Johnnie said. "I am glad to be here." She promised to take every step I was going to take right along with me.

On the day of departure, Daddy, Johnnie, and Helen gathered around me as I stood from my chair in the hospital lobby, walking slowly but surely out the opened door and down the short walkway to the waiting limo. As Daddy helped me in and sat down on the seat next to me, Johnnie waited outside. Leaning in the opened door, she said, "I was going to go with you but God says I don't have to. It is already done. You can do this." She gave me a kiss, closed the door, and we pulled away.

At the airport, an airline representative met us at the limo with a chair. We went down to the gate where my children, Della Jr. and James, joined us. The press was everywhere but Daddy dealt with them so I could be left in peace, my kids coming with me down the ramp to the plane where I stood and walked, slow, with effort, to my seat.

Not a detail in the arrangements had been overlooked. Daddy had stepped into a husband/father role without a hitch, nurturing Dumpsey and Dr. B. as much as he did me. This crisis was extremely hard on my daughter. At twenty years old now, she'd already been through one crisis with the glass door incident. So this had to be like a bad instant replay. It was very hard on James too. Yes, he is a doctor and has witnessed all sides of life and death as part of his profession. But I am his mother and that made a vast difference. Daddy was an anchor to us all.

The plane arrived at 11:30 P.M. that night in Toronto, where we were picked up and driven to London, Ontario.

At seven A.M. the next morning, a man looking every bit like Santa Claus came into my hospital room. He introduced himself as Dr. Drake and spoke with a reassuring, warm smile. Since my ordeal had begun, his was about the first smile (other than from family and friends) that I had seen. Except for that doctor from the arteriograms who had appeared in my room at Midway Hospital, the smile from Dr. Drake was definitely the first medical smile.

He took a few moments to look at my records and X rays, then announced, "These are great X rays. You have a normal female aneurysm."

"Well," I said, "that's nice to know. It's too late in my life to have a male anything bursting in my brain."

Dr. Drake laughed out loud. Oh, it was so good to hear laughter again. And what he said next made him an angel for life. He leaned into my ear, whispering, "I know that I don't do this by myself. God holds my hand."

I said, "Cut me anywhere you want to cut me."

They wheeled me down the corridor on a gurney, my daughter on one side, my son on the other, and Daddy pushing me. Each of them, in their own words, told me I would be fine, and they would be right there waiting for me when it was finished; they each let me know they loved me and they knew that God hadn't brought me this far to leave me now.

At the door to the pre-operative room, they couldn't accompany me any further. As the anesthetist rolled me away, I looked back at the door where their three faces were pressed together against the little square of the glass window. The three of them, Daddy, Dumpsey, and James, were so intent, each wanting me to read on their faces all the love and strength they were sending me. Peering at me through the window were these three pairs of lips smiling hopefully, reassuringly, while tears welled up in their eyes or streamed down their faces. And I could also feel there were tears in their hearts.

As I was rolled away from them, out of their sight, I began to softly sing, "God Is So Wonderful to Me." The anesthetist, looking startled, patted me as if to say, *There, there,* and told me to be quiet.

"Leave her alone," commanded the East Indian nurse assisting him. "She's a singer. I've seen her on Dr. Shuller's program. She loves to sing. Let her sing if she wants to. And you just do your job." She spoke in such a voice of authority, the anesthetist complied absolutely.

He prepared the injection, gave it to me, and told me to count back-wards from one hundred.

A hundred, I thought. *Ninety-nine. Ninety-eight.* That was the last thing I remembered. Nine and a half hours later, I woke up in the recovery room where, in full voice, I was singing, "God Is So Wonderful to Me." The post-op nurses rushed in, looking at me real funny, and quieted me down. But inside, my body kept singing, "God Is So Wonderful to Me."

Later that night, in the darkened recovery room, I opened my eyes briefly and saw Johnnie Colemon sitting in a chair in front of my bed. This was not weird or a drug-induced hallucination or an episode of *Unsolved Mysteries.* Yes, Johnnie was in Chicago. But I saw her. It was Johnnie, flesh and bones, sitting in the chair in the recovery room at the London University Hospital in Ontario, Canada, keeping me company all night until Franklin could be allowed to see me the next morning. There are many pseudo-scientific or spiritual explanations I could give. But, suffice it to say, I believe certain angels, like Mama who came to me after I walked into the glass door, are given the power to transmute form and spirit from the different planes of existence. When they are most needed, I believe, God gives them the ability to do that. And when we are most in need, He gives us the ability to receive our angels, regardless of whether they are no longer living or physically far away.

That first morning after surgery, I awoke back in my hospital room in good, stable condition. It was some fifteen minutes before Daddy would be allowed to see me and I wanted to fluff up as best I could for him. After leaning over and way down to the drawer of my bedside table where I found a mirror, I discovered—to my HORROR—that my hair was all gone and my bald head was covered in a gooey red plastic coating which I immediately began to peel off with vigor.

"Where did you get that mirror?" asked the nurse who had just walked in. When I told her where, she sighed, asking, "Now you have a headache, right?"

"No."

"You leaned all the way down to the drawer and you don't have a headache?"

"No, but what I've got is to get this stuff off my head before my man gets here!"

The nurse waved me off, saying, "Don't worry about that stuff, it will all come off eventually."

"No, I don't think you quite understand. It's bad enough my hair is gone. I don't want Franklin to have to see my head covered with red plastic too."

Before the nurse can reply, the door opens and it's Daddy. And I'm making one of my pleas, saying silently, *Oh, God, don't let this turn him off, please.*

Then Daddy stops in his tracks, cocks his head to get a better look at me, and says the greatest words—other than "I love you"—that I've ever heard. "You've got a perfectly shaped head," he begins. "I never knew that before. You look cute. I want to do a sketch of you before your hair grows back." And he comes to my side with the most amorous tone, saying, "My sweet little bald-head, redheaded baby."

After that, he took me in his arms and together we praised God that we still had each other.

Daddy gave me a handwritten card with pictures he had drawn and a beautiful, loving message in it he'd composed. And every morning after that, he either delivered or had the nurses deliver a new handmade card right as I awakened.

Later that day, after being joined by my much relieved, joyful daughter and son, Dr. Drake stopped in to give me a status report. "So how'd we do, Doc?" I asked, feeling ready to sprint around the hospital. At least in spirit.

"We did great," he said. "The operation was a success. I couldn't have asked for it to go more smoothly." He went on to explain that while they had me opened up, they were able to determine that those other two aneurysms on the other side of my brain were getting ready to burst. Depending on how I was doing, Dr. Drake said, he wanted to schedule a second operation in about ten days so he could correct the problems.

It was just as the expert at UCLA had warned. Thank God I had gotten to Dr. Drake in time.

I really believe—and you can add a hundred *really*s right here—that the only blow that can truly hurt you is the one you don't see coming. The other blows, at least, you can try to dodge, or block. That's why God gives us eyes, so we can see what's coming in time to protect ourselves. But sometimes we can't see. In those times, if we allow Him, God will use His eyes for us. Or those of someone else. In this case, I had been sent the proper medical eyes at the right time to protect me from blows I couldn't have seen coming.

Other eyes were watching out for me.

Over the next week and a half, I woke often during the night, either unable to sleep, or needing to turn over to a more comfortable position. Each of those times that I awakened, Johnnie was sitting in a chair in front of my bed. Saying nothing, only sitting, creating a space of peace and well-being that lulled me back to sleep. In the mornings, she was always gone. At least, from that chair.

As scheduled, the second operation took place ten days later. I was released shortly after that. And ten days later, I was back at work doing a radio spot for Campbell's Soup, for which I was now a commercial spokeswoman.

5

⟜ The principles had worked, God and His angels had delivered me. I came out of that hospital bed *hot to trot,* more infused with spirit than ever before. I had walked on through the valley of the shadow of death, fearing no evil, knowing that God was my shepherd and I had not to want. If ever there had been a question, I knew now beyond certainty that you didn't have to die because somebody or some book said so. I knew that the angel God had chosen as my life partner would stand by me and for me. No matter what the challenge might be. I knew now, beyond certainty, I would marry this man, in God's Time, which is always the right time, and spend the rest of my life with him gladly.

Those feelings only intensified as we returned home and my recuperation began. My biggest discomfort was the healing of the incision at the top of my forehead. Never in my life have I itched like that. I mean, *it-ccchhh-ed.* And I was under the strictest of orders not to scratch. Instead, I had an arsenal of oils and creams with which Daddy would massage my scalp three or four times daily, in addition to the times when the itching woke me up at night.

As my angel of healing, he should have been awarded an honorary doctor's degree. I was amazed at my recovery process. As if none of this had ever happened. There was no part of me that hurt or felt disoriented. The doctors who were overseeing my care during this recovery period were even more amazed than I was. There were regularly expected symptoms or side effects after the kind of stroke I had suffered and the two major brain surgeries I'd been through. But, to the doctors' surprise, these things never happened. No problem with loss of motor control. No problem with paralysis. No problem with loss of sight, hearing, taste, speech, or language skills.

My one pervasive symptom, after the itching was over, was just how tired I was. I slept for weeks. Sometimes I slept so long, Daddy would come in the bedroom to check me and make sure I was still breathing regularly. If I happened to see him in one of my half-awake, half-asleep states, it would completely comfort me just to know he was there. So I slept and slept and slept. Such peace!

Daddy and I initiated a habit we still practice today. To get me out of the bed and out of the house, we'd get up around six or so in the morning and he'd take me for a ride. After a while, we'd stop somewhere to eat. Not a planned place. Just a place we saw that looked interesting. When we returned to the house, I'd go back to bed and until he had to go to his work, he'd sit with me, talking metaphysically and working with me. He made me laugh as he walked with me. He did it all in moments and during feelings no one else ever even knew I was having. We came out of it together, bound more closely than I could have imagined possible.

As for my angel Dr. Charles Drake, I wanted to do something special to thank him. Daddy and I came up with the idea to honor this gifted human being with a concert I would perform as a benefit to raise money for a chair at the university in his name. Once again, Daddy handled everything, working together with others in London—especially Bill Brady, a top radio and television executive—in order to secure a location in a ballroom in London, and arrange for musicians to play for me. The plans had to be made in the utmost of secrecy because Dr. Drake is an individual who doesn't want anyone to make any fuss over him. We quickly found there were many, many other people who wanted to do something to honor him and show their thanks but hadn't, as yet, been able to do it in a way he would accept. Everyone helped out, making the event a certain success. Mrs. Drake told me that in order to ensure it was a surprise, for the first time in her marriage she had to blatantly lie to her husband. When they arrived at the concert, he was surprised, touched, and really overwhelmed by the love so many held for him. Fittingly, the concert was a triumph.

Dr. Drake, whom I love dearly, is a magnificent expression of God, an angel who has deeply touched the lives of remarkably many. From time to time, no matter where I am in the world, I meet people who happen, like me, to have been saved by the skills of Dr. Charles Drake. We consider ourselves a "We Survived" club of very, very blessed people.

Flash forward: The morning of January 12, 1983, a most blessed day, the day I was to become the lawfully wedded wife of Mr. Franklin Thomas Lett, my first and only husband. You might be wondering just how that could be, hmmm? Yes, I told you before about two other men with whom I had been to the altar. But, as far as I'm concerned, that's what the other two were—trips to the altar. This was to be a real marriage, my first. In fact, if I had known before about Daddy and the grand-est, greatest love we would share, he would've married himself the old-est living virgin around. *If,* I say, because of course every relationship I did have in the past had been important to teach and prepare me for my marriage to him, in this perfect time and place. My lessons had been im-portant not only in the area of romantic love, but in all other kinds of relationships—my relationship to God, my relationship to myself, and to several of the friends and angels I have mentioned already. Without these lessons, I knew this blessed wedding day would not have arrived.

At the top of the list of angels was my baby, my daughter Deloreese, who had made a mother of me and whose presence in my life taught me the ins and outs of unconditional love.

Dumpsey had grown into the most beautiful, love-filled, radiant young woman, on her road now to the pursuit of her dreams and inter-ests, moving on soon to her own experiences as a wife and mother.

I beheld her as she arrived that morning, dressed and ready to take part in the ceremony as my maid of honor. It seemed it was only yester-day that I had carried her, a cuddly two-and-a-half-year-old, out of the Sherman House in Chicago, wrapped in my chinchilla coat. Here we were, twenty-two years later, hugging and kissing in celebration of the distance we had come together, tears of happiness already in our eyes. For a moment, I couldn't help thinking about some of the trials we had been through in our journey as mother and daughter. Dumpsey's teens—from about age fourteen to seventeen—were probably the hardest on both of us. Again, thank God for Miss Molly because I wasn't there as much as my daughter needed me to be; and, Lord knows, Dumpsey's friends were there much more than she needed them to be. And many times we had to deal with these issues via international calls going back and forth from places like South Africa, the middle of the Caribbean, Brazil. *Ever-ry-where.* We fought, we argued, we disagreed. But in the end, inevitably, we got together face-to-face, talked it out, cried and hugged and tried again.

At the same time, during her teens Dumpsey broadened our family. There was a student exchange program her school had with a school in Watts, one of the toughest inner-city areas in Los Angeles, and one of the toughest in the country. Of the students who were brought by bus to attend Dumpsey's school, she made five close, long-lasting friends. They spent most of their weekends with us and, in the process of getting to know them, I found myself younger, being a part of this group of young women, to whom I was "Auntie."

When I heard how one of the girls was thrown out of her house by her mother, I tried to call the mother and talk to her on the child's behalf. "Look," I said, "I'm not here to be up in your business. I'm sure you have your reasons for being upset but whatever it is, do you realize that if you put your daughter out like this, it will scar her for life? She'll be gone. You may change your mind after a while but it will too late."

The mother didn't want to hear any of it. So Dumpsey's friend brought her things to our house and stayed with us until she finished college where she received a degree in fine arts. Today, I am so proud to say, my niece is an interior architectural designer. Another one of the group went on to own and run a talent agency, while another has her own travel business.

Being thrown in with these teenage girls kept me young and full of insights about their generation. It also gave me lots of comedy material for my act—to which a good deal of my audience with teenagers of their own could relate. If you've had teens of your own, you'll probably agree that they can really get into some weird and funny stuff.

Earlier, when Dumpsey was about twelve years old, I felt it was time that she meet Delores, Rufus, and their kids, her biological mother, father, sisters, and brothers. We had talked about it for years, Dumpsey and I, and it had never been of interest to her. Although I didn't want to rush it, when I got a two-week gig in Chicago, it seemed like the right opportunity for her to spend time with them.

So Dumpsey came with me to Chicago and I flew my sister-in-law, brother, and family in from Detroit, putting everyone up at a hotel for the duration of my two-week gig. This way, I thought, they could spend quality time with Dumpsey while I worked.

Even though the initial meeting was warm and friendly, I have to admit that it made me nervous. Yes, there was a wiser part of me that knew, of course, my angel and I could never be separated. But there was another, less wise part of me who worried that somehow my baby would choose them over me.

Within a week, Deloreese asked me, "Can we go home early, Mama?"

"Why?" I said, "is something wrong?"

"Not really wrong," my daughter said, "it's just that there's nothing to do or say. I don't know these people. Mama, I just want to go home."

I was so happy to hear those words. The only bummer was that we had to stay the whole two weeks because of my gig. In the years since that meeting, I have urged Della Jr. to stay in touch with Delores and Rufus and the kids, but she has really never been given a reason to do so. And probably nothing anyone could have done would have changed the course that was charted and set from the time she was two and a half years old and placed in my arms. It was a God thing.

My son, James, who was to walk down the aisle with me and give me away, arrived that January morning in 1983 looking most handsome and proud, as if it was his own wedding day.

Daddy's wonderful children, his son, Franklin—or Frank, as he is called—and his daughter, Dominique, were very much in our hearts that day although they had chosen not to come to the wedding, feeling it would hurt their mother. Daddy and I both understood and respected their choice. Not surprisingly, Frank and Dominique are two very attractive, very talented, very intelligent, loving individuals with whom I would become closer in the years to come and whom I adore. Just as Daddy became a father to Dumpsey and James, I now consider his two babies two of my four children. And they call me their "other mother."

There were other new family members for me who were able to attend our wedding celebration, including Franklin's mother, Odessa, and his sister, Denise.

When Daddy and I first started seeing each other, he and his mother weren't in a good place in their relationship. From the time he was a teenager, they'd been at odds about his need for independence and his desire to determine the course of his own life. When I tried to talk to him about it, though he was very sweet in the way he responded, he let me know that his feelings about the situation were definite and, more or less, I should mind my own business about it. "When the time is right," he said, "I'll reestablish a relationship with Mother. But not now."

That day arose a couple of years later. We were in Detroit, for reasons I don't remember, and, without any preface, Daddy informed me he was going over to his mother's to have a talk with her. It was painful for them both, but afterwards a wonderful relationship began to bud.

A short while later, we returned to Detroit to attend Mother's retirement party. The night before the event, Daddy took me to meet Mother. She was five feet of charm, warmth, and feistiness, the cutest and—as Franklin had promised me—the most accomplished manipulator you could meet, but in the smoothest possible way. Mrs. Lett, Sr., still lived in the same house in which Daddy and Denise were raised. Pictures of the two as children were all over the house and I also got a chance to see pictures of Franklin's much-loved, much-missed father, Franklin Thomas Lett, Sr.—a strikingly handsome man who'd passed away some years earlier.

"Della," Mrs. Lett, Sr., began quietly as we found ourselves with a few minutes alone, "just so you know, I'm supportive of my son's feelings towards you. I can see you make him very happy." She went on to say that she felt no special attachment to her son's former wife, nor would she be making any waves about the divorce. She started to enumerate the reasons, in order, she said, to let me know where she stood and why.

"It's all right," I stopped her. "I don't need to know. I have no relationship with his former wife, I don't know the lady, and, to be direct about it, she has no effect on me. They were separated when I met him;

I had no involvement in their marriage, separation, or divorce, and I don't intend to become involved in the future."

She said, "In other words, damn that and look at this."

I said, "That's right."

Then and there we both smiled, just as Daddy returned to the room. He could see already that Mother and I were family. And by the time I left that day, a magnificent mother/daughter relationship had begun. At the retirement party the next day, seeing her surrounded by her employers, fellow employees, family and friends, I saw what a regal, loved woman she was to so many and, from then on out, I called her Queen Mum. Oh, she really loved that.

Queen Mum was a very active woman who belonged to thirteen different clubs, along with a special group of women who comprised a most loving sisterhood. To see the six of them together made you smile. It was the cutest thing. They looked just like Mother, dressed alike, thought alike, talked alike—just like they'd been cut by the same cookie cutter.

Mother soon became as busy—if not busier—than Dot-ski Smith as my number-one fan and top promotions/public relations representative. Whenever I was to appear in a movie, on television, or in the press, Queen Mum got on her hotline, telling everybody she knew, getting them to tell everybody else. She seemed to have an international grapevine.

What a pleasure it was to watch Daddy and his mother grow together. They loved each other so much and they were so alike in their stubborn attitudes. That's right—you heard me—I said, *stub-bb-born.* You cannot tell Daddy what to do. If you ask him, that's a different story; in that case, he'll probably do it. But just don't even attempt to tell him. Mother knew that but she couldn't resist trying to manipulate him. No go. Yet, somehow, they moved beyond that, working it out, bit by bit, long distance, through letters and phone calls. When we let her know we were going to be married and wanted her to come for the wedding, Queen Mum's response was an immediate yes.

Also attending was my new sister-in-law, Denise Lett, whom I would come to love deeply and who was to serve as an important teacher to me in the years ahead.

Our wedding celebration began with the rising of the sun on a gorgeous Southern California January day. It was gorgeous because it was the day God had given us and prepared us for, a day that had been crystal clear in my mind from the time I was young girl. The day Mama had told me about during our last talk together when I was seventeen years old was now upon me and I really did feel all of seventeen. And as part of the celebration I could feel both of my first angels, my mother, Nellie, and my father, Richard, very much in my presence, smiling down on me with all their love and joy.

Our ceremony, which Johnnie Colemon had come in to perform, was held in the Crystal Cathedral in Anaheim, California. True to its name, this architectural wonder is made primarily of glass—the sides and the roof—allowing light to fill the sanctuary from all angles and to seem almost to hang in the air among the clouds.

For the guests who wanted to travel to the cathedral with us, there was parking at the bottom of our hill with shuttles to bring them up to the house. At the appointed time, everyone climbed aboard one of the two luxury buses we had hired. As the chariots transported them to Anaheim, the celebrants were served hors d'oeuvres and champagne so they could party all the way to the wedding.

With Johnnie Colemon presiding, our ceremony was powerful, extraordinarily beautiful, yet simple. It was also symbolic. At the beginning, six children came over the altar carrying baskets of baby's breath which symbolized that we, as bride and groom, brought our love to the altar as children. The nosegay which my daughter Dumpsey carried as maid of honor was made of red roses to symbolize the love we were bringing, while my son, James, and my groom each wore a white rose in his lapel, symbolizing the purity of our love. My bridal bouquet was made of both gardenias, my favorites, and calla lilies—because although they grow from the same root ball, they grow in different directions and each is beautiful in its own direction. My gown was silver gray and all the aforementioned symbols were beaded into the skirt of the gown.

Standing at the altar, listening to Daddy speak the vows that he had written, me preparing to speak the vows that I had written, I experienced a unique floating sensation, as if he and I were floating together amid the clouds which were passing over us, being bathed in the light that was refracted through every pane of glass that surrounded us, being warmed by the love that shines from God and that shone from everyone who was physically or spiritually present sharing with us in our joy.

It was perfect. The angels above were singing, echoing the words of the vows we had written and spoken, the vows which are framed and hanging on the wall at the head of our bed to this day. These are they:

MY SOLEMN OFFERINGS

It is only because I know with certainty about my love for you that I can so freely promise

To give you love each day more than the day before

To give you the security where and when you need it

To give you freedom to decide your own path and goals

And to give you the support to achieve them

To give you both a ready ear and an open mind so that I will be sincerely interested in your thoughts and able to appreciate them

To give you my shoulder upon which to lay your problems when they weary you or to lay your head on during the intimacy of our love

Besides all these I will freely give to you, I further vow to help make life easier for everyone in your family

To make a place for you beside me so that as I climb to new heights and walk to distant horizons there will always be room for you beside me

To place no other person's welfare above yours

To grow with you in our mutual understanding and love of our God.

Given this 12th day of January in the year of our Lord 1983

FRANKLIN THOMAS LETT

Della Reese

MY VOWS TO YOU FOR ALL OF MY LIFE

I will love you without fear

I will always need you, not to fill my emptiness
  but to help me know my fullness

I will always entice you

I will never compel you

I will always embrace you

I will never encircle you

I will trust you without demanding

I will want you without restrictions

I will accept you without change

I will desire you without inhibitions

I will always behold the Christ in you and

I will always be proud to be your lady, your lover, your friend, your wife.

DELOREESE PATRICIA EARLY—*January 12, 1983*

12

If you will kindly think back to the time in the latter part of 1980, after my recuperation from the explosion of my brain, as I was getting back to the business of my life and career and creative pursuits, you may want to stick a pin there. Or, better yet, make it a road sign. And let it read, "Crossroads Just Ahead." At least, that was the kind of sign I could sense coming up along my way, preparing me for a new turn, a new journey.

In my past I had traveled triumphantly to many, many destinations. Of course there had been setbacks and disappointment. At points along the way, I'd sometimes felt unacknowledged, seeing others going to get the Grammys or the Emmys while I was doing time in a Holiday Inn off the beaten track. But now, after almost forty years as a professional, I knew who I was—a working singer, a working actress, a working entertainer. A lot of those people who got the Grammy or the Emmy in the past weren't around anymore. Meanwhile, though I'd certainly had my share of lulls and slowdowns, I continued to work. That road was ongoing, with new destinations continuing to arise, offering new opportunities for growth and learning.

Now, at this crossroads I was approaching, it was another kind of learning which compelled me, another, less determined road that beckoned. Unmarked and unpaved, it pulled me in this new uncertain direction, with no particular destination stated. And, without a need to know where it was taking me, I followed the new road, letting God lead, knowing that He would not bring me back yet again from death's door to lose myself in the wilderness.

At first, there weren't many clues at all. The only thing I knew was that I found myself telling everyone—anyone who would listen—about how the use of my principles had saved my life against all odds; how God's grace had been my sufficiency every step of the way.

Before long, I came to realize that what I had done was through only a little bit of knowledge. And if that little I did know was so effective and so powerful, I wondered, what would happen with more knowledge? I had to have more info; with that, there would be no end to how much I'd be able to do with my life, my affairs, and, yes, my world.

That was my first step in this new path: To find more knowledge. And I didn't have to look far for the right teacher. She was Johnnie Colemon, of course, in Chicago—a plane flight away. So I began studying with her by flying in every weekend that I could to attend church. I devoured every word I heard, hungering to know more, much more. Johnnie taught me and her assistant Helen Carry taught me. After meeting the Reverend Delores McMillan, the church's Bible teacher, I started hounding her with questions too.

Now I was hooked. My weekend fixes weren't enough. I wanted real classes, daily doses. Not a problem. We worked it out so that I could study via a correspondence course. In the summer, I'd be able to attend the intensive seminars and the rest of the time, I could study by mail and phone. I studied with all my might, eating those lessons as fast as they could send them, always worrying Helen Carry to no end about sending me more.

Cut to: Three years later—not long after our wedding celebration—on a Tuesday evening at my home in California where eight students and I were gathered around my dining-room table. Having just received my license to teach, I began this study group and, in effect, founded the interdenominational, interracial entity that would, in time, become a full-fledged church. Those classes were the ground floor and before long, the eight students had multiplied to seventy-five, with numbers growing every Tuesday.

Stepping into the role of teacher was not at all daunting to me. Nope, not for Ma. It was a natural move, a merging of all my interests and abilities—acting, singing, allowing others to laugh and be moved and to think about things in ways they hadn't before, and sometimes change their minds. I drew from my studies and my own life experiences. I loved teaching with every fiber of my being. When I planned a lesson, I let God guide me, letting Him choose the subject. Sometimes, after I'd made all my notes and fallen asleep, He'd wake me up in the middle of the night and have me change the lesson. I was never concerned about finding the right words or with preparing exactly what I was going to say. I knew, as it is written, that if I opened my mouth, God would give me all the right words. He would speak through me.

My students were gifts from God to me and I was learning as they learned.

One Tuesday, a woman who had been attending classes for a few weeks brought her husband. Until that night, I wasn't aware of her situation, nor had I ever met him before, but was informed then that he was dying from terminal cancer. He breathed his anger which he seemed to take out on whomever was in his path—most of all, his wife. Yet that anger, I saw, was a front, a front to cover up how afraid he was of dying.

The good news is that God had understanding ready and waiting at my class for this man. Not knowing he was going to be there, my lesson that night, in fact, was about death. He didn't change outwardly that Tuesday but from then on, he and his wife were class regulars. His anger and fear began to erode while he became sweeter and kinder to her, and to people in general.

Four months later he made his transition, as I and others choose to refer to that stage of life which is called death. The man's wife told me his was a peaceful departure for which they were prepared. "In the last four months," she said, "we got closer and more in love than we probably ever were. He went in peace. I am at peace."

She asked me to conduct the funeral services, which I agreed to do. Before traveling to the gravesite, the services were held at a church where the presiding minister refused to let me use his pulpit, telling me to stand on the floor, behind the piano. Not allowing myself to be rattled, I stood there and spoke to the mourners about the growth I'd witnessed in the deceased during the four months prior to his departure.

"He was afraid at first," I explained, "but within himself he worked out this dying thing and went peacefully, with God inside of him. He made his transition not with fear, but with a great understanding that after life there is just more life."

The mourners stopped crying and the wife was even smiling.

The pastor of the church was neither crying nor smiling. Humphing along, he marched over next to me and proclaimed, "Ashes to ashes, dust to dust. Death is to be feared. Punishment may await. Who can say whether the deceased will find eternal life in Heaven or damnation in Hell or will be lying in the dirt somewhere? What you've heard her say today may be nice to hear, but it means nothing. It is unfounded."

The wife was so angry, after the others had begun filing out, she approached the pastor and asked him not to come to the gravesite.

He was so mad, he changed colors. But he did not come to the burial.

There, as the casket was lowered, I performed the rites, committing the body to the ground. We sang and praised God for the time we had been able to spend with one of His children, celebrating the memory of this man, his life, and his passage home.

Something similar happened when one of my students asked me to conduct her wedding services. She and her fiancé made one request, that during their vows I not use the phrase " 'Til death do us part"; they preferred for me to say, "For so long as we live."

Those were the words I used. But no sooner did I pronounce them man and wife, the minister of the church where they were being married had a pronouncement to make. "Don't you want to be together 'til death do you part?" he said to the couple.

Livid, I shot back, "They will be together as long as they live."

Too late. The minister's interference caused my student to break down in tears, saying in between sobs that her wedding was spoiled.

There was a message in all of this. Clearly, my students and I needed a preacher and a church of our own.

That night I spoke to God, asking Him to choose a minister and send him to us. "We have a flock, Father," I reminded Him, "and now we're ready for someone to lead us. I will supply salary and accommodations for whatever minister you choose."

No answer came from the Father. Not that night, nor the next. So I took the matter up with Johnnie, asking if she could recommend a minister. Surely, I thought, amongst the graduates of her divinity school, there had to be a few excellent candidates.

"Buddy" (that's what we call each other), Johnnie replied, "I would if I could. But at this moment, I know of no one willing to uproot themselves and move to Los Angeles."

I put the phone down and went back to the Father. "We need a minister badly," I began this time. "Please help us find one, Father. As I said before, I'll handle the expenses." No answer. "Father, I know you hear me when I pray. Why don't you tell me what to do? We must have a minister and a church of our own." Still no answer from the Father.

For a month this continued. Then from the depth of sleep one night, I was awakened suddenly—as if someone had been shaking me to wake up. It was three A.M. Daddy was fast asleep beside me. I sat up in the bed, and said, "What is it, Father? Are you going to tell me what to do about a minister?"

God said, "Do it yourself."

"Father, you know I'm not equipped to do this. I'll take care of all the expenses and I'll do everything I can to help whoever you choose."

"I choose you do it yourself."

I mumbled and grumbled but He said nothing more.

What to do now? Wake Daddy up? No, he needed his sleep.

So, I picked up the phone and called Johnnie, reaching her at six-fifteen Chicago time, to tell her what had just happened. She listened closely. "Johnnie, what should I do now?" I asked her.

"He told you what to do, do it. He'll show you the way," she said. She paused for a beat, then told me good-bye and hung up.

Thus, I became conscious of the new road I had begun to travel. What had commenced with a personal, spiritual desire simply to know more and then to becoming a teacher in order to help others was now moving into a second stage, a place of deeper purpose and higher meaning—a place where I could serve God through a ministry, through whatever ways and means He would reveal to me. Back I went to Chicago to study at the Johnnie Colemon Institute. Four years later, I was a licensed minister. During those four years, Johnnie continued to teach and inspire me, as did my very, very much appreciated Bible teacher Delores McMillan. I had never understood nor enjoyed reading the Bible so completely. Most of all, I had never been able to really apply its teachings to my life. With her instruction, now I could, literally. Little did I know in those four years that Reverend Mac would play an even more important part in my spiritual journey later on.

After I received my license, my next step was to find a physical location for the church. This was to be a long stretch of road and a decidedly rocky one. As with the classes which I continued teaching on Tuesday nights in my living room, we now began Sunday services at my home with folding chairs set up around the indoor swimming pool. With the sun shining down through the skylight and the other windows, a softly gurgling fountain over the pool making the beautiful sounds of a natural waterfall, we found ourselves in a most lovely, spiritual setting.

One hitch: the neighbors. They were irate. How dare I have Sunday service in my home? One neighbor in particular gave us all the trouble she could, banding the others together and complaining to the zoning commission. When the inspector and a contingency of the angry neighbors tried to walk in during the middle of a service, Daddy fended them off and forced them to leave. More complaints ensued—including from that one woman who broke into my house and threatened me. So I called the members to a meeting and together we decided to find a place where we could be in peace.

Given the pattern of my own life, it shouldn't have been surprising that for the next several years, our church went on the road, moving from hotel ballroom to building space to another hotel every other Sunday, if not more often. The hotels worked well but they could only rent to us for a week, maybe two, and it proved very difficult to find a building space large enough to hold the growing number of members and guests who were attending each week.

It may be hard to believe but we found that most people would rather any business other than a church move into their area. To date, our church has probably moved more than any other church in existence. Yet in spite of that our membership always managed to increase. A blessing. And even with the ordeal of having to pack up and unpack constantly, it was also a blessing and a joy to watch the fellowship developing, everyone pitching in to help with the boxing and unboxing and carting to and fro each week.

Our first choir was a group I put together and called Brilliance, which featured the very talented singers Mary Clayton, Vermettia Royster, Reverend O. C. Smith, and Eric Strom, along with myself. Larry Farrow, my personal arranger/conductor, a terrific musician and friend, served as the arranger and conductor for Brilliance.

"Reverend Della," said one of the volunteers helping to set up for a seminar and a Brilliance concert one evening, "the person who's supposed to play piano for you today and lead the congregation sing-along hasn't shown up. And we begin in an hour."

Next thing I knew, as we were all trying to find someone capable of playing piano and singing, a tall, attractive man whom I'd seen in my classes before stepped forward and said, "I'll do it for you."

"Wonderful," I said, looking at my watch, noticing it was almost time to begin, "let's get started." I began to walk away and then I turned back and said, "Thank you, I know I've met you, but will you tell me your name again?"

"William," he said with a glorious smile, "William Knight."

William was awe-inspiring, not only as a pianist and leader of the sing-along—with his sensational, soaring voice—but also in helping me, right at my side all day that day, with whatever needed to be done. He really impressed me with his desire and his efforts to see this endeavor succeed. And, indeed, both the seminar and the concert were extremely successful, making for a very spiritual day. Everyone left shouting and praising the Lord.

After the concert was over, William continued to stay at my side, helping me take care of the last bits of packing. I was *ti-i-i-red* and he noticed. "I can see you're beat," he said. "You go on home. I'll handle the rest of this. Don't worry, I'll handle it just like I know you'd want it handled."

On the way home in the car with Daddy, I marveled at what a help William Knight had been to me. And I continue to marvel on a weekly and daily basis, because William has been at my side ever since.

Now I depend on his being there to help—and he's always there, no matter how daunting or mundane the responsibility. An angel through and through, William gives of himself with such conviction and purpose, in such thoughtful ways, I once asked him why he was that way, why he did the unselfish things he did.

William only shrugged and said, "It just seems like the right thing to do."

⟜ With membership constantly growing in my classes on Tuesday nights at home and Sunday service attendance starting to boom, I faced the very important task of doing what was required to establish ourselves as a nonprofit organization. Not only did I not know nothin' 'bout how to do that, I didn't know no one who did. But what I did know, was that God would show me the way—by whichever means He chose to show me.

These were some of my thoughts as I arrived home one Tuesday afternoon around three in the afternoon and went out to get the mail. That was when I noticed an unfamiliar car parked across the street. This was a strange situation. As I mentioned before, I live in a very private neighborhood, off the beaten track, up a windy dead-end road that doesn't get a lot of traffic. Then again, every once in a while people drive up and park for a few minutes to take a look at the view. So, when I saw this car and these two unfamiliar ladies sitting in it, I didn't think it was a big deal.

At about six o'clock I go out to sign for a package delivery and see this car with the two ladies still sitting there. Well. I know the view is beautiful, but not to look at for three hours. So finally, I walk over to the driver side window, which the lady rolls down, as I say, "Can I help you ladies?"

In a pleasant, foreign accent, the lady at the wheel explained, "We're just waiting on the time for class. We drove today from Huntington Beach and we didn't want to get lost."

"You're not lost," I assured them with a smile. Huntington Beach was at the most a two-hour drive. They had to have left around one P.M. to make an eight o'clock class.

The other lady said, "This is where Della Reese's class is, isn't it?" Before I could answer, she said, "Are you Della Reese?"

"Yes I am," I said, and invited them in to wait with me until class began.

As we walked inside, the lady with the accent told me that she had attended an Easter Service I had done in Huntington Beach for fellow minister Peggy Bassett, in which I had mentioned my classes. As we talked further, this lady, who introduced herself as Pat Nilsson, let me know that she was from Denmark. Charming, a little snuggle of a thing, Pat eventually fell prey to my name-changing habit. We all soon started calling her the Danish Dumpling.

She and her friend loved the class and returned the following week. And the next. That Tuesday, I made an announcement that I needed to find someone well-versed in dealing with legal documents, particularly those related to nonprofit organizations and information about how and where to apply for the documents, or, if anyone knew of any companies which specialized in this area.

Everyone shook their heads, unable to make any suggestions. Everyone that is, except for Pat Nilsson, who said, "I know how to do these things," going on to say that she did them for her chapter of Al-Anon, the support organization for families of members who are in Alcoholics Anonymous and Narcotics Anonymous.

The next thing I knew, Pat came in and took over the handling of all our business documents, their registration, the filing necessary to make us a nonprofit organization, and all matters which needed to be addressed to make us a legitimate business operating in accordance with the laws of nonprofit.

The church was now an official entity which we named Understanding Principles for Better Living. The name is what it is because we believe that God wants only the best for all of us and that there are principles to learn so that we can thrive in partnership with God. UP is what we call the church for short, because that is the way we're going—UP, UP in spirituality, in truth which will lift us up in attitude, in faith, in joy, love, peace, health, harmony, and abundance. And, we believe, this movement UP is what Jesus came to show us how to obtain, as it is written, "I have come so that they may have life and that more abundantly."

Pat Nilsson, the darling Danish Dumpling, was responsible for the paperwork that got us started and she continued to handle these duties for two years. Never charged me a dime for it. Had she not decided to move to North Carolina to help take care of her grandchildren there, Pat probably would still be handling these matters today.

In the meantime, my tireless helper, William, had trained as a teacher and was on his way to becoming a minister. At one point, he was the choir director while I was the choir soloist; at another time, it was the reverse. We were both the janitors and the chair-setter-uppers and the preachers and the teachers all at once. We dealt with the whole human experience, teaching that you can do something about your life to make it the way you want it to be, the way God designed you to be: the winner, the victor, and not the victim.

We were sometimes overwhelmed but we held it together and despite our frequent moves, the congregation continued still to grow and grow with people coming from everywhere because lives were being changed for the better.

⌐⌐ In midsummer of 1990, William and I were going over Sunday service priorities, class instruction and organization, and all the many things he would be handling in my absence. To keep an active license as a minister, I was heading back for a five-day intensive seminar at the Johnnie Colemon Institute in Chicago, where I was required to return every two years.

"You know, William . . ." I began, preparing to say something about the fact that we really needed a full-time individual to organize the classes and handle a lot of front office type responsibilities important for a church to run smoothly.

Before I could finish my sentence, William waved to me to say he didn't need to hear what it was, saying, "Yes, Della, I do know. I agree." Besides, he added, neither he nor I were really skilled or experienced in that area.

"And, even if we were," I said, "we're not stay-in-the-office-all-day people."

"No we're not," he echoed. "Neither of us are sit-down-for-long-meetings people, either."

"But I don't want someone who is only an organizer. I want some-one who understands how to structure and schedule classes and events so that they unfold with continuity and go hand in hand with the lessons we're teaching on Sunday morning."

"You're talking about someone who's also a teacher."

"Yep, that's right." Reminding him of a recent conversation about the need for our people to study and understand the Bible, I added, "A Bible teacher."

We were both quiet, not knowing where to even begin looking. Then, a big smile came over my face as the perfect person came to mind.

As soon as I arrived in Chicago at the Institute, I sought that perfect person out—Reverend Delores McMillan. "Reverend Mac," I asked her, "how would you like to come to Los Angeles and help me organize the most spiritually effective church in L.A.?"

She looked at me so strangely and thought for a moment and said, "For real?"

I said, "For really real."

Reverend Mac said, "Let me think about it."

"I'll be here for five days. After that we leave. So you have five days to think about it."

Hers were among the classes I attended over the next days and as I sat in class listening to her teaching—so honest, so simple, and so full of truth information—I knew more than ever that I just had to have her at Understanding Principles.

But I couldn't force the situation. The decision had to be hers. On the last night before I was to leave, since she had yet to say anything, I cor-nered her and asked again if she was interested.

"I've thought about it," Reverend Mac said, "and I think I would like to do it. But, remember, I work for Johnnie and she has my undying loy-alty and I'm not sure if she would let me go or not. Or even how she would feel about it."

"Does that mean that if Reverend Colemon gave her approval, you'd want to come to L.A.?"

She smiled shyly and said, "I think it would be nice."

When I talked to Johnnie that night on the phone, her first response was, "Della, you're asking for my best Bible teacher."

"I know," I said, "but she's who we need. I need for my people to have an understanding of the Bible and its use to us today and I need an organizer and I just know Delores is the perfect one for us."

Johnnie's voice softened as she explained, "Even if I agreed, there remains the question of whether she would really want to uproot her life. Delores is married. She has her own home here. She has lived here for years. She is very much a part of her community. And she has to consider her husband's needs and whether or not he will agree to the move."

Johnnie's concern was well-founded. I understood and thanked her for her words. Then, I hung up the phone and I did a Nellie. That's right, I turned it over to God and accepted that it was already done.

Unbeknownst to Johnnie or to me at that time, Reverend Mac's marriage was over and she had been looking for a decent way to leave it. The cleanest break, she knew, would be to leave Chicago. So, ultimately, she saw that the opportunity to come to Los Angeles might really be perfect for her. After further conversation, I was able to convince her to come for a month to see how she liked it. I put my people at her disposal and left her to experience whatever she felt. Everyone at the church was so loving and appreciative of the knowledge she was offering, she saw clearly how much she was needed. Finally, before she left to go back to Chicago, Reverend Mac told me her decision, saying matter-of-factly, "I'm going back to Chicago to get packed up and coming back as fast as I can. To stay." And so she did.

Was Reverend Delores MacMillan sent as an angel? You better believe it. Not just as my angel but as *ever-ry-body's* at Understanding Principles. With her arrival, I felt wonderful, at last, about the church being fully prepared for the needs of the people. We still had yet to find a location for our permanent home—moving every few weeks, or every few months, or every year. But even though it was so hard for people to find us, those who needed to come were led to us. They came, they learned, they experienced miracles.

Was it extraordinary that they experienced the miraculous? Well, that depends on your interpretation of miracles. I believe that when God supplies your every need or heals you or sends you angels or speaks to you from a burning bush, that's not a miracle. That's what God does all the time; that's His normal mean. The miracle takes place when you realize that you can ask for what you need and know without reservation that He will supply what you have asked for. Miracles are about verbs— the realizing, the asking, the knowing. You see, a miracle is not what God does, a miracle is what you do that allows His blessings to flow to you. A miracle is when you transform the way you think and then transform your life; when you recognize God inside yourself; when you get back in touch with God.

As a teacher, it thrilled me beyond description to witness the transformations of those who were learning the same principles that had guided me in my life's journey.

There was a woman who had been living in cardboard boxes on the street, with her three children. A friend brought her to a service and the lesson that day was about raising your consciousness, raising it from a place of *This is the way it is* to a place of *I can change my mind and change my life*. The woman began taking classes and began to raise her consciousness. She also began to study subjects that would enable her to go back to the working world and soon she applied for the kind of job she'd once thought was far out of her reach. She not only got the job, but both she and her employers found that she was good at it. Promotions came rapidly. Today this same woman drives a late-model Mercedes, owns a nine-room home with a swimming pool, and has happy, healthy children who are doing great in school. All of them, with her success, are living large. The abundance she has claimed for herself and her family isn't the miracle. The miracle came at the moment that the hopelessness to which she had been reduced was replaced by her own realization that she was in charge, that she had the choice to stay in the mud hole or stand up. She stood up and God helped her walk.

Then there was J.Y., a man who became an UP member and moved me very much with the story of his overcomings. Before he came to church, various friends and acquaintances had been telling him about it but he could never seem to find where we were. At that time, he said, he had been suffering for so long from such severe depression that the doctors were in fear for his life. They had tried every possible kind of medication for his depression but nothing worked. Finally, J.Y. said, he went to the doctor one Friday afternoon to ask for something stronger. Afraid to prescribe anything stronger than what J.Y. had already tried, the doctor chose only to give him a little something that might help him go to sleep.

J.Y. said he went outside and sat in his car, outside the doctor's office, and he told himself, *I can't make another day like this. I'll either have to be healed of this today or I'll have to kill myself.* When he arrived home that day, he found on his doorstep one of those free neighborhood newspapers that lists local news and happenings. On the front page was my picture and an article about Understanding Principles for Better Living and where it was going to be that Sunday. J.Y. said he was sure that article was what kept him from killing himself that day and the next because the pills the doctor gave him weren't effective whatsoever, not even for getting some sleep. He made it to Sunday morning, came to church, and never stopped coming.

When I asked J.Y. how he had benefited, he said, first of all, his thinking changed. His feelings of doom and despair melted away; from that day on he never had any more thoughts about killing himself, never. As his thinking changed, so did his life. He turned his job, which he used to dread, into a position he was proud of and one that his employers could not do without. He said he had grown successful in every way—financially, emotionally, and mentally.

The spiritual key he found that first Sunday was hearing me say that none of us have to be the victims, we can all be the victors. A basic principle. Yes, evil deeds and evil thoughts may plague us, but only if we invite or allow them into our mind. From that, J.Y. said, he realized he had been causing his suffering; he had been doing it to himself. The words he heard helped. In fact, J.Y. has said that he's sure he would be dead today if not for the church. But the real miracle was his own powerful realization, his change of mind. It opened the door for him and he never looked back.

Understanding Principles had now been a church on the road a good long while. We rented one beautiful space that became a tour-guide spot for its owner. Not because it was a world-famous location, but because the owner felt he would become world-famous by showing off this marvelous piece of property he owned—during church service. That was really nice. Then we rented from a man who turned out to be certifiably insane, causing us to confront the many trials and tribulations which come from dealing with the insane. We were subjected to challenges from neighborhood block organizations, city councils, and courts of law. And yet, in spite of it all, by using our principles, the people hung together and we grew stronger still.

At last, we found an ideal situation for the church: an office building with rooms for administrative offices, classrooms, and a large meeting hall that was able to contain our Sunday services for a while. When we outgrew it, we kept that building for our offices and classes, and moved Sunday services to a nearby location that has—Thank you, Lord—worked out wonderfully. *Ha-a-a-ppi-ness-sss!!!*

At this writing, we have so many new members and guests attending every week, we know it will be moving time again soon. This time, with money we've been raising for an Understanding Principles for Better Living building fund, we have asked the Father to lead us to a permanent location where we will be able to purchase or build our own building. Thanks in this area must go to Daddy, whose business expertise helped organize and ignite the building fund effort and whose many talents have been lovingly offered in the development of UP.

There are many more gifted individuals whose hands and love have helped to build our spiritual house. One of our newer angels is Assistant

Minister Dr. Charles Brown. During the past few years as my television schedule took me away more frequently, Reverend Knight was so busy handling both his weekly duties as well as mine that we needed someone to take over his areas. One day at the office, an ideal candidate dropped by. It was Dr. Brown, with whom I was acquainted through several mutual friends. Dr. Brown has a long, laureled background in religious studies, including a degree in world religion, a degree in homeopathy from studies in Eastern religions, and a degree in Judaic studies. He has traveled the world living and studying different religions and their various spiritual and cultural practices, in places such as Africa where he worked with the nomadic Masai; in India where he studied Hinduism; in Israel where he lived and learned the practices of Judaism, traveling also with the nomadic Bedouins; studying Islam in the Arabic-speaking countries; living in various countries in Eastern Asia to study Buddhism; along with studying the varying sects and religious practices elsewhere. It is fascinating to hear him speak of his participation in large spiritual processions—in places like Jerusalem, Nepal, Madras, Tibet, in the cathedrals of Russia, Italy, France, and elsewhere. And all of that is only for starters.

When the different holidays and festivals occur, Dr. Brown often acknowledges them in our services, offering prayers for the occasion, explaining to the rest of the congregation the meaning behind the holiday or the rituals attached to it. In this way, all of us at UP broaden our spiritual understanding and continue to live up to the creed we voice each Sunday when we pray:

> *I am one with God;*
> *I am one with all men;*
> *I am one with all life.*

The Understanding Principles congregation truly is a multicultural, multi-everything family. What a joy it is to look around the room on Sundays and see what one visitor to UP described as the way all of America should look. Coming together as one are blacks, whites, Latinos, Asians, all ethnicities, all ages, people from all kinds of religious, spiritual and economic backgrounds. There are straights and gays. There are CEOs and street sweepers. There are newborn babies and ninety-year-olds. There is no judgment, no exclusion. There is acceptance, there is love.

We come together in celebration. We have fun. We have the best house band and the best choir in captivity. We sing, clap, dance, hug. We remember the saying which says that the reason angels can fly is that they take themselves lightly. We *la-a-a-a-u-gh*. And we cry. We lift our voices to the spirit; we join together in silence and meditation. Some come needing a change, looking for healing, transformation, and for lessons in how to overcome the forces that hold them back. Others come to share their healings, transformations, and overcomings, to continue their learning, to praise and thank God and His everlasting goodness.

One of the aspects that I truly love about our fellowship is that so many of our lessons come from the pew as much as they do from the pulpit. Every time someone uses principles to empower themselves, the rest of us learn.

To illustrate my point, let me tell you about Miss Mae. You are looking at one of the sweetest, prettiest, daintiest, most elegant little ladies in the world. Upward in years, Miss Mae first came to church walking with the help of a cane. She needed it to walk and after using it for seven years, understandably, her back and shoulders had rounded over from the leaning. She'd been coming to church for a while when she attended a seminar I gave about healing yourself. After it was over, she went home and began to apply some of the principles she'd learned. Then, one Sunday when I was in my office with William going over paperwork before services, Miss Mae stopped in to say hello.

I gave her a quick hug and turned my attention back to the paperwork.

Miss Mae said, "Do you notice anything different?"

I looked up. "Yes, I do," I said, "what is it? Why, it's your hair, isn't it? You got a pretty new hairdo, right?"

"No." She smiled.

"Oh, that's a new dress. It's awfully pretty."

"No."

"It's that opal you're wearing, I've never seen it before. It's beautiful."

"No."

William, who'd been quietly listening to this exchange, said, "I know what it is. Miss Mae, you don't have your cane and you're not holding on to anything."

"That's right," she said proudly, her body straight as a tree.

I jumped up and hugged her. She told me that a few nights earlier she had a dream that she was running up this hill without her cane. Someone called to her from below, "You left your cane." And in her dream she said, "I'm never comin' back for it. I don't need it," just as she reached the top of the hill.

That was some years ago and she has never needed that cane again.

Then there is the miracle of baby Katherine born to Mary and Carl. This is how Carl tells about his changes:

> *I am 56 years old. I left Flint, Michigan, 3 years ago to find a new life with God as my inspiration. My life in Michigan had many painful memories, my 18-year-old son was killed & my brother and sister-in-law were murdered. I knew no one in L.A. I was led to UP and then God put Mary in my life. She so wanted to be a mother but all the doctors said after 7 operations that it could not be. They were wrong. God blessed us with Mary conceiving. Then Della & UP family prayed and sent healing prayer to guide us thru this. Doctors were saying Mary would have to be in bed for the last 2 months & would be in much pain. Della said let's give this over to God.*
>
> *Well, Mary had no pain and we have an angel child Katherine. Della and our UP family have given us a real family with the Lord as the head . . .*

Mary and Carl brought baby Katherine to church when she was four days old. There was not a dry eye in the house. To know of the tragedies that had preceded Carl's meeting Mary is to understand his overcoming, his miracle; and to know that Mary worked this out just between her and God to defy all the doctors' predictions is to know her miracle. To look at this beautiful, perfect baby Katherine is to behold God's absolute love.

A young man who had been attending Sunday services regularly had a good friend who was a much-sought-after studio musician, a drummer. Although this friend suffered from multiple sclerosis, he had overcome the disease to maintain his musical/professional abilities. That in itself is a major overcoming, given that M.S. can create shaking and nervous sensations in the limbs and that drumming is about keeping a steady rhythm. However, with his illness, the drummer had used morphine and had then become addicted to heroin. The problem had been going on for quite some time when the drummer's friend brought him to a Sunday service. For the drummer who had tried everything to kick his habit, without success, a lesson was waiting that day about letting go and letting God. That day, he turned his burden over to God, knowing and accepting right then, right there, that he was free. And, his friend tells me, he has been drug-free ever since.

That same Sunday, someone else who was brought by a friend changed her mind by choosing to let go. A young woman who for ten years had been trying unsuccessfully to get her recording career off the ground, she was ready to give up hope. But that day, as she stood and heard herself singing with the congregation and the choir, she looked up, reached her arms to God and said, "I give it up to You, Lord." Whether that meant being sent the right messengers to help in her singing career or being guided to move on to some other pursuit, she accepted that God would respond and guide her in whichever way was best for her. Two days later she was signed to a record deal by Sony Records.

One of my more dramatic transformations and overcomings came a few years ago. For a good deal of my younger life I had battled weight gain and then finally accepted myself as I was, whatever size that happened to be. All that frenzy of dieting and exercise seemed to only make me heavier so I quit the worrying. Then, one day as I stepped out of the shower, I literally saw my body. I didn't look at my face in the mirror; I didn't look at myself to dry off. I looked at my physical reality and what I saw shocked me: all this stuff hanging off my body. I really, really, really-really-really SAW it.

And right there I began to pray. I said, "Father, this is not my body. I don't want this body. I want my body back. And I claim my right to have my body back." There were several things about which I was not conscious that were standing in my way to impede my progress to have my body back. Number one, I did not like water. If I drank water, I would disguise the taste with sweetening or fruit. Or I would drink soda pop with ice melted in it. Anything not to drink plain pure water. The other thing was this nighttime habit I had of getting in bed with a dish of Häagen-Dazs Butter Pecan ice cream. But after I finished the ice cream, I didn't like the taste it left. So I would eat potato chips. But I didn't like the taste they left. So I would drink a soda pop before brushing my teeth. Every night.

After I saw my body this day in the bathroom and after I prayed this prayer, I became so thirsty that I went to bed that night and every night to follow with a pitcher of water beside my bed that I woke up and drank throughout the night. I drank water all day long. I was never without one of those larger mountain-spring-water bottles. All I wanted was water, water, water. And I could still eat butter pecan ice cream but after two spoonfuls, if I tried to put another spoonful in my mouth I felt that I would be sick. Same with potato chips. I could have a handful of potato chips and not be able to eat any more—where I used to eat the whole seventy-nine-cent bag.

My diet changed of its own self. My desires changed. I used to love to go to Neiman Marcus in Beverly Hills and buy a box of chocolate turtles and eat them all on the way home. But I no longer had the desire. To this day, I can't eat a lot, though I eat well. Or, as the saying goes, I don't live to eat, I eat to live. I lost eighty-two pounds. Never dieted, never exercised other than my normal daily activity. This was a healing that came about the moment I saw my body and prayed the prayer and accepted God to help me.

Spiritual healing does not always mean a physical healing of the body. Sometimes healing is a release of the physical body. One of the teachers who brought me to this awareness was Dioñ, my much-loved, longtime hairdresser, who—you may recall—was the son of my assistant, Ron.

Dioñ, a sparkling jewel of a person, who was gay, became afflicted by AIDS, this horrendous plague that has ravaged and destroyed the lives of far, far too many of our people throughout the world. It is one thing to know in one's heart and mind that death is never the end of life; but it is another thing altogether to watch any loved one suffer in unspeakable pain and to watch their bodies deteriorate, disappear, and shut down as this virus causes them to do.

Dioñ and I and the many, many who loved him did serious work together, praying for his healing. Dioñ was determined not to be a victim, but to overcome the affliction. Towards the end, I went to visit him in the hospital, to offer him some comfort and prayer. And there, in his bed, as he looked at me through his pain, through the debilitation of his body, his spirit was shining as bright as the most powerful beacon and he told me he had been healed. He had overcome. He was not a victim. Dioñ was prepared to let his body die, knowing and trusting that his soul was something that could never be destroyed.

"I'm not worried, Mama," Dioñ said. "I'm in God's hands. I know wherever I am and wherever I go, He will take care of me." He smiled at me in love and in peace, as if to say, *I'll miss you, but I'll see ya when you get there.*

Two days later Dioñ made his transition.

⟋⟍ Three individuals who taught me the most about the life passage that is called death were Daddy and his sister and his mother.

After Daddy and I were married, Queen Mum remained living in

Detroit where her longtime girlfriends and relatives looked after her with love and caring. My sister-in-law, Denise, was living at that time in Colorado. Then, in the late eighties Denise was diagnosed with ameliodousis, a rare, incurable disease. It is a condition in which excess protein is deposited around the tongue and the throat and eventually around the heart and internal organs, which finally killed Denise.

This period was the one in which I got to know her and I found Denise Lett to be both a most exceptional human and a marvelous teacher. It was Denise who really taught me how to die. Throughout the process, she maintained the greatest attitude possible. She made all the arrangements, planning for the care and continued education of her four children, setting up trust funds, and liquidating her assets. She gave away all of her personal belongings so that no one would have to sort through and clean up the leavings of her life.

Denise never gave up hope. Every day, she deepened her relationship with God, and then, in great peace—the kind that surpasses all human understanding—she left us and went home to Him.

Up until that time, Daddy and Queen Mum had been slowly improving their relationship. With Denise gone, the two realized more than ever their need for one another and thus became even closer.

Mother sold her house on the West Side and moved to an apartment on the far East Side, facing the Detroit River. She hadn't lived there long when she suffered a heart attack and Daddy flew immediately to her side. Although she was soon out of danger, he convinced her to move to Los Angeles where he could be close enough to be there for her when she was in need. This meant leaving her loving group of friends but Queen Mum agreed that the Detroit winters were too harsh for her condition. Independent and feisty as she was, she allowed Daddy to handle the details, packing up her things, closing down her apartment, and bringing her home to our house in Los Angeles where she stayed for almost a year.

"Queen Mum," I told her when she announced it was time to get her own place, "you are welcome to stay with us forever."

"I know," she said, persuasively, "but you can't have two cooks in one kitchen. Besides, I want my own place."

So Daddy found her a place of her own and for the next two and a half years, son and mother got tighter and tighter—a great pleasure for me to witness.

I remember vividly how she took my hands one day and looked at me with the brightest of eyes, saying, "I have never seen Frank so happy. I love you for the joy you've brought him and for the love you two share."

I really loved that. I loved what she taught me by the example she led of always being actively involved in things she cared about, demonstrating a powerful lesson—that you could live a long time and not get old.

Queen Mum became a member of Understanding Principles and everyone there loved her so much they named her First Mother of our church. She baked her fantastic cakes and cookies and sold them on Sundays to raise money for UP's various endeavors, including the choir, her favorite group within the church. Of course, the choir members loved Queen Mum the same way. She never missed one of their refresher rehearsals on Sunday mornings before services.

She remained active in spite of a few serious hospital stays. Queen Mum was a very strong lady.

In 1993, Daddy and I took off for an ocean cruise, looking forward to much needed rest and relaxation. While we were at sea, Queen Mum was stricken. Friends and doctors at the hospital urged her to let them contact us on the boat but Mother refused, saying we worked so hard we deserved to enjoy our vacation uninterrupted. She knew her physical body was in decline but she was determined to hold on to life until she could see her son one more time.

We arrived home to the news that she was in the hospital but doing better and Daddy was able to spend the next several days with her, during which Queen Mum followed Denise's example, preparing for all the arrangements in the event of her death. But she never gave up. She lived in expectancy and she expected to live. And when the doctors offered cautious optimism and said she could go home the next day, Mother, independent as always, in charge as always, got busy making plans for her caretaking when she got back to her place. Late that night, as she was writing out a grocery list so no one would have to concern themselves wondering what she needed, Queen Mum passed away.

Daddy received the call shortly after two in the morning. It was October 26, 1993. He woke me gently. He wore a solemn but peaceful expression as he said softly, "Mother is gone. She has made her transition."

We embraced. He held me as I cried. Then he said he was going on to the hospital to begin taking care of her affairs. I got out of bed, dressed quickly, and went with him, the two of us holding hands tightly as we drove into the foggy night.

The way in which Daddy dealt with every aspect of his mother's leaving moved me deeply. He had Mother cremated, as per her wishes, and together we, our family and friends, boarded a boat large enough to hold us all and took her out to pour her ashes on the ocean. The choir sang all the way, as we sailed out. It was a magnificent day. With choir members' voices and our own reverberating across the water, sea birds glided through the sky above us, a throng of Jet Skis and their riders jumped alongside the boat, doing fanciful tricks, hopping through and over the wake behind the boat, as if they were performing a choreographed dance for the occasion.

When we came to a serene spot, the captain laid anchor and we poured Queen Mum's ashes upon the water and as we did, we watched the sea turn a wondrous, iridescent color, almost a turquoise that glowed and sparkled with white, bright light. And all at once, these seals jumped from out of the turquoise sea, straight up into the air where they fluttered their fins and then jumped back down, swimming deeper and deeper below the surface until they disappeared from sight, along with the last of the shining particles of Mother's ashes.

The choir sang all the way back in to our landing. When we got off, the captain told us he had made that trip many times for other burials at sea but never had he seen such a joyous funeral nor such a good time.

∽⟶ Throughout all the major events that had taken place in my life and in Daddy's—the growth of the church, the ups and downs of our respective careers, the daily doings and concerns of family and friends— we were also working all the while on our marriage, a centerpiece of our lives.

In 1993 we reached the milestone of our ten-year wedding anniversary. Although it seemed we'd known each other for lifetimes, we still really felt like newlyweds. To mark this event, we decided to make new commitments to one another and new goals for the next ten years of our marriage. Unlike our wedding ceremony, we chose to renew our vows by having a few friends over. During our gathering, Johnnie Colemon and some of the other ministers from Christ Universal Temple placed a conference call to us from Chicago and Johnnie did a prayer and blessing service. We wrote new vows for this particular passage. Here are Daddy's to me:

My Offering to You

As two individuals, we came together with only a birthplace and a belief in God in common.

But, as we rooted ourselves more deeply in that belief in God, we became as one . . . as the stem and the flower are one.

We gave away our individual pursuits for a higher common purpose, that of joining two lives together on a shared and upward path.

And as we continue on this journey, I rededicate my life to you:

I Will be the environment around you that provides for your emotional comfort, satisfies your physical needs, guarantees you financial security, and supplies you with intellectual stimulation.

I Will give to you the freedom, to do whatever you need to do.

I Will accept your freedom, without question, without fear.

I Will share with you the glories and accomplishments of my life.

I Will revel in the glories and successes of your life.

I Will offer to you the understanding, help and solace that you need in the building of your church.

I Will gladly participate in the little and the big of your life.

But above all these, I Will love you endlessly.

These offerings I make to you as we make more complete our union in the eyes of God.

The following are mine to Daddy:

My Vows

I have loved you without fear and you have helped me to know my fullness.

You have allowed me to entice you, never needing to compel you.

Speaking from the security of your actions I will continue to trust you without demanding and want you without restrictions.

I accept you and the excitement your dreams cause every day.

I desire you, without inhibitions.

I Will continue always to behold that beautiful piece of Christ living inside of you.

Each day and each moment therein, I Am more than proud to be your lady, your lover, your friend, and your wife.

Since living in your love, I have grown into the woman I always knew I was and wanted to be.

Since living in your love, I have seen myself expand in grace, charm, courage, understanding, nurturing, compromising with compassion.

I offer you now not the same woman that you married ten years ago.

The woman I offer you today has lived in, tested and found true love daily and nightly for ten years.

I Am warmer and more exciting and yet child-like in my maturity.

I Am now your best friend.

I Am now a lover better trained to fulfill your needs and I know from experience how it feels to be loved and cared for and comforted and honored and respected, taught by a Rhodes Scholar.

I have shared laughter that is heartfelt and hearty.

I have slept in the love of one day and awakened in the new love each new day.

I Am of the definite opinion that you will find me more to your loving than when you first married me ten years ago for you have helped reshape me to your specific design.

So here I Am, baby:

Signed by the pen of eternity, sealed by your love, delivered to you by God.

I Am yours and I will love you until there is no love left in this universe which must really be the end of all time.

13

Remember Nellie's mind-reading habit? You may recall my mentioning that sometimes I have it too. Right now is one of those times and I'm pretty sure I can tell what you're thinking at this moment. You're thinking that you've heard about my journeys, you've heard about my lessons, you've heard how I became a singer, an actress, a teacher, a minister, and a blissfully married woman, mother and grandmother. You're thinking that you've heard a lot about all the angels that were sent to me. What you want to know now is how I became an angel. Am I correct? *Absotively, posolutely.* Hello!

Well, it's a *lo-o-o-ong* story that begins with something that may not surprise you. Yes—you are exactly right again—it was a God thing. You probably recall that back in the early eighties, after my brain exploded and after my surgeries, I went through a recuperation period where I was enjoying the delights of sleep, peace, and rest. In those dreamy, meditative, prayerful states I had each morning before opening my eyes, I started to envision new avenues for my work as an actress and singer. The image I began to dream for myself was based on Molly Goldberg, the advice giver I used to love hearing on the radio who was Jewish, wise, loving, and funny, and who helped people solve their problems. The character I was dreaming of in my bed was like a cross between Molly Goldberg and Nellie Early. I dreamt about her so much, even creating scenes with dialogue, I think God must have decided to collaborate and do some creating of his own.

In the meantime, after getting back on my feet and starting off on my spiritual journey, the matter of my livelihood became a priority. Unworried, I asked for the Father to provide work, knowing that He would deliver just what I needed.

Although the seventies had seen my TV acting work really take off, there were usually only three types I was ever considered for—the singer, the aunt, or the mother/neighbor type. God knew how much I wanted to branch out of those three categories and show what else I could do as an actress. And, of course, that's what manifested: a series regular role on a wonderful comedy called *It Takes Two* in which I played a judge, a real change of pace. The show followed the lives of the Quinn family, which included the father, a surgeon, played by Richard Crenna; the mother, an assistant district attorney, played by Patty Duke; and the two Quinn kids were played by Helen Hunt and Anthony Edwards. A stellar cast it was and a loving group of people. My role as judge and friend to Patty Duke's character was enjoyable and different from the kind of stuff I had been doing. But after only a few episodes ABC decided to drop the show. I wasn't very happy with the network for doing that.

But God kept the pump pumping as singing and acting opportunities continued to come my way, through all channels—live performance, stage work, television musical variety shows, and guest star shots on episodic shows and sitcoms. The one area I really wanted to do more of was feature films. And I began to see myself doing movies where I was holding my own with top talent in really juicy acting parts. Something so on the other side of the spectrum from what I usually did, no one would say I was just playing myself. I wanted to be able to say, "You see, that's not me. I am an actress."

Well, let me tell you. When it comes to our wants and needs, God is so bountiful, so generous, so extravagant. He really takes us at our literal word.

A few years later, I got just the part. Thanks to Eddie Murphy, I landed the role of a trash-talking, ass-kicking, law-breaking madam in *Harlem Nights,* which Eddie wrote, directed, and starred in. When I went to read for the part, it was so different from what I'd been doing, none of the producers or casting people wanted me. But Eddie Murphy—who is undoubtedly one of the great comic geniuses of our time and a loving young man to me—insisted no one could play the role but Della Reese. It was exactly what I had prayed for. When the movie was released in 1989, however, not only did no one suggest that I was playing myself, certain people in the religious community were outraged that a minister of my reputation would play a role like that. Even Johnnie Colemon, who stood by my side during the uproar, wasn't happy about it. My answer was simple, "That's not me. I am an actress."

This wasn't quite the context I'd hoped for. Nor was the controversy what I'd hoped for. Still, I wasn't upset by the criticism and am to this day very proud of the movie and my work in it.

As I moved into the nineties, approaching my sixtieth birthday, not far from the traditional age of retirement, but light years away from when I wanted to retire, my dreams and goals for work began to shift. It wasn't so important anymore to prove what I could do as an actress. I had done that. What I wanted now was simpler and it was more in sync with what motivated me as a teacher and minister. I didn't want to play sidekicks or supporting characters; I wanted to play leading roles in stories that mattered, in stories that touched people's lives. Stage, TV, movies, the whole deal.

Are you getting the drift here? I think you are.

Once I got clear about my goals, I found that the seeds for their fulfillment were already being planted. In fact, they were being planted right on the set of *Harlem Nights*. First of all, it was such a pleasure to act with the likes of Eddie Murphy, and the other stars, including Redd Foxx and Richard Pryor. The laughter never stopped. One day in particular, while shooting a scene around a meeting table, in between takes, those off-camera zingers and one-liners were really flying.

They started when Redd referred to our prop mistress, whose name was Renita, by asking, "Where is that broad?"

I say, "Excuse me? The woman has a name. Her name is Renita."

Redd says, "Where is that broad, Renuzit?"

"Redd, that is the name of a room deodorant. Her name is Renita."

"Oh, Renita, Renuzit—what difference does it make?"

I say, "Then I can call you chartreuse and magenta, though your name is Redd. What difference does it make?"

Now Richard Pryor, signifier that he is, starts goading Redd: "Man, you gonna let the woman talk to you that way?"

I say, "I'll talk any way I like."

Richard says, "Mmmmm, mmmmmm . . ."

And before we know it, the three of us are capping each other, topping line for line with sarcasm and feigned disgust, having the best time.

Eddie laughed so hard he could barely direct the rest of the scene. "This is a damn TV show," he said, and when he went back to his trailer during a break, he wrote it down. And that became a pilot for the TV show Eddie created for Redd and me called *Royal Family*, which went on the air two years later.

This was a literal interpretation of that which I had desired. Yes, it was a lead role and the stories which dealt with the day-to-day struggles of a black family who used humor and love to overcome touched the lives of many, many viewers. In its 1991–92 debut season, the show was off to a promising start. There was one nagging problem. One of the producers was extremely antagonistic towards Redd. It apparently began when Redd didn't like one of the lines the producer had written for an episode. The producer insisted that Redd say it; Redd adamantly refused.

Let me say this. Redd Foxx had come up the hard way, making dimes as a teenager doing comedy stand-up on street corners. An admirable human being who gave back from his success to other young people of all colors, Redd ran a club for struggling comedians and performers to help them get their start; he went to prisons and did shows he paid for out of his own pocket. As I understand it, no other performer has worked in the prisons to the extent Redd Foxx did. He knew about pain and struggle. And he knew about what was funny and what wasn't. He was the author of an acclaimed book on humor, a veteran of a long-running hit TV show, *Sanford and Son,* and he had earned a level of respect that this producer was not giving him.

One morning when we were rehearsing a scene and Redd was busy in another part of the studio doing an interview for one of the entertainment TV shows, this producer pulled him out of his interview to come to the rehearsal for his part which was simply to walk through the scene and mug at the camera. Redd was irate. Rightfully so. Any stand-in could have done that for him. And everyone knew it. He returned to his interview and a short while later came back to the rehearsal for the next scene he was in. Agitated as he was, he was a professional and got down to work right away. At the beginning of his line he looked as if he was going to fall down and then he grabbed onto a chair. For a few seconds we all thought it was some kind of pratfall, a typical Redd Foxx bit. Not so. In the next instant, he hit the floor. It was a heart attack. I ran to his side and held him in my arms praying until the studio medics arrived. They worked on reviving him but when the hospital paramedics came and got him into the ambulance, they pronounced him dead. Mrs. Foxx, who was there, and the rest of our extended family on the show, began to pray, all of us getting into our cars and rushing with the ambulance to the hospital. When we arrived in the waiting room outside the intensive care unit, the doctor said that Redd was not dead. And for the next four and a half hours, as we all waited, the producers and network executives looking grim, the rest of us comforting each other in prayer, Redd hung on.

Then the doctor came out to the waiting area and told Mrs. Foxx, "I'm sorry." He paused with that look that says whatever needs to be said to let someone know that their loved one has made their transition, then told her the details, assuring her that he was not in pain but had gone peacefully. She had remained fairly stoic but at this point began to softly cry. Crying myself, I went to her side and held her. At that moment, not three feet away from us, the producers began talking about what was going to happen to the series and how they could replace Redd and what they could do to assure the network it wasn't a lost cause. I was so mad I didn't know whether to cry or cuss. When Mrs. Foxx and her family left, I turned to the producers and went ballistic. Now, you know where I come from. You know I know how to pitch a bitch. You know my slums love a chance to get out and show themselves. But as a teacher and minister now, I mustered every ounce of restraint I could and, between hisses, told them that the least they could have done would have been to offer Mrs. Foxx a few words of condolence.

Driving home from the hospital, I swore out loud that if they ever did to Franklin what they did to Mrs. Foxx, I'd have to come back from the grave and blow up the TV studio.

Over the next few days I did some thinking and when we regrouped to discuss the future of the show, the producers explained that they were bringing in a new character to be played by Jackee Harry. At first she was supposed to be my daughter, which didn't work at all. Then they changed her to my sister. The show was now going to focus on the sister relationship. No disrespect to the lovely, talented Jackee, but to fill the shoes of Redd Foxx would've been impossible for anyone. Besides, as I told the producers and writers, the reality of my character, a woman who has been married for forty-two years and has never worked now coping with the loss of her husband was an ideal premise to work with. How would she earn money? How would she deal with her kids and grandkids?

How would she heal? Would she date? There was humor and pathos there that I knew audiences would be moved by.

As a matter of fact, I received boxes and boxes of letters from fans who felt I really had lost my husband, offering sympathy and suggestions for ways to get on with my life in *Royal Family*. Some who wrote were women who had coped with such losses and found healing through working with children, or people with disabilities, or seniors in nursing homes.

This premise was ignored by the decision-makers but we did produce a beautiful, poignant memorial show for Redd Foxx's character. The network executive who came to the taping was so touched he cried. And because of that, he determined, "We can't put it on the air. It even made *me* cry."

This floored me. As if feeling strong emotions for the loss of someone as great as Redd Foxx was a no-no. They did air the episode but it was edited and retooled so much that it was no longer the emotionally effective memorial we had wanted.

The show went further downhill from there. After it was canceled, I decided never to do a television series again. The whole corporate atmosphere was just too dehumanizing. But, like the song says, even though a door had closed, another window had just been opened. As it happened, these were the years that NBC was seriously dominating in the ratings. ABC wasn't getting too hurt but CBS was getting out-and-out killed. For some reason, I remember that every time I was watching TV and it was CBS, I'd talk to the television set and I'd say, "CBS, you need me. You really need me. I could help you. I could really help you and your ratings."

This was what I had been saying a lot when, somewhere in early '94, it was time for Daddy to take me on our annual honeymoon. Yes—that's what I said—my husband takes me on a honeymoon every year. So I call my agent to tell him I'd be unavailable for work for a week or so because of my honeymoon.

My agent asks me how do I think I'd like Wilmington, North Carolina, for my honeymoon? He describes it to me—how lovely it will be that time of year. Not too hot. Not too cold. "And," he says, "all the azalea bushes will be in bloom and in color all over the city, and, oh, by the way, you've been offered this part in a pilot for a series that they're making there."

Unenthusiastic as I was after my last experience, I started to say we'd best pass on it when he assured me that the pilot probably wouldn't fly, and this was just a way to make a little pocket money, he said, maybe buy myself a couple of new pairs of shoes. That was his joke, of course, because anyone who knows me knows I have more shoes in my closet than the entire populations of certain very small nations.

"Well, okay," I said, still feeling skittish, "how many zeroes in the figure, and what's the part like?"

My agent proceeded to describe what boiled down to a black Molly Goldberg, a woman who was wise, loving, and funny, and who helped people solve their problems.

It was my dream role, the one I'd dreamt up laying in my bed recuperating from brain surgery thirteen years earlier. "I like it," I chuckled.

"Oh," he added, "she's an angel."

"I like it even better," I said, laughing and shaking my head. As I have witnessed here for you these many pages, I did know a thing or two about angels. But then, remembering my firm decision to avoid TV series, I tossed it off. Sure, I'd do the pilot and buy some shoes. Or maybe something extravagant for my grandson Sean, then age nine, or my grandson Brandon, then twelve.

The pilot for the show, created by John Masius, turned out to be a joy, mainly because I met Roma Downey on it. In the pilot, Tess (my role) and Monica (her role) didn't get on so well. In real life, we clicked so immediately that I was certain we'd known each other in a previous lifetime. Sweet, real, beautiful, and a wonderful actress, Roma and I became instant family. Her mother had died when she was ten and she felt I was a kind of mother to her. And you know me, the one they called Ma at the age of three, I love mothering anyone as loving as Roma.

After we finished the pilot, we said our good-byes and exchanged words of hope that we'd see each other again. Hopefully sooner than later, we said. If I was a betting woman, I wouldn't have necessarily put my money on sooner.

But sooner it was. Not only that, when I got the news that the show was being bought, I found out that the network which was taking the series on was none other than CBS.

"See, Daddy," I said to my husband, "I told you the TV could hear me when I talked to it. And it transmitted the message to CBS. They know they need me. CBS knows they need me and that I can really help them with their ratings."

Franklin only laughed, knowing there was always a method in the madness.

The role was a dream, Roma was a dream, and the fact that it was CBS a good sign. But I still had strong reservations about doing a television series. At my age, as busy as I was in my roles as teacher and minister, and at that stage in my career where I would just as soon sing, do my own act, tell my own stories, and touch others in that way, did I really need or want a TV show? Hadn't I already seen that, done that, been there? Well, not according to Martha Williamson, the executive producer CBS had brought in to retool the show. At a meeting which Roma and I attended, along with others who would be working on the show, Martha became very impassioned telling us how this television series was going to be different from anything else on TV. At one point, she looked right at me and said, "I just want you to know that the show is going to talk about God and the word of God and God's love and about faith and trust in God. Is that all right with you?"

I laughed out loud. She was asking me, a preacher who'd been singing gospel since I could talk, if it was okay. "Yes, Martha," I said, "God's all right with me, has been for a long time."

Now I was confused. I thought the Father and I had been over the subject of TV series and agreed they didn't work for me. Not only that but CBS had only ordered six episodes and there was a rumor going around that everyone knew it was dead in the water after that. Then again, this was my black Molly Goldberg character as an angel named Tess giving advice helping to solve people's problems in a show that dared to put God front and center and praise His name; it was a lead role in stories that would touch people's lives, stories that mattered. And it was CBS, whom I had so boldly boasted before that I could really help.

After leaving the meeting, I went home, went into my bedroom, closed the door, and went directly to my bed and said, "Father, I don't want to do this. You know I don't like the structure, all that corporate stuff. I just want to sing, just make a living."

And He said, "Do it for me."

I said, "C'mon, Father, a TV show . . ."

He said, "Do this for me. And you can retire in ten years."

That was my decision. Period, the end.

A lot of people continued to subscribe to the notion that the life span of the series was going to be six episodes. Not me. When we got ready to leave for Salt Lake City where the show was going to be filmed, we had to go have this health exam we're required to take when traveling to work in out-of-state locations. The insurance company won't insure the production if the actors have any serious health concerns.

The tests are so routine, you have to have something really acute not to pass. I was in fine health. But when they handed me my form to sign, I said, "Excuse me, I can't sign this." Not unless, I insisted, they changed what they had typed in for the length of time I was expected to be working. They had typed in the amount of time they expected it would take to shoot six episodes. I wanted it changed to say ten years. The nurse thought this was unreasonable. I only shrugged and said, "It's a God thing."

When the nurses asked Martha Williamson what to do, she said, "If Della says it's a God thing, it's best to go along with her."

Touched by an Angel has definitely been sent its share of help from above. After those six episodes, a few more were ordered and then a few more, and with preempting and scheduling changes the series managed to last the season. That first year the ratings weren't impressive and the critics were skeptical. When talk of cancellation came up, a massive grass-roots campaign was mounted with letter writing from fans and friends of and on the show. Guest stars from the first season even got together and paid for an ad that said if Anne Rice could take an ad out for vampires, they could take out an ad for angels, to which they signed their names. And we were brought back from would-be angel retirement for the '95–'96 season. That year we really started to soar. By the third season, the show was a smash, often rating third or fourth for the week and rarely going below one of the top ten shows for the week. See, CBS, I told you.

During that third season, John Dye joined the cast, adding a powerful dynamic by taking a new approach in his role as Andrew, the angel of death. Without the love and warmth which John exudes as Andrew, the character would not work as successfully as it does. Instead of portraying death and its angel as ominous or shadowy, Andrew appears in the same peaceful, heavenly glow of light in which Tess and Monica are illuminated.

Offscreen one of our differences is that when either Roma or I fly on airplanes, most of the passengers are very happy to see us on the flight with them. John, on the other hand, says that sometimes people get a little nervous when they see him boarding their flight.

John is not only a superb actor, he is a true southern gentleman—in only the best sense of that term—thoughtful, considerate, polite. With John it's a constant litany of concern: "Della, can I get you a chair?" "Something to drink?" "After you . . ."

Meanwhile, Roma and I have only grown closer and more fond of each other as time has gone on. With that lovely Irish lilt, she really is as charming as the TV character she portrays. And, yes—you're a step ahead of me—Roma Downey is an angel in my life. It is no accident that our paths have crossed. Being in Salt Lake City, away from Dumpsey, who is an adult now and busy with her own family, I know that the Father has given me Roma as a spiritual daughter to fill that absence.

Roma, too, has given me yet one more angel. After honoring me by asking me to preside at her marriage ceremony, she went on to bless me, not with a grandchild, but with a God-child, a precious baby girl, Reilly Marie.

But I'm somewhat concerned about my goddaughter. Roma, talent that she is, cannot sing and she has this habit of trying to croon lullabies to baby Reilly. "Do not sing," I've told Roma, over and over. "Unless you want that child to grow up tone-deaf, please do not sing." Roma may laugh but I'm serious. I think Reilly has a lot of musical promise. So if Roma starts up again, I repeat, "Don't sing to that child. You let me do the singing."

There is one number, however, that I can't interrupt if Roma decides to perform it. When she's really excited or on long days when we're all hot and tired and wanting to go home, Roma may opt to invigorate the troops by singing and doing this choreographed dance routine to the song, "Disco Inferno." Not exactly the type of song you'd expect an angel to sing. But to see this angelic Roma dancing her heart out to those raucous lyrics is an experience I wouldn't miss for anything.

What is it that I do on those long hot days on the set when I'd rather be at home in my bed with my husband? Well, sometimes I do what I did one late afternoon back in our first season. After several hours of shooting in the desert—under blazing blue skies and a temperature of 104°—production had come to a grinding halt. We'd been sitting and waiting forever for something or other to get fixed so we could finish the day. Tempers were starting to flare. Mine included. So, I centered myself and talked out loud to the Father, saying, "Lord, we're hot. We need a cloud."

Within fifteen minutes the sky turned from blue to gray and the clouds which blanketed it quickly brought down the temperature at least ten degrees. What can I tell you? It's a God thing.

Touched by an Angel's cast and crew are my most loving family, as close to me as my family at Understanding Principles. We have been blessed with some of the best actors in the business in the roles of our recurring angels and as our guest stars. Never before this experience have I worked on a TV series where stars have told me how happy they are to be doing the show and how much they had been wanting to do it. And I think they give us an extra portion of themselves. Darren McGavin, for instance, not only did his part, he actually gave acting lessons during rehearsals and on camera, generously making sure everyone got their due and their moments. The fabulous Diane Ladd was another who worked with regulars and extras alike, making for a fantastic show. This is exactly what a God thing is, a training ground for everyone to learn something they can use.

Most of all, it has been with this show that all my many roads seemed to have merged and come together. God bless Martha and the other writers and producers who never overlook an opportunity for Tess to sing, including—yes, you got it again—the theme song. It's singing and it's acting, funny and dramatic. It's learning, it's teaching, it's changing people's minds and changing their lives. It's part and parcel of the work I do as a minister.

We receive truckloads of mail weekly from viewers and fans who tell us how the show has impacted on them. People approach me whenever I am out and about to thank me for the messages *Touched by an Angel* has brought them.

One such person spoke to me at the Salt Lake City airport on my way back to Los Angeles after a *lo-o-o-ong* work week. It was a Friday night and we were catching the last flight out and all I could think about was flying home and getting into my bed. That's when the lady at the ticket counter saw me, and came over to me in the waiting lounge, and said, "I just want to tell you how much I appreciate the show."

"Thank you very much," I said, tired as I was. I have never had a problem talking to fans because they're the ones that feed me. After all, if they don't like me, I don't work and then I don't eat. I learned about that many moons ago from Mahalia Jackson. So this was not a problem and I listened as the lady told me how the show had helped her marriage.

It had gotten into a rut, she told me. She and her husband had stopped really talking to each other, other than the regular *good morning*s and the *what's for dinner*s and the *will you pass the butter*s.

"I don't remember how, but I stumbled on *Touched by an Angel*," she said. The show she saw was about a marriage in trouble that was as much the wife's problem as it was the husband's. And the wife had always blamed the husband and never seen what she could have done to make it better. The lady at the airport said, "That was the first time that had ever occurred to me. I'd been making it all my husband's fault for years." So she changed her mind and she started trying to do more, instead of expecting him to do more. And somehow or other, her husband stumbled in the living room and he started watching the show. Then her children came in and they started watching it too.

One day, not very long after that, this lady said that her five-year-old came up to her to say, "You know, Mommy, I think you and Daddy are beginning to like each other because you started talking to each other." The lady told me it was so and, as a result, her life was better.

On another plane trip, as we settled into the last row of first class—Franklin on the aisle and me by the window—this woman leaned forward out of business class, over my husband, and said to me, "I want to thank you because your television show saved my life."

Now, I'm trying to be gracious. But inside I'm saying, *Give me a break, ain't no way a TV show gonna save your life, you takin' this a little too far.*

And the woman seemed to sense that. She said, "No, really, your television show has saved my life. Six months ago my husband died." She explained that he was a young man, healthy and strong, and one day just up and died. "I didn't know how to handle it," she said. "I couldn't find a way to help myself and, therefore, couldn't help my children." And that was when she saw a show where a man was dying, much older than her husband, and at a time of dying, but the man was so happy and up and so glad about dying, while the family stood around the bed singing. While she was watching that on TV, she said that she realized that because of the kind of person her husband was, he would be happy wherever he was and he wouldn't have gone if he hadn't wanted to go. "It relieved me," she said, smiling, "and I was finally able to pick myself up, help myself, and my children. And we're doing fine now." With that, she went on back to her seat.

A policeman wrote to say that after watching an episode about police corruption, he was troubled so much by an actual incidence of corruption he knew about that, at the risk of harm to himself, he reported the police officers he knew to be involved, and retired from the force.

Again, I have received more wonderful, inspiring letters than could fill many volumes. The one letter I would like to share with you comes from Kathy, a most special lady:

Dear Ms. Reese:

I am writing to tell you how much I enjoy your show. I have come from an abusive family so I can relate to so much of the pain on your show. You give me hope to continue on. I have healed so much watching your show. Years of counseling have not been able to do what your show has been able to do for me. Last week's show about the inmates on death row hit so close to home. Me being abused and molested, seeing my nieces and nephews going through the same thing I did. Seeing the authorities' hands tied. Me trying to do better with my children, only to see my son have a child and watch so much abuse with my grandson that my insides seem to not take it anymore. Your show last Sunday gave me hope to keep going, to keep having faith, to not give up . . . I would like to have you as my role model. To try to help someone else. The people who play Tess, Monica, and Andrew are angels to me. Because they seem to be so warm and caring. That isn't something they teach you in acting school, it comes from the heart . . . Thank you for the good you are doing. I hope I can pass on what I have learned from you to others. God bless you.

You see what I mean about all the facets of my life coming together? If you think that I'd just gotten real lucky all at once, let my share with you one of the great lines that Tess had to say a while back: "Luck is when God wishes to remain anonymous."

In so many ways, *Touched by an Angel* is an extension of my ministry. Not because I write or direct the contents of the script but because the same principles are at work.

They're not what most people consider religious principles. They're spiritual principles. They are universal principles.

As angels on the show, we don't come to fix people in trouble. We come to teach them how to fix themselves. And to reassure them that they are never alone, that God loves them, unconditionally and forever. God wants only the best for them but God can't make them do anything. Human beings have been given free will and the choice is always ours.

In the same way, at my church, as I have said, I teach that we are in charge of the miracles, that we can heal ourselves in partnership with God. I don't teach that there is one way and one way only to salvation, nor that one denomination is more truthful than another. I may be the only other minister besides Johnnie Colemon to say this, but I believe and teach that you don't need a church to pray; I teach that you don't need a minister to pray. I teach that you don't have to call God what I call Him in order to be in touch with Him. Or Her. I teach that Father/Mother God loves you with infinite love and loves to hear from you and talk to you no matter what's on your mind.

It doesn't have to be serious business. Do you know that God has the best sense of humor? I know it because I know you have to have a great sense of humor to create something as funny as a platypus or an orangutan.

The power of prayer is so phenomenal. For example, some years ago I went to God and I said, "Father, I don't hear my music on the streets anymore. I really want to hear my music on the streets again. Thank you, Father."

Lo and behold, the Father asked me to do *Touched by an Angel* for Him, and in return blessed me in abundance, including the answer to my desire to hear my music on the streets. Once the show became a hit, every record company and label I had ever recorded for started putting out rereleases of almost every record I'd ever made. What a joy it is to hear my music out there again, alive and well these many years later. But one thing I forgot to say when I prayed to the Father was that I wanted to have some money attached to it. That's right, the way recording contracts used to be, anything rereleased later on would not pay royalties to the artists. This time, when I release my next new album, I might pray a bit more specifically.

⌒— May, 1997. Ah, hiatus! Which means for the next two and half months I won't be flying back and forth from Salt Lake City but will focus my energies on an active summer for UP, as well as having a few more romantic evenings with Daddy, possibly even catching a movie or two. Oh, and then there's the next few weeks to finish up this book. After that, I'll spend whatever extra time I can find trying to organize my house after all the construction that's been going on. Then again, there's my work to do as honorary chairperson for the National Stroke Association. And did I mention that Franklin's writing and producing a movie about my early years touring with Mahalia, in which I will be playing my great mentor? P.S. And there's the next book I'm going to write.

I love it. A reviewer recently came to the set of *Touched by an Angel* and after finding out that I had such a busy schedule, she asked what I did for fun. I laughed. "This," I said. "Everything I do, I do for fun."

Writing can be a fun thing too. And sometimes a necessary thing. From the time I was twelve years old, I've written about what was going on in my day-to-day world. You might call it a kind of journal although what I wrote could take many forms, sometimes prose, sometimes poetry, even songs. Writing was an outlet, a tool for learning and making sense of my world. Especially whenever I was in a problem, or off on the road without a friend to listen to me, I wrote it down and wrote it out. Or I wrote songs so that I could sing it out.

As I sit today at my computer, gathering my thoughts for these last pages, I look out at the majesty of life on this cool, blue-skied sunny morning. A feeling of peaceful joy is present, a feeling that all is well with me and with the world.

Where did I find this understanding that everything was ultimately going to be all right? From Nellie, of course, of whom I was born.

On a recent morning, during my early-hours communion with God, I flashed on that time Mama took care of me when I was stricken with rheumatic fever. I remembered that my mother never told me how the doctors told her I might die or never walk. And something I had forgotten came back to me from that time in vivid images. It took place in the middle of the night in my small bedroom when I was having a bad night and awoke to see this picture on the wall in front of my bed. There on the wall I saw the figure of a man projected as if on a movie screen and he was smiling at me and it didn't frighten me. It made me feel better when he smiled and pointed at me and said, "It's all right, everything is all right." I believed him.

Mama opened the door to enter and she saw this picture fade as she entered. She knew who it was and she prayed as she hugged me. I didn't understand it then, but now, looking back, I know it was my first meeting with Jesus Christ.

Thank you, Father, for your Son, and for all your angels.

Epilogue

As you have seen, my life is such an adventure. And writing this book has allowed me to understand that more completely and to look back at the way God has always foreseen what I needed for life and that more abundantly.

Even though I refused to listen sometimes.

Even though I went directly against His express wishes, which I did. And when I did, of course, I'd fall and He would pick me up and dust me off and start me out all over again.

Whatever, wherever, whenever, forever, God has been my sufficiency in all things whether I recognized it and/or used that knowledge or allowed myself to wallow in the muck of it. When I, like the prodigal son, arose and went home to my Father, the proper changes would take place. The proper people would enter my life with what I needed or where to get what I needed or how to get what I needed.

I have made it from 984 East Vernor Highway in Detroit, Michigan's, slums to the top of Bel Air Road in Los Angeles—the *crème de la crème* of residential areas. In more ways I have survived the blows I took and have seen those who struck the blows reap what they sowed, for the most part.

I have loved and truly been loved in return.

I am loved and truly loving in return.

I am caring and I am cared for.

I've learned the art of forgiveness.

I've learned patience and determination.

I've learned the Christ in me will never leave me or forsake me because God assigned it to take care of me as its sole and main function.

My faith is not only the substance of things hoped for; my faith is a reality through the use and success of my faith in my life.

I've learned to trust the Lord completely and to marvel at the way He keeps me safe and staid in His power and His mercy and His peace that surpasses understanding.

My life has been marvelous. It's at times seemed disappointing. It's been sunshine of the greatest brilliance. It's been the storm to end all storms. It's been an exciting adventure. It's been a dull lull. It's been all that I could desire. It's been a nightmare of great demons. It's been a trip. It's been a magic carpet ride that has brought me to this wonderful place of living.

As I told you when we started this journey which has now come full circle, I am at the perfection of life: Where I want to be, with who I want to be; I am doing just what I want to do, with who I want to do it; I am free of the fears of my youth and I am settled in the assurance which only comes from surviving and turning the stumbling blocks into stepping stones. The bigger the blocks, the higher the step provided by the stone.

Of course, as my steps took me higher, I needed more assistance in the day-to-day management of life and God sent another angel to take care of me. Guess what? From the day we met she called me Mama. She had been abused by father, family, husband, and a host of supposed friends. She had raised a family of fourteen by herself as she worked her way through school. She was mad, she was hostile, she was belligerent and argumentative to a fault. She always felt attacked, was gun-shy of everything, and, in self-defense, she trusted no one. She is now my first assistant. She is now the most loving person you'd want to know; she is charming, sweet, intelligent, and she takes good care of me, Daddy, the house, and the doggy babies.

God, looking out for me as usual, knew that I would need someone to help take care of me, and so six years ago He sent me this caring angel, Shirley, a licensed nurse. No, I am not ill or incapacitated in any way. But sometimes the days are so long I do need a back rub or a leg rub every once in a while.

Confidence in God's constant provision of what and who we need comes with experience. Confidence in yourself comes from experiences you have dealt with successfully and lessons you've learned by dealing with them. I've learned the lessons and now I'm receiving the blessings.

I'm writing this down for Dumpsey and Jim and Dominique and Frank III and for my loving husband. And because Putnam's checks don't bounce. Yet more than that, I am writing because I believe if each of you would look back over your life, you would see God's hand in it and, in His hand, your hand—or you would have never made it this far.

I think if you do this and accept His presence in your life whatever is happening to you at this time, at this very moment, will be easier to handle because of the confidence you will feel in His love and the re-membering of those times when you thought it was the end of the world and He stepped in and made the world new and safe again for you.

Please know also that God has no respect of person. We are all the same to Him. So I was not picked out special. In His eyes, we are all spe-cial. He doesn't think any more of me than He does of you, so all He has done for me and more He is ready, willing, and able to do for you—if you will just trust Him.

Be of good courage and do what you wanna do. Relax in the reality and the joy that you are empowered with the spirit of God. Allow yourself to be as wonderful as you really already are.

Get firmly planted in, relaxed in, comfortable in your power. Don't ever be afraid to use it. Be proud you have it and use it every chance you get. Create your own reality; don't fall for the propaganda.

No, I wasn't always this sure of my convictions and the power therein but I am now. I learned day by day, trial by trial, victory by victory, disappointment by disappointment. I've had some major disappointments.

Serious business.

I never gave Franklin sons. I would have liked to have given him at least four.

I didn't give birth to Dumpsey or Jim.

I was not there when my grandson Sean was born.

I was never Ray Charles's favorite singer. I have never sung with Gladys Knight. Quincy Jones has never arranged for me. Luther Vandross hasn't asked me to sing with him when we would make such beautiful music together.

I haven't as yet been able to build the church building that I want to build so much.

I don't have my Academy Award yet or my Emmy. I haven't had my long run on Broadway ending in a Tony award.

There was a time when I would have felt sad at sixty-six not having accomplished these things. Now I realize this is what I have to look forward to in my future.

These things are part of the new adventures of my life.

Let me say to the young people, hold onto your dream. Dreams do come true.

Find something you like to do so much you would do it even if you weren't paid for it, something that the joy of it is all that makes you love to do it. And it will make you wealthy. Not just rich but wealthy with the contentment it brings you, with the commitment you are able to make to it, and the financial profits it will bring you. He didn't say it would be easy; He said it would be worth your while.

Just as there have been angels along the way to watch over me, there are angels watching over you right this second.

I want to leave you with something that is really what I have always believed. And because I did believe it, I found it worked for me and I always found my way out. I wish I could take credit for writing it—this is so absolutely correct—but it was written by my most gifted musical director of UP's house band, musician and songwriter T. C. Campbell, along with talented songwriter Robbie Long. It is called "A Window Open":

> *When the key won't turn*
> *And the locks seem broke*
> *And you're running round in circles*
> *With your dreams up in smoke*
> *Just take a good look around*
> *And you might be surprised*
> *That there's a new way*
> *If you're willing to try.*
>
> *For each door that closes, the good Lord*
> *Leaves a window open.*
>
> *There comes a time*
> *That inside you know*
> *Some of the games you're playing*
> *You just have to let go*
> *Might feel lonely and lost*
> *The walls caving in*
> *But what seems like the end*
> *Can be your chance to begin*

'Cause for each door that closes,
The good Lord leaves a window open.

So step on up, make no excuse
You've got a power, just beggin' to get loose
There is a light, shining for you
It is in your heart, and it will lead you through
'Cause when you're stuck in a rut
And you think you can't cope
Just call on the spirit and don't give up hope.

'Cause for each door that closes,
The good Lord leaves a window open.

So, pick yourself up . . . and make no excuse
Work that power . . . that's crying to get loose
Just look in your heart. . . . for that speck of light
An open window that will lead you right.

So when you take that first step
Hold your head up high
Take courage in knowing
That the Lord will provide.

'Cause for each door that closes,
The good Lord will leave a window open!!!!!!

Don't worry about the doors, keep your eyes open for the windows of life that lead you to the new horizons the Lord has planned for you.

Thank you for letting me share some of my life with you. It helped me to do so and I hope, in some way or another, it helped you.

I place you lovingly in the hands of God. I do that because God alone has love to surround us all individually and He has power to protect us individually and He has that peace that surpasses all understanding and He will watch between me and thee while we are absent one from the other.